SAP® HANA Advanced Modeling

Dominique Alfermann
Stefan Hartmann
Benedikt Engel

Thank you for purchasing this book from Espresso Tutorials!

Like a cup of espresso coffee, Espresso Tutorials SAP books are concise and effective. We know that your time is valuable and we deliver information in a succinct and straightforward manner. It only takes our readers a short amount of time to consume SAP concepts. Our books are well recognized in the industry for leveraging tutorial-style instruction and videos to show you step by step how to successfully work with SAP.

Check out our YouTube channel to watch our videos at
https://www.youtube.com/user/EspressoTutorials.

If you are interested in SAP Finance and Controlling, join us at
http://www.fico-forum.com/forum2/
to get your SAP questions answered and contribute to discussions.

Related titles from Espresso Tutorials:

- ▶ Ingo Brenckmann & Mathias Pöhling: The SAP® HANA Project Guide
  http://5009.espresso-tutorials.com
- ▶ Janet Salmon & Ulrich Schlüter: SAP® HANA for ERP Financials, 2nd edition
  http://5092.espresso-tutorials.com
- ▶ Rob Frye, Joe Darlak, Dr. Bjarne Berg: The SAP® BW to HANA Migration Handbook
  http://5109.espresso-tutorials.com

Dominique Alfermann, Stefan Hartmann, Benedikt Engel
SAP® HANA Advanced Modeling

ISBN:	978-1-51710106-0
Editor:	Alice Adams
Proofreading:	Tracey Duffy
Cover Design:	Philip Esch, Martin Munzel
Cover Photo:	fotolia #50865078 (c) carloscastilla
Interior Design:	Johann-Christian Hanke

All rights reserved.

1st Edition 2015, Gleichen

© 2015 by Espresso Tutorials GmbH

URL: *www.espresso-tutorials.com*

All rights reserved. Neither this publication nor any part of it may be copied or reproduced in any form or by any means or translated into another language without the prior consent of Espresso Tutorials GmbH, Zum Gelenberg 11, 37130 Gleichen, Germany.

Espresso Tutorials makes no warranties or representations with respects to the content hereof and specifically disclaims any implied warranties of merchantability or fitness for any particular purpose. Espresso Tutorials assumes no responsibility for any errors that may appear in this publication.

Feedback
We greatly appreciate any kind of feedback you have concerning this book. Please mail us at *info@espresso-tutorials.com*.

Table of Contents

Preface   **7**

1 Introduction   **11**
    1.1   Intention   11
    1.2   Objective   12
    1.3   In and out of scope   12
    1.4   Content   13
    1.5   Data model definition and terms   15

2 Case study and hardware setup   **17**
    2.1   The demand for SAP HANA native solutions   17
    2.2   SAP HANA native project introduction   19
    2.3   System landscape and configuration   27
    2.4   Test approach   28
    2.5   Summary and conclusion   32

3 Create the data model   **33**
    3.1   Persistency versus virtualization   33
    3.2   Modeling approaches   43
    3.3   Engine utilization   53
    3.4   PlanViz   57
    3.5   Test scenarios   65

4 High-performing information views   **87**
    4.1   Attribute view   88
    4.2   Analytic view   98
    4.3   Calculation views   132

5 Advanced modeling techniques — 191
- 5.1 Development perspective — 191
- 5.2 Core Data Services — 192
- 5.3 Challenges in SAP HANA modeling — 197
- 5.4 Development methods — 223

6 Best practices and recommendations — 233
- 6.1 SAP view strategy — 233
- 6.2 SAP HANA table design — 234
- 6.3 Joins — 235
- 6.4 Calculations — 240
- 6.5 Currency and unit conversion — 243
- 6.6 Filters — 246
- 6.7 General SAP HANA design aspects — 249
- 6.8 Summary — 253

7 Operational reporting on SAP HANA — 255
- 7.1 Operational versus strategic reporting — 255
- 7.2 Specifics of operational reporting — 257
- 7.3 Operational reporting scenario — 266
- 7.4 Operational reporting optimization — 269
- 7.5 SAP HANA Live — 272
- 7.6 Summary — 280

8 Conclusions and outlook — 283
- 8.1 Conclusion — 283
- 8.2 Outlook — 285

A About the Authors — 292

B Index — 295

C Disclaimer — 298

Preface

This book introduces you to advanced modeling techniques based on actual project experience as well as field tests. Our aim is to provide clear modeling recommendations for setting up data models, optimizing performance, using the SAP HANA modeler and development perspective, as well as efficiently solving complex requirements in SAP HANA.

The target audience of this book is SAP HANA developers and architects acquainted with the methods and options for implementing logic in SAP HANA. The reader should possess a solid understanding of general SAP HANA objects.

In our world, technologies evolve at an extraordinary pace and new market opportunities develop just as quickly. Companies face the challenge of adapting to unfamiliar technologies and markets with different rules and key players. While businesses adapt, IT departments face similar struggles with constantly changing business requirements and new technologies. In these hectic times, it is essential to have a good reporting foundation available to keep track of existing and also new business.

SAP is one of the big players in business software and is currently developing new products and promoting new product suites at a speed previously unknown to most customers. A central element to all of these products is SAP HANA. Most IT departments have seen SAP HANA in sales presentations, or even implemented the software in a proof of concept (PoC). However, few companies truly consider SAP HANA an alternative to existing databases or data warehouses.

In this book, we go one step further and take a closer look at how to build reporting views in an SAP HANA native environment. We not only take a close look at SAP HANA design elements and patterns, but also evaluate these patterns and provide recommendations and best practices for modeling in SAP HANA. The evaluation is based on critical factors such as performance and storage consumption, as well as on ease of use. In the course of the chapters, we examine possible implementation elements or variants in the different types of information views and their impact on the evaluation factors. The evaluation is performed using test scenarios and is based on our practical experience and results in recommendations and best practices. In order to complete the picture, we demonstrate how to solve complex problems and calculations in SAP

HANA. Finally, the book discusses new challenges in integrating operational reporting into the operational system while avoiding redundancy. We hope you enjoy reading this book and collecting insights into SAP HANA native.

Dominique & Stefan & Ben

Personal dedication

Writing a book like this is also the result of encouraging support and contributions from our friends, families, and colleagues. Their numerous ideas, hints, and discussions helped us to greatly enrich each chapter. We are truly grateful to them. We especially want to mention our employer Capgemini Deutschland GmbH, including Kai-Oliver Schaefer and Thomas Schroeder, who inspired us to go ahead with this book project. Last but not least, we want to say thank you to the Espresso Tutorials team, especially to Alice Adams, who patiently advised us in formalizing and completing the book.

We have added a few icons to highlight important information. These include:

Tips

Tips highlight information concerning more details about the subject being described and/or additional background information.

INTRODUCTION

Examples	
	Examples help illustrate a topic better by relating it to real world scenarios.

Attention	
	Attention notices draw attention to information that you should be aware of when you go through the examples from this book on your own.

⇨ Link codes	
	For long hyperlinks we include a consecutive number ⇨1 (link code) with the link. Visit *http://4110.espresso-tutorials.com* to find a dynamic list of links that you can click on to easily access information.

Finally, a note concerning the copyright: all screenshots printed in this book are the copyright of SAP SE. All rights are reserved by SAP SE. Copyright pertains to all SAP images in this publication. For simplification, we will not mention this specifically underneath every screenshot.

1 Introduction

In this chapter, we clarify and emphasize the reasons for writing this book. Furthermore, we explain the overall scope of the book and provide a brief introduction to its content. We conclude the chapter by defining frequently used terms.

1.1 Intention

One key element to the successful management of a company consists of a solid business intelligence (BI) solution and highly available business applications. The evolution of new technologies constantly challenges IT management to balance the need for innovation with the demand for consistent and accurately working system processes. One of these new technologies enabled by the decreasing cost of main memory is the in-memory database. In-memory databases not only result in performance improvements for reporting, but also impact the holistic BI strategy. Introducing in-memory databases to the IT landscape offers completely new possibilities to IT and end users and requires a rethinking of existing principles and processes. A further aspect to be taken into consideration for the business is that getting the right information at the right time to the right decision makers becomes increasingly important. Today especially, decisions have to be made in near real time and based on a massive amount of data. SAP is positioning its in-memory database product SAP HANA to fulfill the requirement of real-time reporting and enable new business opportunities. This product represents the foundation for many SAP products and the basis for high-performing data processing and reporting.

SAP HANA delivers a wide range of inherent functionalities that enable it to be leveraged for reporting, making it far superior to the average database. The approach of developing reporting based on the HANA database directly is called *SAP HANA native* development. For this purpose, SAP HANA provides a comprehensive set of out-of-the-box solutions for structured and unstructured data, classical database queries, predictions, and text or fuzzy algorithms. Furthermore, SAP is continuously improving SAP HANA and with each release new features are distributed to the customers. This in turn results in a large and growing number of possible ways to implement a reporting solution based on SAP HANA native. The idea of this book is to provide a cookbook that you can use to build your high-performing SAP HANA native data model in order to lift your solution into the champions' league of existing HANA solutions.

1.2 Objective

This book introduces you to SAP HANA advanced modeling techniques based on actual project experiences as well as field tests. The goal is to provide clear modeling recommendations for setting up data models, optimizing performance, using the SAP HANA modeler and development perspectives, as well as solving complex requirements efficiently in SAP HANA.

1.3 In and out of scope

In contrast to other publications, the aim of this book is not to provide an introduction to SAP HANA and its possibilities, but to supply the reader with clear recommendations on how to improve both modeling in SAP HANA and creating a development environment on SAP HANA. These recommendations are divided into five areas:

1. Virtualization versus persistency (see Chapter 3)
2. Evaluation of HANA design elements by performance and memory consumption (see Chapters 3 and 4)
3. Advanced modeling techniques (see Chapter 5)
4. Best practice recommendations (see Chapter 6)
5. Operational reporting (see Chapter 7)

The first area examines where persistency is still required in a normally read-optimized in-memory environment. The outcome of the evaluation regarding the second area (2) is a list of design options and their impact on the noted evaluation factors. The third area (3) reviews common challenges during implementations and how to solve these challenges in SAP HANA. Recommendation area four (4) results from the second area (2) and field experience, whereas the final area (5) comprises operational reporting as well as experience from projects.

For the purposes of this book, decision tables, analytic privileges, hardware-related performance tuning, and the consumption of views by different client tools (e.g., SAP BusinessObjects) are out of scope. Furthermore, this book does not explain basic concepts of views or tables in SAP HANA, as an understanding of these concepts is a prerequisite for reading this publication.

1.4 Content

To provide you with a consistent storyline, the book merges a case study with a structured evaluation of SAP HANA design elements and options. After the introduction to the case study (which is referenced in all of the chapters), you will be acquainted with the major considerations for starting your development in SAP HANA in the chapter on the technical foundation (see Chapter 3). Furthermore, we discuss several architectural options that can be applied to the case study. We verify these using test cases which identify the SAP HANA design patterns with the best balance between performance, memory consumption, and maintainability. We walk you through advanced modeling techniques for implementing this architecture and for solving further common business problems. Chapter 6 then covers best practices gathered throughout the previous chapters. The final chapter discusses operational reporting in terms of in-memory databases. The book closes with a conclusion and a review of topics for further investigation. Figure 1.1 provides an overview of the structure of this book.

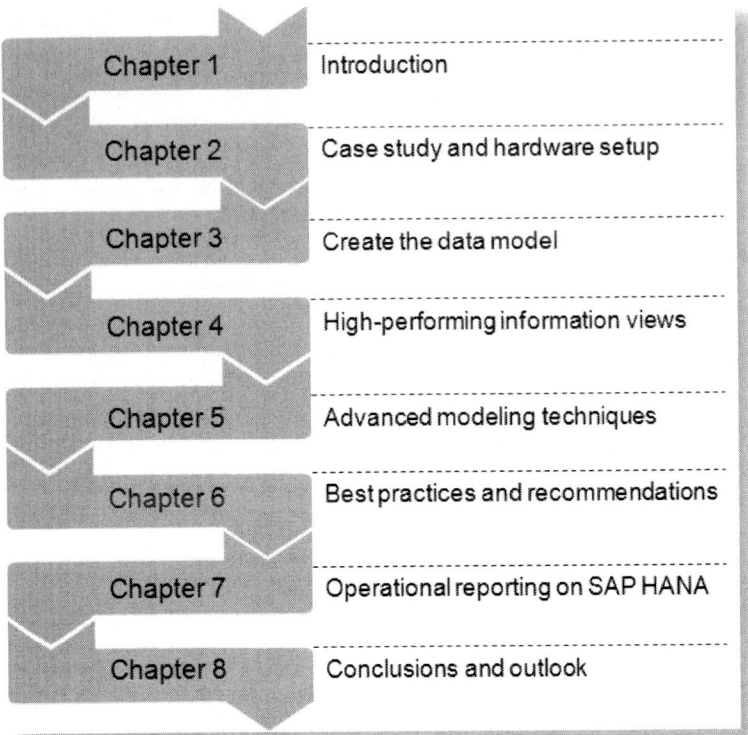

Figure 1.1: Book structure

Let's take a brief look at the focus of each chapter.

Chapter 2: The SAP case study presents the reader with a business case and the (hardware) setup used for the implementation of this business case. Business entities and their correlations are highlighted. To prepare the basis for our test cases, this chapter presents the SAP HANA solution, including the size of the data model and consequently the available hardware. It also discusses a common test approach.

Chapter 3: Create the data model looks at data persistency versus virtualization and uses these considerations to create physical tables. This chapter also presents first test scenarios to the reader. These test scenarios evaluate the impact of various physical architectural elements on performance and space consumption.

Chapter 4: High-performing information views are structured using the different information views provided in SAP HANA Studio. Through various test scenarios, we take a closer look at the different types of information views to understand the performance impact of the SAP HANA design patterns provided in these information views. We thereby create a set of guidelines and recommendations for various features of SAP HANA Studio, as well as for the general use of different view types.

Chapter 5: Advanced modeling techniques provides detailed insights into the aggregation behavior in SAP HANA which is ultimately the basis for solving difficult calculation problems in SAP HANA. The chapter then focuses on the SAP HANA development perspective, including *Core Data Services (CDS)*, and the use of this perspective for data modeling. Furthermore, this chapter examines common problems within daily work along with solutions to these problems. The chapter concludes by looking at and explaining the topics of parallel development and agility aspects.

Chapter 6: Best practice recommendations leverages the insights gained from the previous chapters, multiple test scenarios, and real implementation experience to provide best practice recommendations.

Chapter 7: Operational reporting with SAP HANA describes the special requirements resulting from an SAP Business Suite on HANA implementation, focusing on SAP HANA Live as well as reporting. The chapter also examines the new possibilities arising from SAP HANA as an operational database.

Chapter 8: Conclusion & outlook summarizes the results and learnings from the previous chapters. Within this chapter, we address how the goals of the book have been achieved. This chapter also gives you an overview of some ideas for further topics that may be interesting to follow up on.

1.5 Data model definition and terms

In this book you will come across terms that we need to clarify in advance. In general, we will follow the concepts of the conceptual, logical, and physical data model and clarify the meaning of HANA information views. In the world of SAP HANA native, the concepts of the three different types of data modeling are still applicable. The *conceptual data model* describes the highest level of relationships between different entities, which means that this type of model shows only business terms and how they are connected. No key relationships are shown. The *logical data model* describes the data at a finer level of granularity without taking into account how it is implemented physically with SAP HANA native. The logical data model already depicts tables and their reciprocal relationships. The *physical data model* reflects the way the data model will be implemented in the database. This includes all table structures and their characteristics, such as column names, data types, key fields, and the table relations. In our case, we introduce an additional split at this level: we add the concepts of *virtual* and *persistent*. The persistent data model comprises everything storing data in a physical way, such as a table. In contrast, the virtual data model does not store the data physically but instead supplies it only virtually when queried, e.g., through information views. The third chapter of this book contains a deep dive discussion on the topic of virtualization versus persistency.

Information views are the central components of the solution you develop in your SAP HANA environment. There are three different types of information views in SAP HANA:

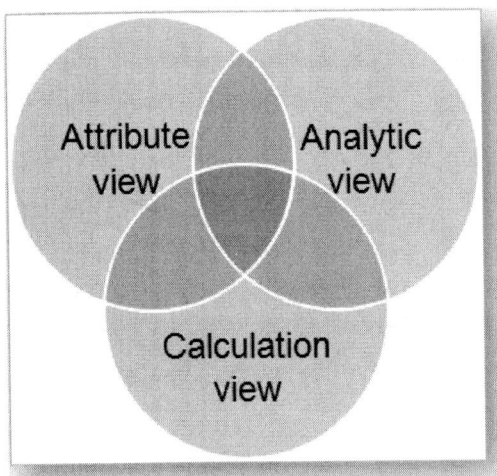

Figure 1.2: Information views

In simple terms, HANA information views are just the metadata definition of how data is transformed. For example, in the view you simply define how a calculation has to be performed; the result of the actual calculation is not yet stored physically within the data. This means that everything is virtualized and all aggregations and calculations are performed on the fly when the view is executed.

2 Case study and hardware setup

In this chapter, we use a case study to explain how to implement an SAP HANA native solution. We describe the as-is situation, including known issues with the current business warehouse, develop an entity relationship model, and propose a system landscape. This analysis will serve as the basis for the planned solution. The chapter concludes with a high-level view of our test approach.

2.1 The demand for SAP HANA native solutions

Through our daily project work with clients in recent years, we have noticed an increasing demand for real-time reporting and flexible data warehouse solutions. The need for real-time reporting in areas such as logistics, planning processes, market basket analyses, and next best action recommendations emphasizes the numerous use cases. These examples underscore the demand for a wide range of reporting solutions. Given the reporting requirements, clients are likely to invest in these types of technologies. Furthermore, many research facilities regularly analyze reporting needs and user experience. Gartner, Inc. recently published an analysis stating that by using real-time reporting in consumer businesses, for example by sales representatives leveraging data on a daily basis, revenue increased by up to 17%. The corresponding analysis can be found in the article *Fast-Fashion Retailer Boosts Sales With Real-Time Big Data Analysis* by Alicia Fiorletta in Retail TouchPoints.[1]

Based on the fashion retailer Bohme, the article analyzes and highlights the benefits of real-time reporting.[2] According to the article, the retailer achieved a 15% increase in sales shortly after implementing a real-time reporting solution. The company's employees had to deliver an unreasonable amount of work in order to handle warehouse stock and maintain operations. The article states that "tracking and analyzing the sheer

---

[1] http://www.retailtouchpoints.com/topics/store-operations/fast-fashion-retailer-boosts-sales-with-real-time-big-data-analysis ⇨1

[2] http://www.risual.com/retail

variety and velocity of data became too cumbersome."[3] Once the company implemented a real-time reporting solution, they achieved a turnaround. Using different visualization types, such as dashboards to report relevant KPIs etc., improved collaboration between the shop floor (production team) and management significantly.

The development of real-time data for sales representatives had a positive impact on the company's revenue.

Best practice emphasizes the importance of real-time reporting for the effective management of companies, as well as for their daily business. Above all, it shows that there is a vast market for real-time data analysis that can be used for different industries and approaches.

Since SAP announced its new SAP HANA technology, these topics have received higher visibility within companies already using SAP, as well as those considering implementing SAP in their IT environment. However, whether or not a company should commit to SAP HANA, particularly an SAP HANA native implementation, is a question that is occupying many decision makers.

SAP Societas Europaea (SE) dedicated itself to this question in a concerted effort with its customers and analyzed their motivations for choosing an SAP HANA native solution. They identified the following key aspects (see Figure 2.1).

Speed is one of the main arguments for an SAP HANA native implementation. This was outlined by Mr. Akihiko Nakamura, the Corporate Senior Vice President of the Nomura Research Institute: *"Now and in the future, speed is the key to adapting to an ever-changing business environment. The speed SAP HANA enables is sudden and significant, and has the potential to transform entire business models."* [4]

In addition, agility, as described by SAP, enables real-time interactions across a company's value chain.

---

[3] CEO BOHME *http://www.retailtouchpoints.com/topics/store-operations/fast-fashion-retailer-boosts-sales-with-real-time-big-data-analysis* ⇨2

[4] SAP Top 10 Reason *http://www.tyconz.com/more/Top10Reasons CustomersChooseSAPHANA.pdf* ⇨3

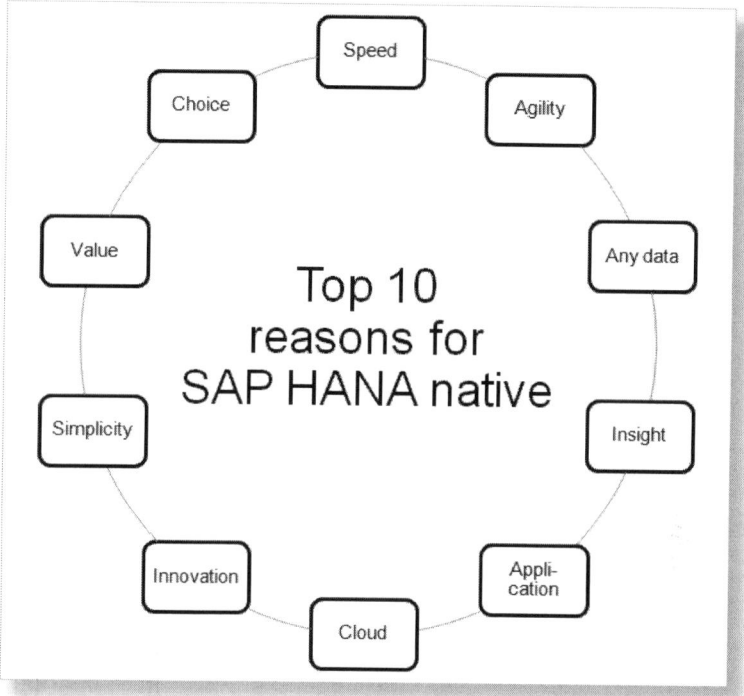

Figure 2.1: Top 10 reasons for SAP HANA native

Another argument for SAP HANA native is the ability to build interfaces for structured and unstructured data. In other words, it enables various heterogeneous data sources to be connected. One of the main benefits of this solution is *insight*, enabling faster response times and consequently, better planning and predictions. Finally, *simplicity* implies the ability to quickly and easily create data flows as long as complex logic is not required. Other aspects such as costs and utilization have to be considered, as well as the return on investment (ROI). SAP clients keep asking questions such as *why should I use SAP HANA native and not some other in-memory solution?"*.

2.2 SAP HANA native project introduction

The customer in our case study is a well-known retail company. Their customer analytics department is tasked with focusing on customer behavior. Their analysis looks at a variety of questions, such as the average purchase price per city, repeat customer profiles, and products that sell well.

Our retail company is the market leader in analyzing data and predicting future shopping behavior and trends. They want to sustain a solid market share growth and therefore, the business department intends to implement a real-time reporting solution. In the CIO's opinion, SAP HANA native provides a suitable approach for their end users in the business department.

The IT department is often in conflict with the business department regarding the required reporting processes. The business department intends to analyze the buying patterns of consumers, as brands often invest in marketing campaigns such as discounts and bonus programs in order to incentivize customers to buy their products. However, the most valuable clients are not the one-time purchasers but those buying the brand more frequently. This is actually the most challenging target. For that reason, the business department wants to improve the quality of their analysis in order to increase their performance.

The IT Director decides to set up a new project to implement SAP HANA native in order to provide the business department with the foundation for real-time reporting.

Therefore, the IT Director introduces a simple process grouped into the three clusters noted in Figure 2.2.

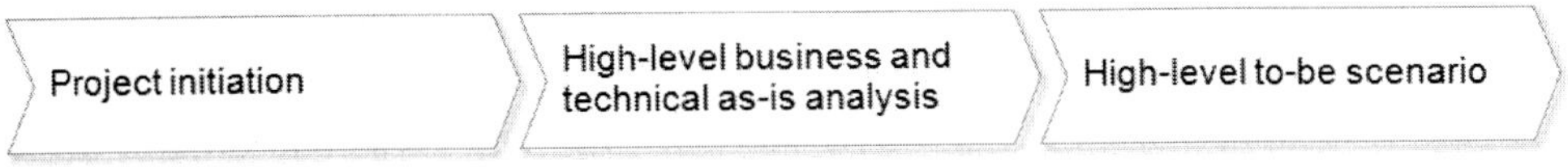

| Project initiation | High-level business and technical as-is analysis | High-level to-be scenario |

Figure 2.2: Project process

The project initiation represents the project's vision and provides an overall picture of the project. Of course, the IT Director has to convince each stakeholder that he or she is a part of the project and supports the overall vision.

Based on an employee survey and data analysis, the as-is situation is evaluated and the requirements are defined. The final future scenario is described in an entity relationship model (ERM) which is considered the foundation for the SAP HANA native solution.

2.2.1 Project initiation

In our case study, the IT Director wants to provide the business department with a best-in-class reporting solution for their daily work. The aim of this project is to replace the existing SAP business warehouse (BW) with the SAP HANA native solution.

Figure 2.3 shows the current system landscape at a high level. We will cover the solution in more detail when we discuss the future scenario.

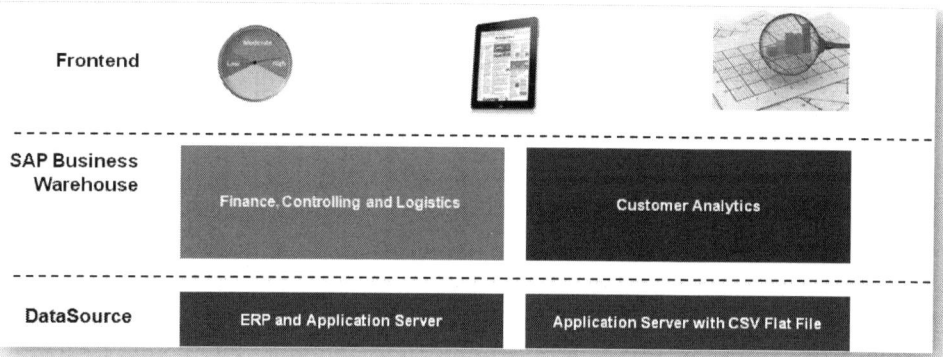

Figure 2.3: High-level SAP BW architecture

The relevant aspect of this project will be the customer analytics data model and the underlying source data. This data model will be reconstructed and adapted to a solution based on SAP HANA native.

The customer analytics will be provided in the SAP HANA Cloud and the new system landscape will be built from scratch. The selected approach should be stable for the next couple of years. To obtain the buy-in of all employees involved, the IT Director demonstrates the strengths of the solution using an SAP HANA native prototype developed within Cloud Services by an IT consulting company. As all stakeholders agree to this solution and the project scope has been defined accordingly, the project can now start.

In the next section, we will take a closer look at the as-is situation. This includes the reporting environment as well as the data itself which serves as the basis for reporting.

2.2.2 As-is analyis

The SAP Business Warehouse shown in Figure 2.3 was implemented following the standard Layered Scalable Architecture (LSA) recommended by SAP. During the implementation, many developers worked on enhancements and made adjustments to the data model. As a result, complexity and inconsistency increased dramatically. The Business Warehouse is characterized by various unused objects, complex transformations, and missing documentation.

To understand the weaknesses of the existing solution, the IT Director conducted an employee opinion survey. The results identified six key issues (see Figure 2.4).

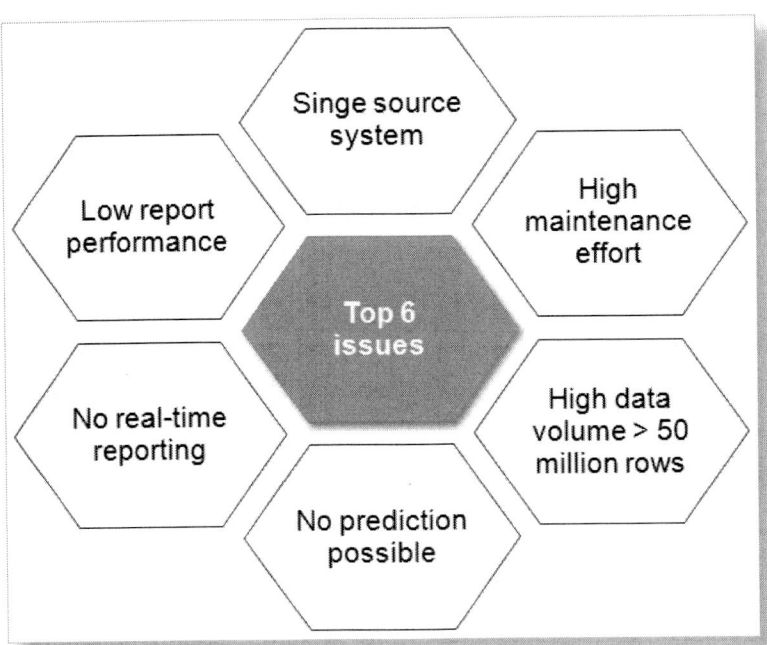

Figure 2.4: Top six issues in the existing IT landscape

Let us take a look at each issue in more detail:

- **Single source system:** The most common interface on the customer side is a flat file interface. Generally, the data is delivered automatically to a NetWeaver Application Server in a comma separated values (.csv) file format via a software solution.

- **High maintenance effort:** The complexity of the data model has increased significantly over the years. Therefore, maintenance involves lengthy processing times, time-consuming testing, and requires in-depth knowledge of the data model and the business. Thus, maintenance costs are very high.
- **High data volume >50 million rows and no real-time reporting:** As a consequence of high data volumes, data loads can only be executed at night (otherwise the system response times are unacceptable). Hence, no real-time reporting is possible and even standard reporting is difficult as response times are mostly above one minute. Furthermore, drilling down to a more detailed level is almost impossible.
- **Low report performance and user acceptance:** Due to the large volume of data being stored in the system and the complex analyses required, reporting performance is poor. The query execution times generated through the reporting tool were checked and compared to the overall execution time to ensure that the issue was not with the reporting tool. Due to these issues, user acceptance of the system is very low and this is reinforced by actual system usage—the number of reports run daily is very low.
- **No prediction possible:** Advanced analytics with predictions for future trends is impossible with the current system setup.

2.2.3 Implications of the tool selection

Based on these observations, the IT department endorses the proposed SAP HANA native solution as the most suitable solution for the customer analytics team. It is clear that the requested points such as real-time reporting, managing high data volumes, and predictive functionality can be fulfilled by the SAP HANA native solution.

2.2.4 Analysis of the source data

The next step is to analyze the different business entities that are currently built in the business warehouse. These entities are used in historical transactions, offers, and current transactions as shown in Figure 2.5.

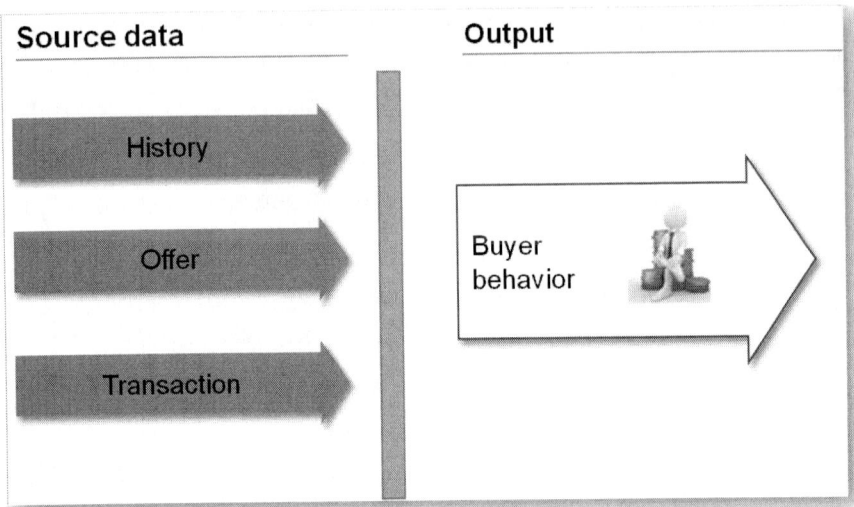

Figure 2.5: Data sources

Each data block reflects one CSV file that is automatically transferred to the system.

The *history data block* consists of a unique customer, a store chain, an offer, and a geographical region. The number of purchases made by a customer is also included. Finally, it contains the date on which the offer was send out/made to the customer.

The *transaction data block* includes the store chain, as well as an explicit transaction, product category, company, brand number, and the purchase date. The following key figures are also included: product size, product unit, purchase amount, and purchase quantity.

The *offer data block* includes offers, category, brand, and the company number. In addition, the values for the key figures and the quantity of offers are included.

The numerated files contain only anonymized transactional data. To put the data into context, master data is added.

Based on the as-is analyses from the business and technical points of view, the following situation ensues:

- ▶ The IT department initiates the SAP HANA native project.
- ▶ The business is convinced and supports the project's targets.
- ▶ The challenges and expectations are clear.
- ▶ The relevant reporting data is identified.

The IT department proceeds to evaluate the future scenario.

2.2.5 Future scenario

Bearing the six main pain points of the existing Business Intelligence (BI) solution in mind, the design of the new backend solution has to ensure easy maintainability, flexibility and simplicity.

As already mentioned, the SAP Business Warehouse will be replaced by the SAP HANA native solution. The significant difference here is that this solution is based in the cloud, which will be explained in detail in the upcoming section (refer to Section 2.3).

Based on the delivered and elaborated data, the IT Director developed an entity relationship model with his team. As a result of the data analysis, the following business entities and their relationships were determined:

- ▶ A customer has an address.
- ▶ A store has an address.
- ▶ A customer makes several purchases.
- ▶ A purchase can include several promotions (e.g., buy one get one free).
- ▶ A store makes several offers.
- ▶ A store sells several products.
- ▶ An offer can contain one or more products.

The ERM model developed serves as a fundamental basis for implementing the data model in SAP HANA Studio (see Figure 2.6).

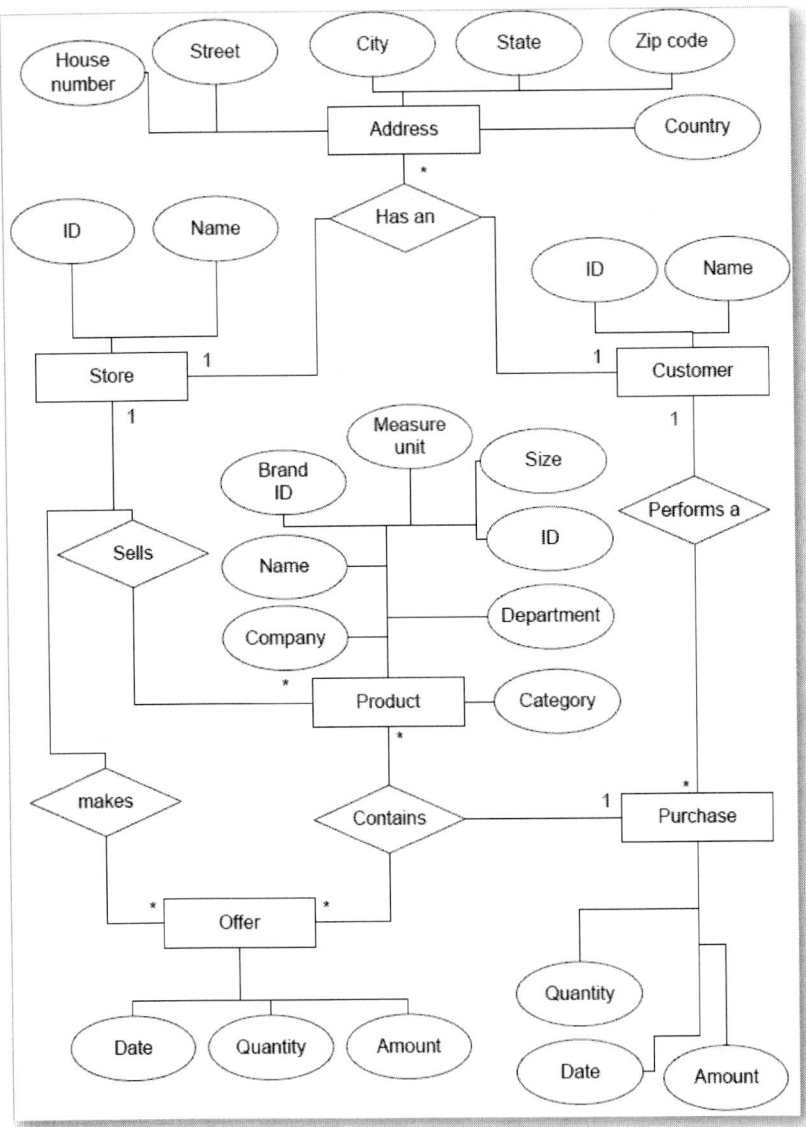

Figure 2.6: Entity relationship model

Using the entity relationship model in Figure 2.6, the IT department fulfills the data requirements identified by the business department. Any enhancements made should keep the model simple and flexible to ensure that the challenges described in the as-is situation do not occur again.

SAP HANA information views are the main method of implementation for realizing the future scenario.

Next, we will walk through the applied technology on a high level to ensure that you have a basis for comparing the tests and implementations with another HANA system.

2.3 System landscape and configuration

Since October 2012[5] it is possible to use SAP HANA based on a cloud provided by Amazon Web Services (AWS). SAP is working with Amazon to establish the cloud appliance library (CAL) which makes it possible to run SAP HANA in the cloud. Amazon is one of the biggest cloud computing providers in the world.[6] They are currently building a computer center in Germany. This demonstrates that Amazon is committed to strengthening their position in the German market. Within the scope of these activities, Amazon has to follow the data security guidelines defined by the German government.

In addition to the points mentioned above, one advantage of this solution for the IT department is that costs would be billed hourly. If the business department needs reporting for certain time periods only, the costs can be reduced by shutting down the SAP HANA instance. Due to the advantages mentioned, the IT department decides to use Amazon Web Services (AWS). They select the following configuration as a starting point for providing the business with a suitable solution (see Table 2.1).

Configuration	Key figures
Cores/threads	8/16
Storage volumes	6
Storage (total)	151 GB
Main memory	68.4 GB

Table 2.1: SAP HANA AWS configuration

---

[5] http://aws.amazon.com/blogs/aws/sap-hana-now-available-for-production-use/ ⇨ 4

[6] Wirtschaftswoche – Der Preis des Terrors; Edition 42, Page 9, 2014

An advantage of this type of solution is that the required hardware can be adjusted at any time. For example, the instance type can be changed to another instance type with more main memory and CPU power with just a few mouse clicks. EBS storage volumes can be added, or the main memory increased easily. The IT department decides that the development should be based on SAP HANA SPS9 and the operation system is a SUSE Linux Enterprise Server 11 SP2.[7]

This configuration was selected because of the expected data volume of approximately 30 GB.

Now that we have explored the future landscape, the next section focuses on the test approach we will use in this book. These tests compare different design patterns in SAP HANA to identify which design elements are most suitable for our purposes and which design decisions have what kind of impact. Design elements can be different information view types, or also simply functionalities within views such as calculated columns. We will evaluate performance impacts and reusability.

2.4 Test approach

The test approach presented in this book provides the basis for testing design elements in an SAP HANA native implementation. Since the same goal can be achieved using different designs, the test strategy must ensure that these designs are evaluated in the same way.

To ensure a consistent level of quality and comparability, all test scenarios are structured in the same way and follow a similar process. We will walk you through this process in the following section step by step.

The process is illustrated in Figure 2.7.

Each test will be performed based on the three steps noted in Figure 2.7. First, the scenario and procedure are prepared (1). Next, the tests are executed and the results are documented (2). Last, the test is completed by gathering and comparing the results (3).

---

[7] *https://aws.amazon.com/marketplace/pp/B009KA3CRY/ref= mkt_ste_sap_micro_SAPHana1* ⇨ 5

CASE STUDY AND HARDWARE SETUP

1. Scenario and procedure	2. Execution and result	3. Conclusion
• Title and number • Test categorization • Scenario description • Outlook	• Test execution • Gathering results	• Result recap • Data model outlook

Figure 2.7: Testing process

To prepare the test scenario (1), key metadata including title, numbering, and categorization is provided.

> **Test scenario structure**
>
>  **Structure:**
> Chapter number and test scenario title
> Test scenario number
> **Example:**
> 4.1.2 Calculated columns in attribute views
> Test scenario 4A.2

In addition, we record the test category, the scenario description, and the expected result in the scenario overview. We also include the architectural elements used to perform the test, e. g., the functionality *calculated columns* in an attribute view (ATV).

Table 2.2 shows a sample test scenario for calculated columns.

Test focus:	Calculated columns
Scenario description:	Analysis of the impact of calculated columns on the performance of attribute views
Expected result:	1. An overview of the performance impact of calculated columns by data type 2. An overview of the impact of several calculated columns on the attribute view performance, also combining data types in correlation to the findings of (1).
Architectural elements:	Calculated columns in attribute views

Table 2.2: Test scenario example

29

Subsequently, we provide a high level overview of the procedure and detail the individual process steps (see Table 2.3).

Step	Testing detail
1	Use the same attribute view several times to create different calculated columns with different formats to ensure that the performance measurement is performed on the same dataset.
2	Combine the calculated columns in one attribute view and measure the outcome.

Table 2.3: Test scenario procedure

The test is executed step by step based on this test scenario. The results are then depicted in a separate table. After the test execution, we summarize the outcome and provide recommendations for modeling your own performance-optimized information view.

Figure 2.8 provides an overview of the test areas in each chapter. The test areas are clustered into data model creation and the performance optimization of information views. The information view area is grouped into attribute, analytical, and calculation views. These areas are then summarized and compared in the last section.

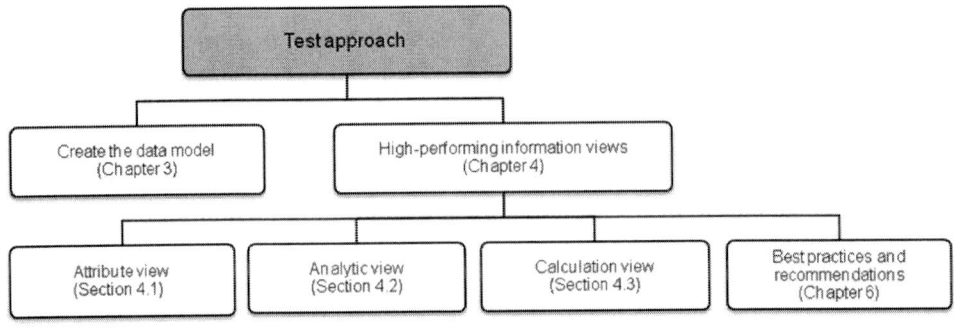

Figure 2.8: Test approach

2.4.1 Create the data model

The test area **Create the data model** focuses on recommendations for creating tables in SAP HANA native. Due to the fact that the data model is implemented from scratch, we also have to clarify which data storage approach should be used for faster reporting. For this reason, we will compare normalization and the star schema. This test area also looks at the join performance of primary keys (PK) and foreign keys (FK), different data types, and unique values with regard to saving space. Accordingly, we will also do a first test on the performance of data loading. In addition, we will compare virtualization and persistency.

2.4.2 Optimizing information view performance

Once the data model is successfully implemented, we will continue with tests on information views. In doing so, we will evaluate the implementation of different design elements, such as currency conversion, variables, and input parameters. This will serve as a type of catalog for your future SAP HANA native project as we provide recommendations and design principles for the data modeling based on the test results (see Figure 2.9).

The **attribute view** considers aspects such as the join performance, selections, and filters. Furthermore, different data types and their conversion are evaluated here. The testing around **analytic views** (ANV) covers topics such as the data foundation and investigates the logical joins, including currency conversion, calculation before aggregation, and the different data types. With regard to the data foundation, we analyze the join options.

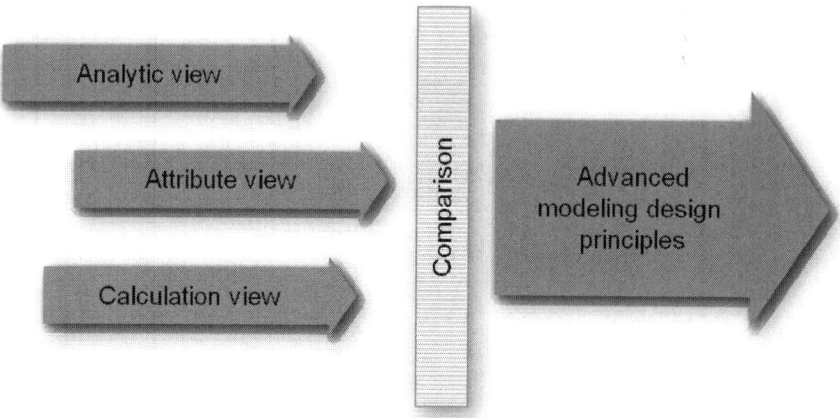

Figure 2.9: View comparison

Next, in the **calculation view** test, we cover different nodes, such as projection and aggregation nodes. In addition, we focus on calculated columns, metrics, currency and unit conversion, as well as filtering. To conclude the test scenarios, we analyze the different join variants, scripted calculation views, and parallelization in the calculation view design.

The chapter closes with a summary of the results.

2.5 Summary and conclusion

This chapter walked you through the case study and explained the anticipated bottlenecks for the future solution. The ERM developed represents the foundation for the data model implementation within SAP HANA Studio later on.

We also presented the system landscape and explained the test approach.

The next chapter covers the implementation of the data model in detail.

3 Create the data model

This chapter covers key concepts for defining an SAP HANA data model. The most frequently asked questions we hear have to do with data virtualization and persistency. In this chapter we elaborate on these topics and take a closer look at the general strengths and weaknesses of both, as well as approaches for creating persistency and the limitations of virtualizations. To create the data model for our case study, we perform the first test scenarios to illustrate the setup of our data model.

3.1 Persistency versus virtualization

SAP HANA supports on one hand the physical storage and provision of data in tables, and on the other hand, the preparation and runtime access of data via information views (e.g., analytic view, calculation view). A critical consideration is whether to store data physically (*persistency*) or use the tremendous in-memory power of SAP HANA for runtime calculations (*virtualization*). This question arises whenever you set up a new data model or change an existing one. There are many voices calling for a completely virtual data modeling approach when it comes to reporting. The most common ideas are either to build virtual layers directly on the transactional systems, or create one common replicated data layer as the foundation for what will probably become a virtual enterprise data warehouse. We are convinced that a clever balance between data virtualization and persistency will provide you with the best cost benefit, or cost performance ratio, and we will prove this in the course of this book.

To start the discussion around data persistency and virtualization, we have summarized some of the key arguments in Table 3.1.

	Persistency	**Virtualization**
Strengths	▶ Storage of historical data ▶ Provision of historical truth ▶ Maintenance of time-dependent data ▶ Storage of intermediate results of complex data transformations ▶ Reconciliation of data/audit trail	▶ Performance support for (near) real-time queries ▶ Sourcing the single version of truth ▶ Data consistency ▶ Ease of data recovery ▶ Sizing requirements
Weaknesses	▶ Limited support of real-time processing ▶ Costs of data storage ▶ Redundancy of data	▶ Creation and maintenance of complex data transformations ▶ Data model management ▶ Risk of failure

Table 3.1: Strengths and weaknesses of virtualization versus persistency

3.1.1 Strengths of persistency

This section covers the strengths and benefits of physical data storage per layer.

Storage of historical data

One of the fundamental drivers for persisting data comes from the demand for historical data to be available. Transactional systems do not typically provide the entire history of data that may be necessary for reporting or analysis requirements. There is generally no option available to regenerate historical data on the fly. Thus, you must identify a physical location for keeping the requested raw data history available. This can also be a kind of persistent corporate memory as suggested in the SAP *Layered Scalable Architecture LSA++* approach.

> **Resources for Layered Scalable Architecture LSA++**
>
> Further details on the Layered Scalable Architecture approach in SAP HANA databases (LSA++) are available at
>
> *http://help.sap.com/saphelp_nw74/helpdata/en/22/ad6fad9 6b547c199adb588107e6412/content.htm?frameset=/en/76/0a0f65cca14 e369fa8df4b77367b4b/frameset.htm&current_toc=/en/ad/6b023b6069d2 2ee10000000a11402f/plain.htm&node_id=12&show_children=false* ⇨6

Provision of historical truth

Building on the previous section, the requirements regarding the provision of historical truth are also possible drivers for storing data physically in their original structures. Essentially, there are three types of requirements for reporting historical data.

1. *Show historical data using (master data) structures valid today.* This approach uses the (physical) representation of the historical raw data and applies the (master data) structures valid at the time of the query (e.g., an organizational hierarchy). In this approach, the structural information is applied to the (physically) stored raw data during runtime. Therefore, no additional physical storage of transactional data is normally required.

2. *Show historical data using (master data) structures valid on the posting date (historical truth).* For this requirement, the historical transactional data is often directly combined and stored together with the structural information valid at a specific point in time (e.g., at the time of posting). Depending on the complexity and type of structural changes, it is also best practice in a HANA-based environment to store the historical structural information physically as part of the transactional data. The main reasons for this approach are maintainability of the data model, reproducibility, and durability of the data. SAP HANA supports this approach with the *history table* concept, which also covers time-dependency of data.

3. *The user decides on a point of time/version of historical data.* This variant is a combination of the second approach with a user-defined parameter. The user chooses a value or key date for which the requested data will be shown.

Maintenance of time-dependent data

When it comes to the time dependency of data, one of SAP HANA's out-of-the-box solutions is history tables. Generating timestamps virtually or on the fly is not something that can be maintained in large analytical scenarios. History tables automatically add timestamps to each data record (VALIDFROM and VALIDTO). Write operations always insert a new version of a record in the table (instead of overwriting existing records). Update and deletion operations also result in new versions with updated timestamps of the existing records. The original records are invalidated in parallel.

Storage of intermediate results of complex data transformations

One of the most crucial points in data modeling is how to best generate and approach the results of complex data transformations. What is a complex transformation? Unfortunately, there isn't an obvious answer to this question (we also don't have an easy answer). However, there are good reasons from numerous SAP HANA implementations for storing the results of complex data transformations physically. SAP HANA is capable of performing every transformation requirement at the point of query execution/data access (at least when you scale your hardware accordingly). We recommend storing (intermediate) results of complex transformations physically, opposing the requirement of a short query response time at one extreme and covering the complexity of necessary transformations, calculations, or enhancements of data at the other.

This applies especially when very short query response times are expected with comprehensive data transformation logics in parallel. However, when it comes to (near) real-time reporting needs, this approach does not fit; the costs over time for storing the intermediate results are inappropriate and too high.

> **SAP HANA Enterprise Information Management (EIM)**
>
> An interesting approach in this context is provided by SAP HANA Enterprise Information Management (EIM). Available since SPS 9, this option provides valuable features for enhancing, cleaning, and transforming data in order to make it more accurate and useful. Further information and details of current limitations are available at: *http://help.sap.com/hana_options_eim*.

Reconciling the data/audit trail

For quality assurance purposes, data for reporting or analysis demands is regularly compared to the original data (e. g., in a transactional source system). In particular, SAP HANA systems subject to external audits require that data is easily reconcilable and traceable. To achieve reliable, transparent, and sustainable data reconciliation, the physical persistence of data best supports traceability. This is also valid for SAP HANA-based scenarios. Virtual approaches generally do not provide sufficient support for versioning of their definitions because previous data states cannot be restored exactly, and consequently, cannot be audited.

3.1.2 Virtualization strengths

As SAP continuously showcases the capabilities and power of SAP HANA, the vision of processing a huge quantity of data on the fly is on everyone's mind. This section highlights how virtualization can empower your data model in this regard.

Performance—support of (near) real-time queries

SAP HANA enables high-performance operations on inconceivably huge volumes of data. Its column-based approach best supports read operations on large data volumes. That is why column-based tables are used

37

for reporting and analysis requirements. The downside of this approach is the reduced speed of insert and update operations. Thus it is best practice, especially for the realization of (near) real-time reporting scenarios, to implement all necessary data transformations and calculations only with SAP HANA's virtual concept of information views. The costs of any physical write or update operation (e. g., to store the result of a complex data transformation) might lead to a failure of the expected query response time. In any case, the demand for (near) real-time response time has always been referenced with the necessary complexity of data transformation. The more complex the transformation logic for preparing the data for the expected outcome, the less likely that (near) real-time reporting will be achievable (even in a completely virtual scenario). A (near) real-time scenario can nevertheless combine a physical real-time-capable data replication (e. g., by using *SAP Landscape Transformation Server (SLT), Sybase Replication Server (SRS),* or *SAP HANA EIM*) with data transformations and calculations implemented in information views on top of the replicated data layer.

Sourcing the single version of truth

Searching for the single version of truth is an ongoing challenge in today's information landscape. Each and every time data is copied, transferred, or transformed there is a potential risk of failure. Failures can be of a technical nature (e. g., outage of a source system), or can occur on the application level (e. g., faulty transformation rule, missing look-up information). It takes significant effort to identify the root causes of data mismatches and to (re-)establish the desired single version of truth. The fewer physical copies and layers used to prepare the data for its intended use, the fewer sources of error that exist. Virtualization, especially when paired with the in-memory capabilities of SAP HANA, can strongly support achieving a single version of the truth. SAP HANA can combine various data operations within a single information view and can execute multiple transformations in a sequence to provide data in the requested output format. It is no longer necessary to design step-by-step transformations with several physically stored intermediate results in between. Thus, virtualization in in-memory environments leads to fewer layers in the data model and to less physical storage and duplication of data. Using data replication engines such as SLT or EIM is a good complement to virtual concepts for data transformation. The one-to-one replication of source data into a reporting environment builds a solid and (in terms of transaction security) valid foundation for setting up virtual layers on top acting as a central entry point to access the single version of truth.

Data consistency

Traditional, relational databases provide transaction security according to the *ACID principle* (atomicity, consistency, isolation, and durability). In reporting environments, many sources (e. g., database tables) are combined to display the complete and correct result of a reporting request. Therefore, the data of involved sources is normally physically copied, transferred, and transformed accordingly. For each source, these data operation processes must successfully complete (database commitment for each table) before any database query can be executed. As we have learned, virtualization in in-memory environments helps to reduce the number of (physical) layers in a data model and, therefore, reduces the number of physical database operations. Furthermore, virtualization enables direct access to source tables. In this scenario, the correctness of the data across the entire solution is based on the transactional consistency of the source system., The source system is the foundation for all data transformations (e. g., implemented in information views) to generate the expected result. From a technical perspective, *Smart Data Access (SDA)* is a promising approach for directly accessing source system data with a remote database connection (no physical copy of data in the target environment). The need to ensure overall transactional security is thereby pushed down to the source level.

Ease of data recovery

A key aspect of virtualization is the simplification of the data model, especially due to the reduced number of layers with physical data storage. Thus, in case of a system outage or any kind of data failure, the recovery process to restore the latest valid status of data is less costly as data is ideally only stored physically once. Therefore, as soon as the physical data layer is rebuilt, the virtual concepts definition can easily be recreated. In this way, the consolidated view of the (reporting) data is available directly again.

Sizing requirements

The added value of virtualization with regard to the sizing of an SAP HANA instance is debatable. The fewer the physical layers a data model has and the lower the volumes of data that have to be physically stored, the lower the (RAM) sizing figures of the corresponding SAP HANA solution. In this context, virtualization saves money. However, the use of virtualization should not be exaggerated on this account (as will be further emphasized in the course of this book). Moreover, to enable the calculation of the results of virtual concepts such as information views or remote access to data via SDA, additional memory space has to be provided and considered in the sizing exercise. Overall, the lower the volume of data stored physically (and in turn, the greater the volume modeled using virtual concepts), the smaller your SAP HANA machine will need to be.

3.1.3 Weaknesses of persistency

As well as providing strengths and opportunities, data persistency also has some weaknesses that have to be considered. Now let us look at the main aspects of persistency in SAP HANA.

Limited support of real-time processing

Storing data physically as a result of data transformation processes is reminiscent of classical ETL batch processing (*extraction, transformation, and loading – ETL*). Nowadays, various vendors expend a lot of effort in the pursuit of the end of batch processing. But that day has not yet fully arrived. When it comes to complex data transformation requirements, physically storing transformation results and, therefore, a batch-like data processing approach, is still valid. In any case, we have listed this characteristic as a weakness of persistency as the market trend is moving increasingly in the direction of real-time reporting. Our understanding is that batch-like processing of data will still be justifiable. A downside in SAP HANA environments is how to actually realize, maintain, and monitor the processing steps ending in physical storage of the transformation results. At this point in time, there is no real best practice available. Tools such as SAP Data Services and SAP HANA EIM can support this approach.

Costs of data storage

The volume of data (persistently stored), along with other aspects, such as CPU power or RAM, builds the basis for sizing an SAP HANA instance. The greater the volume of data maintained on a physical level, the higher the sizing figures will be. The sizing impacts on one hand the cost of licenses, and on the other hand, the scaling and price of the required hardware. Identifying the correct SAP HANA hardware sizing is crucial to ensuring a solid and high-performing environment. SAP's Quick Sizer tool gives a good indication of the expected sizing. Based on the results, the hardware costs can be determined together with certified hardware vendors. Aside from SAP Quick Sizer, SAP provides additional tools for calculating the expected SAP HANA size (e.g., database scripts and ABAP reports). Depending on the intended use of the SAP HANA instance, we recommend that you leverage these specific tools for the sizing exercise.

> **SAP HANA sizing resources**
>
> For sizing questions see SAP Notes 1514966, 1736976, 1872170, and 1637145.

The costs of data storage are not only linked to license and hardware prices, but also to the cost of data maintenance. Each physical data layer must be maintained and manual operations may be needed to adjust or delete data before the correct data can be reloaded in the case of failures. Thus, the effort for daily operations (to keep the system running) and corresponding costs for internal man-days or consultancy support has to be taken into account according to the number of physical data representations in SAP HANA. A highly virtualized approach requires additional RAM and CPU.

Redundancy of data

Preparing data for specific purposes such as reporting may require the physical storage of the results of complex data transformations. This leads to a type of data redundancy in your SAP HANA environment. As we discussed, virtualization is the extreme opposite to avoiding data redundancy. The correct trade-off between persistent storage of data and utilization of virtual concepts is one of the key challenges in designing SAP HANA data models. We included redundancy of data in this section on the weaknesses of persistency because it leads to additional effort in maintaining your data in daily operations and presents a potential risk of data inconsistency. In our opinion, these two arguments are crucial in making a decision on how to define a design model.

3.1.4 Virtualization weaknesses

This section highlights the shortcomings of virtualization. Here we describe the key arguments to consider when designing an SAP HANA data model.

Creation and maintenance of complex data transformations

Based on our project experience to date, we continue to see a need for building complex transformation logics to address business or external needs for reporting or data representation purposes. SAP HANA virtual concepts, namely the information views, can be designed either graphically or with *SQLScript*. Graphical views are limited in their out-of-the-box functionalities. Additional custom programming (e.g., capsulated in procedures or scripted views) can be added to realize any kind of transformation or calculation. However, we consider the requirement of implementing complex data transformations as a weakness of virtualization, especially due to the significant amount of coding needed to be controlled, versioned, and maintained. Furthermore, debugging a transformation step by step or restarting a data transfer for a specific data record is not supported, or only partially supported. Finally, to ensure that the implemented transformation functions are transparent, a very well-structured and disciplined method of programming (especially when working in parallel or distributed teams) is essential.

Data model management

The main aspect of managing a virtual data model consisting only of virtual concepts is transparency. A *virtual data model* means that the data model is realized using virtual concepts such as information views without physical storage of results in the final stages. We see a big challenge (especially in growing SAP HANA implementations) in maintaining a clear overview of which transformation logic is located in which information view, which dependencies exist between the information views, and which components are reused in the data model. There are certain restrictions to reusing artifacts in virtual SAP HANA data models (e.g., information views can be reused easily, but components of an information view are not automatically ready for reuse). Thus, keeping the virtual data model consistent and understanding the correlation between its building blocks is a key success factor for utilizing virtual concepts.

Risk of failure

A data model built on virtual concepts lacks the ability to handle failures in the execution of the information view in an appropriate way. For instance, in the case of a data quality issue (e. g., values do not match the expected data type), the entire view execution fails and the reporting application breaks down. Therefore, any agreed SLA on real-time reporting will be missed. Up until now, there has not been an option for sorting valid and invalid data within an information view (e. g., similar to ETL tools, so that at least suitable data is propagated to the end user). Therefore, any kind of error handling has to be custom-programmed in a virtual environment.

3.2 Modeling approaches

The following sections provide principles for using data persistency and virtualization effectively. In addition to the fundamental aspects of different implementation approaches, we also cover known limitations.

3.2.1 Using data virtualization

In general, virtualization is about simplifying an application landscape. This chapter illustrates virtualization concepts in SAP HANA: we distinguish between accessing remote data (data that is physically stored outside of the SAP HANA database and accessed on demand) and data processing and transformation within the SAP HANA database using information views.

Virtual access to remote data

SAP introduced *Smart Data Access (SDA)* in SAP HANA SPS 06. SDA is a feature that provides remote read access to relational and non-relational data sources. Within the SAP HANA Studio environment, the tool creates an additional ODBC connection to a remote data source such as Oracle, DB2, Microsoft SQL Server, or Hadoop. The objects of the remote database (e. g., tables and views) are accessed directly from SAP HANA (Studio). The remote data is processed in SAP HANA, just like data from local SAP HANA objects. Thus, the data can be combined with local data, transformed, and distributed to any downstream application via information views. A query running on the SAP HANA database can easily include data from remote sources in real time.

Using SDA means that data ownership remains with the remote database because no data is physically copied (stored) to the SAP HANA database. Thus, there is no consumption of physical storage on the SAP HANA side.

> **Smart Data Access**
>
> Smart Data Access (SDA) works as a cache for remote data on the SAP HANA side. Therefore, when sizing your SAP HANA environment, the expected volume of data accessed via SDA has to be considered in your memory consumption.

SDA is not yet a very mature or common technology, but it has already proven its potential in numerous research labs and proofs of concept. SDA is a good choice for simplifying your application landscape, especially for operational reporting. It makes other (SAP HANA) databases or data warehouses transparent to SAP HANA. Thus, it supports the consolidation of your data warehouse landscape with the goal of a single version of truth. SDA also addresses security concepts and enables unified security, as security roles are maintained only once in SAP HANA. For this purpose, SAP HANA needs only one technical user to connect to the remote database. Thus, there is no need to create an account for each and every (reporting) user on the remote database.

In addition, you should take into account that SDA also works in parallel with replication mechanisms such as SLT and SRS (see Section 3.2.2). By establishing ETL processes based on SDA tables, SDA provides for a non-disruptive evolution from virtual tables to persistent data structures. As you can see, using SDA provides a wide variety of scenarios for enriching your SAP HANA landscape with virtual concepts.

Data processing with virtual concepts

SAP HANA provides three types of information models for accessing, processing, and providing data from tables and views. All three types of information models can be reused in the SAP HANA environment.

1. *Attribute views* are used to represent master data. They access physical tables with master data or text information which can be joined in the definition of an attribute view. There are several parameters which have to be defined in order to create an attribute view (e.g., type of attribute view (standard, time, derived), type of table join (inner join, left/right outer, referential, text)). Attribute views are an essential building block in designing analytic views.

2. *Analytic views* represent transactional data in a multidimensional view. They combine fact table data with dimensional information from attribute views (star schema approach). Analytic views consist of at least one key figure (measure) and the descriptive qualitative characteristics (attributes). The classification of a field as a key figure or characteristic is done during build time. In the same way as for attribute views, you can specify parameters such as join type and cardinality. Analytic views are optimized for mass data processing and aggregation.

> **Attribute views for master data**
>
> We strongly recommend using attribute views to define the master data/dimension views. On one hand, the definition of an attribute view can be easily reused in an SAP HANA data model and on the other hand, attribute views create a layer of abstraction from the physical tables.

3. *Calculation views* provide the most powerful approach for preparing and calculating data in an SAP HANA data model. In a calculation view, you can combine data directly from (SAP HANA) tables, attribute views, analytic views, or even other calculation views. You can define a calculation view in SAP HANA Studio using the graphical modeling perspective or by writing an SQLScript statement using either Calculation Engine (CE) functions or Standard SQL. We recommend the graphical approach.

45

> **Development and governance rules**
>
> The default features for transforming and processing data in the graphical design for calculation views are limited and the CE function vocabulary is not yet very sophisticated. In order to build complex transformations, you have to create custom scripts or procedures. Strict development and governance rules must be considered with regard to keeping transparency, performance, and maintainability of the defined information models at a high level. We will elaborate on key aspects of these rules during the course of this book.

Despite the execution optimization of SAP HANA views, SAP HANA is not automatically always fast or able to cope with any kind of application scenario. Complex transformation scenarios in the calculation (e.g., with numerous time-dependent structures) may require storage of intermediate results as well as a guarantee of a high level of performance reporting for the end user.

All types of information views can be built on top of remote tables which are accessed via SDA. However, please consider that SDA acts like a cache and requires memory space from your SAP HANA instance. Furthermore, each transformation step performed via an information view is calculated in-memory and will eat up your available SAP HANA memory. More details about the best approaches for creating SAP HANA models will be explained in combination with concrete recommendations in the subsequent chapters.

3.2.2 Use of data persistency

To store data persistently in SAP HANA, we need to concentrate on three general ways of generating physical data representations:

1. Data replication
2. Data transformation (ETL)
3. Storing the results of an information view

Let us take a closer look at the three types.

Data replication

Data replication is the process of synchronizing and therefore copying data between various locations. Replication is executed on a frequent or scheduled basis right up to (near) real-time updates. It is usually capable of full and delta updates. Although some replication tools offer options for executing some light-weight transformations during the actual replication (e.g., data format adjustments, concatenation of fields), we strongly recommend that you use replication only for one-to-one data transfers. Two key reasons are:

- ▶ Reconciliation of data: in the case of a data mismatch between the source system and a query executed on the target system, the corresponding root cause analysis and troubleshooting is simplified because no data manipulation is done during the replication step. Thus, the source export layer data and the target import layer must be identical and the error search has to take place in only one specific location: the source system. The actual transformation of data should take place in dedicated, subsequent processing steps.

- ▶ Restart of replication: the reason for relaunching a failed replication process (e.g., broken network connectivity) is easier to identify if data is not manipulated/transformed during the replication process. The last correct updated record in the target looks exactly the same as in the source. In addition, this helps to clean up the data target before you restart the replication.

In the SAP HANA environment, replication is currently best supported by *SAP Landscape Transformation (SLT)* and *Sybase Replication Server (SRS)*. Both tools provide (near) real-time capabilities for data replication.

- ▶ The SAP Landscape Transformation Server (SLT) is the default (and currently most widely used) replication engine for SAP HANA. It allows trigger-based, near real-time replication from SAP and non-SAP sources such as Oracle, DB2, or Microsoft SQL Server into SAP HANA. For SAP sources, the read modules reside directly in the source system, leveraging database triggers based on the *change data capture (CDC)* concept. The data is replicated to the SLT server (RFC connection) and sequenced to the SAP HANA system (database connection). For a non-SAP scenario, the read module is located in the SLT system only and receives data changes via DB connection from the source logging tables. SLT can be managed directly from SAP HANA Studio.

SLT replication setup

Details about the technical SLT setup are provided in the document *Real-Time Data Replication with SAP Landscape Transformation Replication Server*, which can be found at http://www.saphana.com/docs/DOC-4713.

SLT real-time replication

SLT provides (near) real-time replication of data by default. Our practical experiences (on version 2.0 SP 8) show that a very short update cycle (e. g., one second) can create such a workload on the source system that on one hand the source system can no longer be used for its intended purpose, and on the other hand, the source system cannot provide the changed data (delta) within the one second update cycle. Thus, the source system cannot provide the data within the configured timeframe and is never able to deliver the defined threshold. Hence, update cycles of between ten seconds and one minute are normally selected in productive environments.

SLT transactional consistency

With regard to the replication of data from non-SAP sources, there is currently (Version 2.0 SP 8) no guarantee of transactional integrity/consistency. This means that there may be data inconsistencies, e. g., due to missing records in the target system. SAP has announced that they plan to provide transactional consistency in upcoming SLT releases.

- ▶ Sybase Replication Server (SRS) uses a log-based replication mechanism and provides real-time data replication. It supports common databases such as Oracle, DB2, Sybase ASE, and Microsoft SQL Server as the replication source. SRS requires a *replication agent* in the source database which natively looks for changes in the requested database tables. It uses the native log API provided by the database itself. In this regard, this replication approach is very efficient and does not share the weaknesses noted for SLT (e.g., lower latency time and less overhead than the SLT trigger-based approach). In fact, transactional consistency is guaranteed for any database supported. SRS copies the data to the SAP HANA database using the *Express Connector for SAP HANA (ECH)*. ECH is a native HANA ODBC connector for SRS and links directly to the SAP HANA ODBC driver (libodbcHDB). Thus, no intermediate gateway (which may have an impact on performance) is required. Our practical experience emphasizes the high level of reliability and maturity of SRS.

> **Sybase Replication Server setup**
>
> Details about the features, configuration, and setup of Sybase Replication Server are provided in *Replicating transactional data to SAP HANA using Sybase Replication Server*, which can be found at http://help.sap.com/replication-server.

Data transformation (ETL)

The classical process of data transformation, especially in the context of data warehousing, comprises the following three steps: *data extraction, transformation, and loading (ETL)*. There are many tools available that provide a rich set of components to support any kind of (complex) data transformation resulting in physical storage of the transformation result into a database. The same concept is applicable for SAP HANA. The ETL tool of choice in an SAP HANA landscape is *SAP Data Services*, which provides the deepest integration with SAP HANA. Other ETL tools such as Informatica also offer good interaction with SAP HANA. Using SAP Data Services, you have the option to transfer and transform data from heterogeneous sources (SAP and non-SAP) into SAP HANA. This tool can also leverage the full power of SAP HANA by pushing down SQL statements or calculations directly to the database. For SAP HANA, the data transformation is changed and optimized for the ELT sequence (extraction, load, transformation). Thus, data is first transferred to SAP HANA and then transformed in-memory using internally created calculation views or database procedures.

We recommend SAP Data Services as the best data provisioning option for ELT/ETL batch processing. It provides sophisticated concepts for data transformation, data validation, and data cleansing. Moreover, its graphical user interface, customization options, and transformation step debugging are helpful features during development and runtime activities.

SAP Data Services setup

The latest information about SAP Data Services can be found at *http://help.sap.com/bods*. For specific information on SAP HANA support of SAP Data Services, see also:

http://wiki.scn.sap.com/wiki/display/EIM/SAP+Data+Services+Support+of+HANA.

SAP HANA for SAP Data Services

Assign an SAP HANA instance as a temporary workspace to your SAP Data Services server. This allows you to also benefit from the high-performance capabilities of SAP HANA during the actual data transformation processes.

SAP Data Services real time

Although there are real-time features available in SAP Data Services, they are currently (Version 4.2 SP05) not designed for handling large volumes of data. SAP has announced close interaction with Sybase Replication Server and SAP Landscape Transformation for specific (real-time) scenarios in upcoming releases.

As well as third party ETL tools, the classic *SAP Business Warehouse (SAP BW)* can also act as a data transformation tool for SAP HANA. With release SAP BW 7.4, the known transformation object can be compiled as a database procedure and executed in SAP HANA. Furthermore, the transformation results generated (usually stored in DataStore objects (DSO)) can easily be accessed in SAP HANA, either by going directly to the corresponding active table of the DSO or by using the (automatically) generated analytic view in DSO. (Note: it may be necessary to consider the type of change log with the first option, e.g., calculated change log versus persistent change log. Based on our practical experiences we recommend the persistent change log.) For the sake of completeness, the reverse is also possible—publishing data from SAP HANA to SAP BW (e.g., via analytical index and transient provider).

Storing the results of an information view

Data persistency can also be created by storing the results of an SAP HANA information view physically. This approach combines the features of transforming and processing data with SAP HANA-owned concepts with the advantages of physical data storage.

To achieve this storage function, execute an SQL statement inserting the result of an information view into a table. The following statement is an example:

```
INSERT INTO <table>
SELECT [Columns] FROM <information_view>
GROUP BY [Columns];
```

This statement can, for instance, be part of an SAP HANA procedure for controlling data processing steps.

> **Development and governance rules**
>
> If you have many parallel or sequential data transformation steps across numerous information views, using scripted processes still requires strong development, governance, and documentation rules to maintain the transparency of the entire application.

Another option, and in our opinion a more convenient one, is to use an ETL tool to trigger the SAP HANA view execution to further process or store the result in a table. SAP BW can also consume and store the results of SAP HANA information views.

3.2.3 Comparison of data virtualization and data persistency

The best approach for your scenario depends on how you rank and rate multiple criteria. Table 3.2 provides a guide for determining the best approach and way forward for your specific use case.

	Data virtualization	Data persistency
Complexity of data transformation logic	Only lightweight transformation logic should be implemented.	Complex transformation logic stores dedicated result sets persistently.
Real-time data provisioning requirement	Real-time needs should refer to virtual concepts as much as possible.	Storing data persistently will not support genuine real-time demands.
Consumption of (in-memory) space	The utilization of virtual concepts occupies memory only for calculating the results and the storage of intermediate results.	Physically stored data (which is loaded into memory) steadily reduces memory space. Calculations on this data access additional memory.
Data ownership	In a purely virtual reporting environment, data ownership clearly remains with the source system as no physical copy of the data is stored elsewhere.	The typical question of who is the owner of the data arises and has to be clarified, as data is copied and transformed from its origin.
Application maintainability	Extensive use of virtual concepts with a high number of dependencies and scripted calculation logics can easily lead to a lack of transparency and, therefore, to high maintenance costs. Clear governance rules have to be established.	A useful modeling concept of only a few physical layers can help to structure and maintain a clear picture of the overall data model. Governance rules are still mandatory.
Audit trail	Auditing is hardly possible.	Data persistency provides a good audit trail foundation.

Table 3.2: Data virtualization and persistency comparison

3.3 Engine utilization

SAP HANA information models can be created on top of database tables (either on local SAP HANA tables or remote tables leveraging SDA). The SAP HANA information models are used to implement business logic for processing and preparing the data for any kind of reporting or analysis scenario. Thus, they represent the core of SAP HANA application development.

The SAP HANA information models can be accessed and consumed in various ways:

- ▶ HTML- or Javascript-based applications (e. g., UI5-based forms)
- ▶ SAP HANA native applications (e. g., custom-built applications in the SAP HANA development perspective)
- ▶ SAP standard reporting tools (e. g., Analysis for Office)
- ▶ Third party tools (e. g., Microsoft Excel, MicroStrategy)

Information views are used to leverage the capabilities of SAP HANA. They are dependent on the tool and type of connection used to access an SAP HANA system and you should consider that the range of supported SAP HANA functions may vary. Nevertheless, the way information views are processed in SAP HANA is independent of the tool selected.

We already know that there are three types of information views. By default, each view is executed in a specific type of SAP HANA in-memory engine to achieve the best possible performance. Figure 3.1 provides a high-level overview of important architectural components of the SAP HANA index server.

The primary SAP HANA database management component is called the *index server* and it contains the persistency layer and the engines for processing the data. Each request to the SAP HANA database is redirected to the corresponding engines for calculation. The *optimizer and plan generator* orchestrates the execution of a query. SQL, SQLScript, MDX, or requests via the BICS interface are common ways of interacting with SAP HANA. The *OLAP engine* and the *calculation engine* perform their operations directly in the database. The OLAP engine is optimized to aggregate mass data based on a star schema, whereas the calculation engine offers a rich set of special operators for more complex scenarios (e. g., currency conversions, predefined business logic, large hierarchies). There are also additional engines such as the graph engine (for geospatial data), text engine (for text processing), and planning engine (for planning functions). The latter engines mentioned are not in scope for this book.

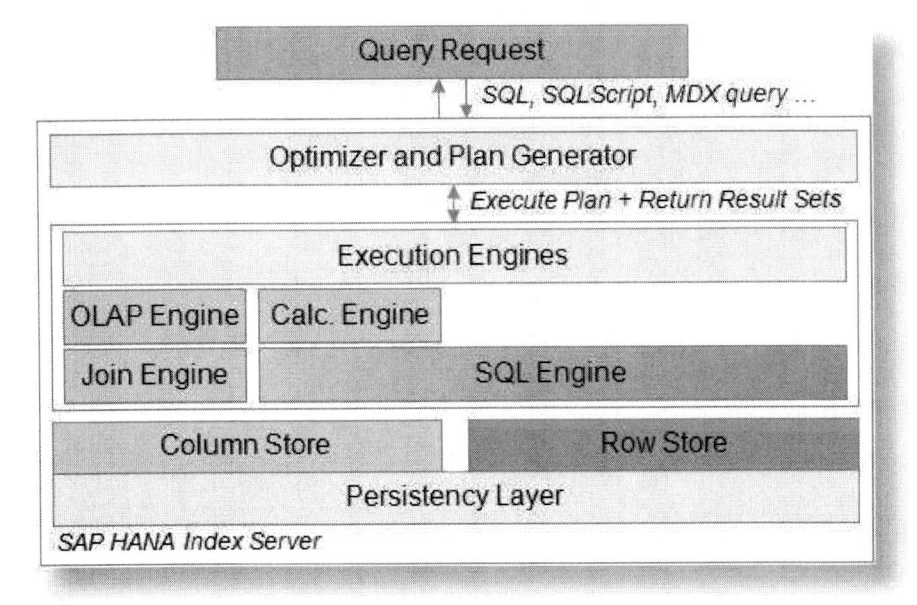

Figure 3.1: Components of the SAP HANA index server

Type-specific engines are available for calculations on row-based and column-based data (*row engine* for row-stored data and *column engine* for column-stored data). Both types of data organization use the same *persistence layer*. The *join engine* is optimized for join operations on column-stored data.

To create well-designed information views, you have to understand which engine is leveraged by which kind of view or which type of query design. Let us look at the general classification:

▶ Attribute views are designed for preparing and processing master data. Master data joins and text tables are the most common operations in an attribute view. The join engine is responsible for the calculation of the result set. The join engine and column store SQL engine are often interpreted as one component that is not separately distinguishable. You can also use the join engine when you run plain SQL directly on database tables. However, we do not recommend that you **combine row and column store objects in your SQL query** as this leads to poor performance. The intermediate result sets of your query (from row-based and column-based storage) have to be materialized first and shifted between the various engines. If your query also accesses analytic views or calculation views, additional engines will be incorporated and this is explained below.

- Analytic views are used for presenting transactional data enriched with dimensional information. They constitute a multidimensional or star schema-like view and are primarily used for read and aggregate operations on mass data. Analytic views (without calculated columns) are executed in the OLAP engine. The OLAP engine is specifically designed for executing star schema queries. The query optimization therefore understands the scenario set up in principle and optimizes accordingly. Joins to attribute views or to database tables will be included in the runtime object of the analytic view. This takes place during the activation process. Thus, only the OLAP engine needs to be accessed when an analytic view is run (and not additionally the join engine, for instance). A downside of this approach is that analytic views do not always create the optimal execution plan for join operations.

- Calculation views are used for query requirements which cannot be realized within attribute views or analytic views. This means that they provide the richest set of functionalities for processing data. Calculation views and analytic views with calculated columns are executed in the calculation engine. This is valid for both graphical and scripted calculation views. To best leverage the calculation engine, do not mix SQL, SQLScript, or CE functions in a single query. As an initial recommendation, consider using analytic views instead of calculation views in your first attempt. The processing performance of the calculation engine can be significantly slower for the same scenario in a calculation view compared to an analytic view. For analytic views with calculated columns, the calculation engine will always be accessed even if the calculated column is not part of a specific query request. For specific scenarios in graphical calculation views, execution in the SQL engine (column store) can be faster. You can force the execution in the SQL engine in the properties of a calculation view ('Execute In'). If you do so, the calculation engine tries to generate an SQL statement out of each node during runtime and combines these individual statements into one big SQL statement. This is passed on to the SQL engine which has a larger set of optimization rules than the calculation engine. There are some restrictions to consider when using this option and these are described in detail in SAP Note 1857202.

> **SQL execution of calculation views**
>
> In some cases, the execution of a graphical calculation view is faster when switching to the SQL engine. The prerequisites and impact are described in SAP Note 1857202 (SQL Execution of Calculation Views).

When using the scripted calculation view, please keep in mind that there are SQL statements that are not supported by the calculation engine. In this case, SAP HANA switches to the row engine to calculate the result. This has an impact on the performance of your query. SAP Note 1764658 is also helpful for a basic understanding of calculation engine behavior.

> **SAP HANA calculation engine instantiation process**
>
> The SAP HANA calculation engine does not behave like a typical SQL user would expect. SAP Note 1764658 (SAP HANA calculation engine instantiation process) refers to several valuable documents explaining the nature of the calculation engine. See Chapter 5 for more information.

As you can see, there are many concepts and parameters to understand and consider when designing queries that perform well. The essential groundwork is to have a solid understanding of which engines are involved in calculating the requested result. The *Explain Plan* function or the *Plan Visualization (PlanViz)* of your model provides insight into which type of operations will be executed (e. g., table scan, join operation, filter assignment) and which engines are used.

- ▶ Explain Plan provides initial information about which engine is used (column EXECUTION_ENGINE). It is a simple analysis tool which focuses on costs and estimated cardinalities (number of rows). The disadvantages are poor formatting and the fact that it cannot be used for modeled views (SQL only).

▶ PlanViz is a graphical tool which is built into SAP HANA Studio (PlanViz perspective) and it is SAP's tool of choice for analyzing query runtimes. It provides estimations and runtime statistics, e. g., for memory and CPU time.

> **SAP HANA query execution plan**
>
> Details of the execution plan of a query in SAP HANA are provided in the SAP HANA Development Guide located at *http://help.sap.com/hana/SAP_HANA_Developer_Guide_en.pdf*.

3.4 PlanViz

We will take a look at the PlanViz tool using a simple example which we would normally not implement in this manner. However, it serves as a useful example. This functionality finds critical paths, analyzes execution times, views engine execution, and finally checks filtering.

3.4.1 The PlanViz sample view

> **Sales comparison for four cities**
>
> One of our regional managers wants to compare the quantity sold and amount sold per city in a certain timeframe. Therefore, he decides to build a report that always compares the four cities to one another.

For the sake of this example, let us assume that the table structure is already clear and we have an analytic view that contains the central fact table as well as attribute views that add some master data information to the fact table in a classical *star schema* manner. The fact table also contains the purchase date and has two *input parameters* which enable the user to choose a start and end date to define the reporting timeframe.

To achieve the goal of comparing four cities and leave the user with a choice of what cities he or she wants to compare, we will use four *projec-*

CREATE THE DATA MODEL

tion nodes in a calculation view and *input parameters* for filtering the city selected by the user. Each projection node then uses one input parameter for filtering on the city selected by the user. The projection nodes each use the same analytic view that we have just discussed. Finally, the four projection nodes are merged using a union node as shown in Figure 3.2.

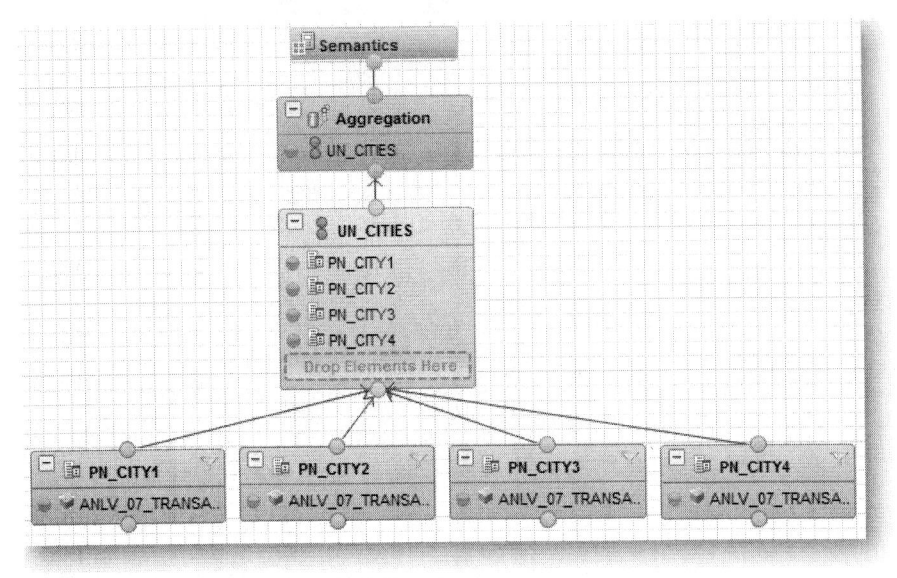

Figure 3.2: PlanViz sample calculation view

This view leverages *input parameter mapping* for mapping the start and end date input parameters from the analytic view to the calculation view.

Coming back to PlanViz, we will now use a simple SQL to run a select statement on the calculation view.

> **PlanViz execution**
>
> At this point in time (SAP HANA SPS09), PlanViz can only be run on an SQL statement. It is not possible to simply see how a calculation view performs using PlanViz on a graphical calculation view because HANA behaves differently for each SQL statement executed.

This SQL statement contains *placeholder syntax* for replacing the input parameters with concrete values. In this case, we used 05/03/2015 –

58

05/10/2015 as the reporting timeframe and Dublin, Brooklyn, Sudley, and San Jose as the cities to be compared. The statement uses the amounts and quantities supplied by the four projection nodes. There is a total for the amount and quantities on a product level. You can see the SQL statement in the code box below.

```sql
SELECT TOP 20000 DISTINCT "CATEGORY_ID",
SUM("PURCHASE_QUANTITY_CITY1") AS "PURCHASE_QUANTITY_CITY1_SUM",
SUM("PURCHASE_AMOUNT_CITY1") AS "PURCHASE_AMOUNT_CITY1_SUM",
SUM("PURCHASE_QUANTITY_CITY2") AS "PURCHASE_QUANTITY_CITY2_SUM",
SUM("PURCHASE_AMOUNT_CITY2") AS "PURCHASE_AMOUNT_CITY2_SUM",
SUM("PURCHASE_QUANTITY_CITY3") AS "PURCHASE_QUANTITY_CITY3_SUM",
SUM("PURCHASE_AMOUNT_CITY3") AS "PURCHASE_AMOUNT_CITY3_SUM",
SUM("PURCHASE_QUANTITY_CITY4") AS "PURCHASE_QUANTITY_CITY4_SUM",
SUM("PURCHASE_AMOUNT_CITY4") AS "PURCHASE_AMOUNT_CITY4_SUM"
FROM "_SYS_BIC"."Advanced_Modeling/CALC_03_PLANVIZ_EXAMPLE"
('PLACEHOLDER' = ('$$INP_PURCHASE_DATE_FROM$$', '2015-05-03'),
'PLACEHOLDER' = ('$$INP_PURCHASE_DATE_TO$$', '2015-05-10'),
'PLACEHOLDER' = ('$$INP_CITY_2$$', 'San Jose'),
'PLACEHOLDER' = ('$$INP_CITY_3$$', 'Brooklyn'), 'PLACEHOLDER' =
('$$INP_CITY_1$$', 'Dublin'), 'PLACEHOLDER' = ('$$INP_CITY_4$$',
'Sudley'))
GROUP BY "CATEGORY_ID"
ORDER BY "CATEGORY_ID" ASC
```

Once the SQL statement has been written, we call the PlanViz functionality.

> **Calling the PlanViz functionality**
>
> To leverage the PlanViz functionality, you first have to right-click on the SQL statement and select VISUALIZE PLAN. This opens the PlanViz view. Once there, right-click again on the project and select EXECUTE. This will supply real execution information.

PlanViz now offers a graphical overview of the *execution plan*. Click the arrow-shaped symbol in the top right corner of the box to analyze a specific node. Furthermore, users can see additional PlanViz perspective-related views/tabs such as CONSOLE, TIMELINE, and OPERATOR LIST. Let us start with the graphical execution plan.

CREATE THE DATA MODEL

3.4.2 Graphical execution plan

The graphical execution plan in PlanViz provides the user with an understanding of the SAP HANA execution process and the engine utilization. First, let's check the sample query and identify whether the supplied input parameters really filtered the data on the lowest level, thereby significantly reducing the amount of data being pulled. After clicking our way through PlanViz, we find out that the filters were indeed applied on the table level, as shown in Figure 3.3.

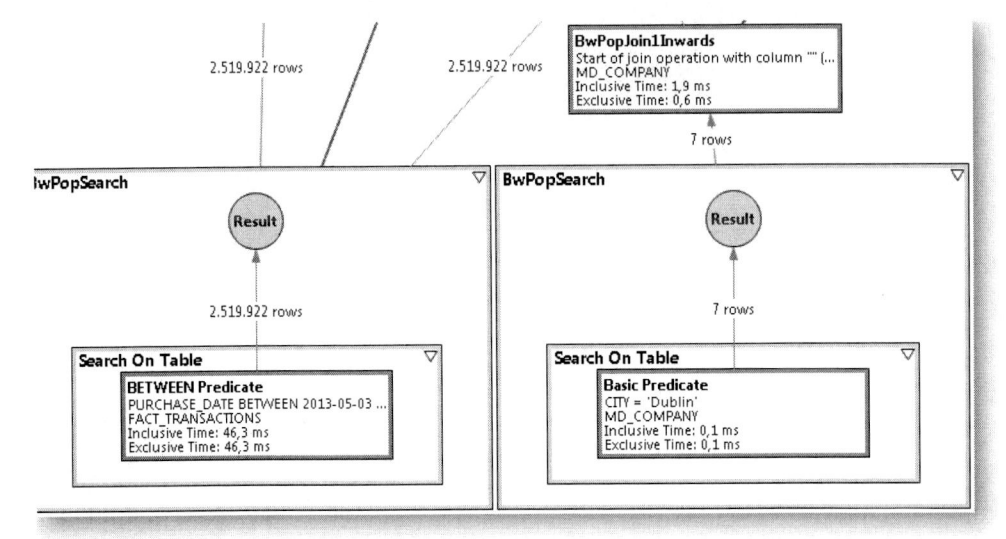

Figure 3.3: Checking filters in PlanViz

Not only can we see that the `between` predicate was applied on the table level for the transaction table, but also how many rows were passed from one operation to another. This is very important for analyzing causes of issues as it enables a second analysis of how many rows should be passed versus how many rows are actually passed. Furthermore, the information about the number of rows can help performance optimization because you can see which operations output or input a large number of rows. The larger the number of rows, the lower the performance will naturally be. Finally, when looking toward advanced analytics, you can run checks to establish which tables being joined to the central fact table are causing duplicates.

Execution time

Another useful piece of information is the inclusive and exclusive execution time for each operation. The *exclusive time* describes the execution time of a single operation, whereas the *inclusive time* considers the time of the lower level operations as well. Figure 3.4 shows the inclusive and exclusive join time.

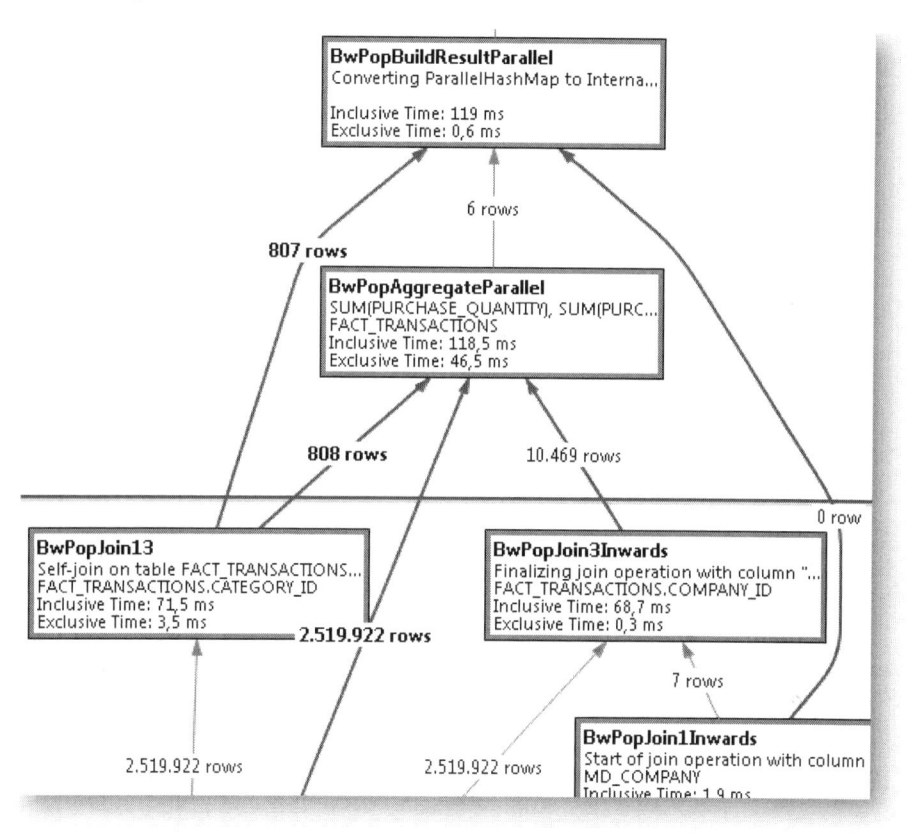

Figure 3.4: Inclusive and exclusive operation times

Critical path

Another useful PlanViz feature is the visualization of the critical path in the execution. It shows the combination of operations that take the longest time in the execution. This can be especially useful if one path is taking considerably longer than other paths. You can then try to reduce the execution time of that path by eliminating operations in the information views or reducing complexity. Figure 3.5 shows the critical path.

61

Create the Data Model

[Figure diagram showing PlanViz critical path with boxes: BwPopAggregateParallel (SUM(PURCHASE_QUANTITY), SUM(PURC..., FACT_TRANSACTIONS, Inclusive Time: 122,1 ms, Exclusive Time: 46,9 ms), connected via 808 rows and 10.469 rows to Join (0 row), BwPopJoin13 (Self-join on table FACT_TRANSACTIONS..., FACT_TRANSACTIONS.CATEGORY_ID, Inclusive Time: 74,7 ms, Exclusive Time: 3,6 ms), BwPopJoin3Inwards (Finalizing join operation with column "..., FACT_TRANSACTIONS.COMPANY_ID, Inclusive Time: 72 ms, Exclusive Time: 0,4 ms), 2.519.922 rows, 2.519.922 rows, 2.519.922 rows, 6 rows, BwPopSearch (Filtering entries in table FACT_TRANSA..., FACT_TRANSACTIONS, Inclusive Time: 71,1 ms, Exclusive Time: 71,1 ms), BwPopJoin1Inwards (Start of join operation with column "" (..., MD_COMPANY, Inclusive Time: 2,2 ms, Exclusive Time: 0,7 ms)]

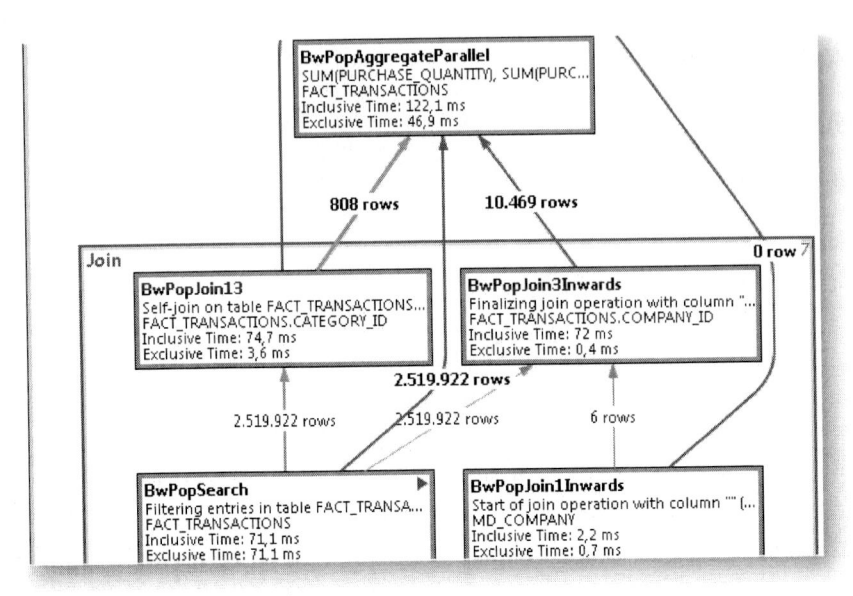

Figure 3.5: Critical path in PlanViz

Engine utilization

The operations themselves also supply useful information when you hover over them with the mouse, including the operation name. In the example in Figure 3.5, all nodes start with a **Bw** prefix. This implies that the operation is performed in the analytical engine. We would also like to note here that when you create an analytic view, the joins with attribute views are integrated into the analytic view. Thus, only the analytical engine is used, even when you use attribute views for joins. In general, the prefixes are:

- Je – Join engine
- Bw – OLAP engine
- Ce – Calculation engine

3.4.3 PlanViz perspective views

As we have explained, PlanViz comes with additional views/tabs as shown in Figure 3.6. They include:

- Neighbor
- Network

CREATE THE DATA MODEL

- Operator List
- Performance Trace
- Tables Used
- Timeline

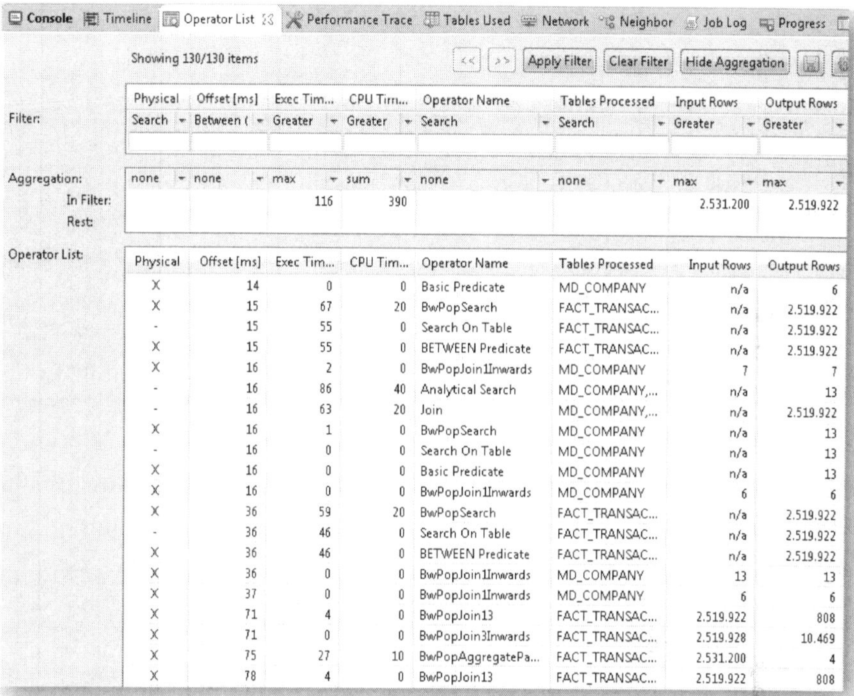

Figure 3.6: PlanViz views and operator list

Each of these views supplies information about the plan execution. In SAP HANA Rev. 91, the most useful views are the OPERATOR LIST and the TIMELINE. Figure 3.6 shows part of the OPERATOR LIST view. This list supplies the user with all of the operations in the PlanViz graph in a table format including some additional columns. The additional columns include the actual execution of a statement, the number of output rows, or the tables that were processed. You can sort the table, for example by execution time, to easily find the most expensive statements. Finally, whenever a certain node in the execution plan is marked, the OPERATOR LIST view automatically jumps to the relevant line in the table. However, this does not work in reverse.

63

The TIMELINE view is a very useful tool that allows you to see the exact composition of the total execution time of a statement. You can see which actions were executed in parallel and which actions were performed sequentially. The TIMELINE view shows the graph in the form of a Gantt chart. As with the operator list, whenever a certain node in the PlanViz graph is selected, the correct bar is highlighted in the timeline Gantt chart.

The other views are of limited use from our perspective:

- The NEIGHBOR view shows only the predecessors and successors of a node, so a part of the large graph.
- The TABLES USED view shows which tables were accessed, how often, and how much time it took to access the tables overall.
- The PERFORMANCE TRACE view lists all of the nodes and SAP HANA internal information that is not really helpful to a user unfamiliar with the engine's internal coding.
- The NETWORK view visualizes the network transfers and the execution time for data being transferred between different servers.

3.4.4 PlanViz highlights

In summary, PlanViz is very helpful for understanding the inner workings of SAP HANA for optimizing query performance.

The help offered by PlanViz includes:

- Details of the number of rows being transferred between nodes, which are a great help when analyzing problems
- Details of the execution times, which shows the nodes that consume the most time in execution
- The critical path, which helps you to optimize inefficient view or query design
- Possibilities for deeper analysis via the views, e.g., operator list and timeline

3.5 Test scenarios

Now that we understand the fundamental options for handling and storing data in SAP HANA, we are ready to take the next step to build a high-performing data model. We start our test series to investigate the storage and performance behavior of SAP HANA depending on specific design criteria of the data model.

3.5.1 Denormalization versus star schema

For years, star, snowflake, or galaxy schemas were well-established approaches for ensuring that your data is organized in the data warehouse such that reporting is optimized. The organization of the data following the third normal form is also a key goal of some modeling approaches in this regard. However, the IT department is questioning whether a star schema, snowflake schema, or third normal form is still adequate for designing a high-performing analytical solution? In-memory technology offers new capabilities and opportunities for handling and quickly processing large volumes of data. Thus, the IT department decides to run the first set of tests with a focus on this question.

> **Denormalization versus star schema**
>
> The IT department would like to understand if it is still appropriate to design complex star/snowflake schemata to ensure a high-performing reporting application. In this test example, they build a scenario using a classic star schema approach and compare memory size and performance with one large columnar table overarching all of the attributes of the star schema involved (denormalized data organization).

To summarize the test scenario, the structure shown in Table 3.3 is used as a template throughout this book.

Test category:	3 – The physical data model
Test focus:	Physical data modeling – storage and performance
Scenario description:	Analysis of the effect on performance and storage when creating a denormalized data model versus a star schema with dimension tables divided by topic area
Expected result:	A performance and storage comparison of the same data modeled in a star schema and in a denormalized manner
Architecture elements:	Column tables, attribute views, analytic views

Table 3.3: Test scenario 3.1: denormalization vs. star schema

The test procedure is divided into six steps:

1. Create star schema tables
2. Create one overarching table
3. Compare memory consumption
4. Create ATV for normalized table
5. Create ANV on normalized + denormalized table
6. Compare performance of both ANVs

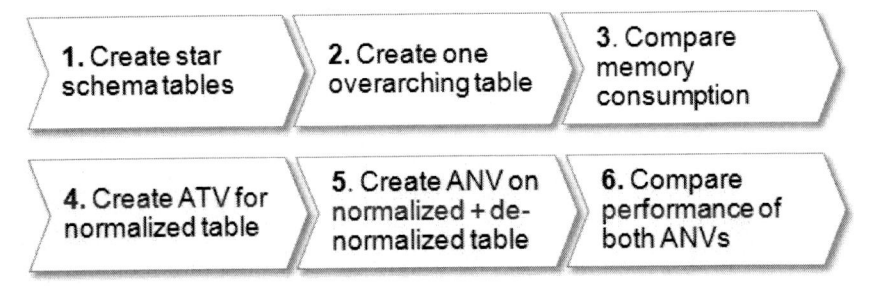

Figure 3.7: Steps for test scenario 3.1

First, the IT department creates physical database tables according to star schema guidelines. Second, they create one overarching physical database table (covering all attributes of the star schema approach). After filling all tables, they analyze and compare the overall memory consumption of both approaches. Fourth, they create an attribute view (ATV) on top of the normalized tables. In addition, they implement two analytic views (ANV) (the fifth step), one using the normalized and one using the denormalized solution. To obtain the analysis results, the IT department records and compresses the performance of the views.

For this test, the IT department uses the fact table FACT_TRANSACTIONS, with around 50 million records, and the master data tables MD_CUSTOMER (65,000 entries), MD_COMPANY (10,000 entries), MD_CHAIN (30 entries), and MD_REGION (34 entries). At the same time, these tables

CREATE THE DATA MODEL

build the foundation for the star schema because they can be joined with the fact table FACT_TRANSACTIONS via ID columns. The IT department also creates one large fact table FACT_TRANSACTIONS_ALL which contains all attributes of the master data tables (MD_*). To analyze the memory consumption, the IT department queries the view "SYS"."M_CS_ALL_COLUMNS":

```
select TABLE_NAME, round(sum(MEMORY_SIZE_IN_TOTAL)/1024,0)
"TOTAL_MEM_KB",
round(avg(COMPRESSION_RATIO_IN_PERCENTAGE),2) "AVG_COMPR_%"
from SYS.M_CS_ALL_COLUMNS
where SCHEMA_NAME ='AM_SCENARIOS' and TABLE_NAME in
('FACT_TRANSACTIONS_ALL')
group by TABLE_NAME, LOADED
```

Table 3.4 and Table 3.5 show the results.

TABLE_NAME	TOTAL_MEM_KB	AVG_COMPR_%
FACT_TRANSACTIONS	3,476,501 KB	25.53%
MD_CHAIN	349 KB	721.28%
MD_COMPANY	569 KB	105.86%
MD_CUSTOMER	6,402 KB	50.82%
MD_REGION	302 KB	1,158.87%
SUM SCENARIO STAR SCHEMA	3,484,123 KB	25.76% (weighted)

Table 3.4: Test scenario 3.1 result: memory consumption for a star schema

TABLE_NAME	TOTAL_MEM_KB	AVG_COMPR_%
FACT_TRANSACTIONS_ALL	4,431,236 KB	12.85%
SUM SCENARIO DENORMALIZED	4,431,236 KB	12.85%

Table 3.5: Test scenario 3.1 result: memory consumption for a denormalized scenario

In our scenario, it appears that the SAP HANA system can leverage its compression capabilities better using the star schema approach. The alternative approach using one large, denormalized database table needs almost one GB of additional space compared to the star schema solution (see Table 3.4 and Table 3.5).

In the next step, the IT department wants to review the query performance for these two approaches. Therefore, they execute steps four to six of this test scenario. First, they execute the analytic view querying the denormalized fact table in its full width and with all records. The average server processing time is 24.8 seconds. For the star schema scenario, the analytic view with the fact table and joins to the corresponding attribute views is also executed by accessing all of the attributes provided. The server processing time recorded averages 36.3 seconds.

Summarizing the insights, the denormalization of the data model helps significantly in terms of performance. The downside is the higher consumption of memory. Another limitation arises in terms of changes or corrections in the master data which is directly attached to the transactional data. Thus, the IT department decides to move forward with the data model approach based on a star schema.

3.5.2 Data types

Finding and defining the correct data type to store a specific type of information is essential for the accuracy and performance of a reporting solution. Thus, the IT department wants to find out how using specific data types impacts the storage consumption and performance of the SAP HANA system. They also investigate the benefits and weaknesses of using additional indices.

> **Using different data types**
>
> The IT department needs to understand how different data types impact the storage and performance of the SAP HANA solution. Previously, the approach was to create (artificial) integer-like IDs in order to improve join performance. This was substantiated by the fact that joins on numeric columns were faster than on alphanumeric data types. As SAP HANA can keep all table data in memory and thereby uses various compression algorithms to optimize read access, the validity of the paradigm needs to be proven again for SAP HANA.

This test scenario is summarized in Table 3.6.

Test category:	3 – The physical data model
Test focus:	Physical data modeling — storage and performance
Scenario description:	Analysis of the effect on performance and storage of using different data types and additional indices
Expected result:	A performance and storage comparison of the same data using different data types; a clear understanding of how the definition of indices influences storage and performance
Architecture elements:	Column tables

Table 3.6: Test scenario 3.2: different data types

The test procedure comprises the following steps:

1. Create a table with 8 columns
2. Alter columns using various char. data types
3. Alter columns using various int. data types
4. Compare columnar storage consumption

Figure 3.8: Steps for test scenario 3.2

For this test scenario, the IT department needs to create a table with eight columns. The first four columns are defined as integer data types using BIGINT, INTEGER, SMALLINT, and TINYINT (step 2). The other columns are defined as character data types (VARCHAR, NVARCHAR, ALPHANUM, SHORTTEXT). The final step in this test is to compare the storage consumption on the column level.

Before the test is executed, the team needs to collect detailed information about the different data types in SAP HANA.

> **SAP HANA data types and conversions**
>
> A good overview of the data types available in SAP HANA can be found at:
>
> https://help.sap.com/saphelp_hanaplatform/helpdata/en/20/a1569875191014b507cf392724b7eb/content.htm. ⇨7
>
> The corresponding functions for converting data between various data types are explained in the SAP Help at:
>
> http://help.sap.com/saphelp_hanaplatform/helpdata/en/20/9ddefe751910 14ac249bf78ba2a1e9/content.htm. ⇨8

To execute this test, the IT department uses a subset of the customer master data (MD_CUSTOMER) and creates a separate table. The table consists of around 20 million records. Each character-based column contains an alphanumeric value with 15 characters. The integer-based columns are all filled with identical figures per row. This setup enables a reliable test basis.

The comparison per column in terms of storage consumption (in bytes) and compression rate (percentage) is summarized in Table 3.7. The data is collected from the view `"SYS"."M_CS_ALL_COLUMNS"`.

COLUMN_NAME	TOTAL_MEM_B	AVG_COMPR_%
C_INT	43,648 Bytes	0.05%
C_BIGINT	44,444 Bytes	0.03%
C_TINYINT	43,648 Bytes	0.05%
C_SMALLINT	43,648 Bytes	0.05%
C_VARCHAR	74,217 Bytes	0.02%
C_NVARCHAR	74,217 Bytes	0.02%
C_ALPHANUM	125,762 Bytes	0.07%
C_SHORTTEXT	74,217 Bytes	0.02%

Table 3.7: Test scenario 3.2 result: memory consumption for different data types

The IT department summarizes that for all integer data types, the memory consumption is equal except for the BIGINT data type. BIGINT allocates slightly more memory for the same information. Looking at the character-based data types, the first thing that is evident is that data type ALPHANUM requires approximately 70% more space in memory. Furthermore, the view M_CS_ALL_COLUMNS also reveals that for the SHORTTEXT data type, an internal shadow column labeled $_SYS_SHADOW_C_SHORTTEXT$ is generated. When this is loaded into memory, it allocates an additional 484 MB of memory. This is due to the full text search option, which is automatically enabled for columns of data type SHORTTEXT.

There are two more columns to mention that are used only for SAP HANA internal operations: $rowid$ (1.5 MB) and $trex_udiv$ (7 MB).

Based on this test scenario, the IT department analyzes the difference between running join operations on integer type columns and running them on character type columns. Thus, they execute several left outer join operations on the same table created earlier in this test scenario in combination with a new secondary table containing a data subset of the primary table. For each data type in the scope of this test, a join operation between the two tables is set up. This means that, for example, the integer-based column of the primary table is joined with the corresponding integer type column in the second table. As each join test in this scenario runs on the same tables and each column possesses exactly the same values (independent from their data type), a comparison of the runtimes is possible. The resulting server processing times are shown in Table 3.8.

Data type of join column	Server processing time
INT	9.4 s
VARCHAR	11.3 s
NVARCHAR	11.4 s

Table 3.8: Test scenario 3.2 result: runtime of joins for different data types

Summarizing the results of this test scenario, it is clear that integer-based data types helps significantly in terms of storage consumption and the runtime of join operations.

3.5.3 Partitioning

Relational databases provide various options for defining how data from one table can be spread across several partitions. Similarly, SAP HANA offers hash, round robin, and range partitioning functionality. The first two options (hash and round robin) do not require deep knowledge of the content of the data itself and strive for equal distribution of the records. In contrast, range partitioning is used based on specific criteria for the distribution of the data (e.g., calendar year). As the number of records per calendar years may vary, this approach is unsuitable for even load distribution. However, the advantage of having a set distribution is that the partitioning does not have to be recalculated with each insert.

> **Partitioning**
>
> **eg** The IT department wants to gain some practical knowledge on using SAP HANA's partitioning solutions and their impact on performance. As they have to deal with large data volumes later and do not have a clear view of how SAP HANA will handle a high number of records, the IT department is considering partitioning as a possible solution statement with a preferably even distribution of the data. As a hash-based distribution can be defined on specific columns and is generally more beneficial than round robin, the IT department focuses on the hash-based approach only. The second reason for this decision is that round robin is not applicable for tables with primary keys (PK).

Thus, the IT department creates an additional test scenario for hash partitioning, as summarized in Table 3.9.

CREATE THE DATA MODEL

Test category:	3 – The physical data model
Test focus:	Physical data modeling — storage and performance
Scenario description:	Analysis of the effect on performance and storage of distributing data over several partitions
Expected result:	A performance and storage comparison of the same data using the hash data partitioning approach
Architecture elements:	Column tables

Table 3.9: Test scenario 3.3: usage of data partitioning

The test procedure is divided into the steps outlined in Figure 3.9:

> 1. Create a table with two identical columns → 2. Load different datasets into each column → 3. Compare compression and memory usage

Figure 3.9: Steps for test scenario 3.3

First of all, the IT department executes an SQL statement using a left outer join between the fact table FACT_TRANSACTIONS and the master data table MD_CUSTOMER. The second step consists of partitioning the table by the TRANSACTION ID column using the hash partition algorithm. To conclude this test, the team executes the same join operation again and compares the runtimes (steps 3 and 4).

Table status	TOTAL_MEM_KB	Join runtime
Unpartitioned	2,141 KB	11.2 s
Partitioned	1,716 KB	5.7 s

Table 3.10: Test scenario 3.3 result: partitioning

The results show that partitioning the table improves both the overall memory consumption as well the join operation of the test scenario significantly. Looking more closely at the statistics of the SAP HANA machine, the IT department realizes that all four FACT_TRANSACTIONS table partitions have almost the same size (see Table 3.11).

73

Table partition	TOTAL_MEM_KB
Partition 1	428,995 KB
Partition 2	428,871 KB
Partition 3	429,194 KB
Partition 4	429,129 KB

Table 3.11: Test scenario 3.3 result: partitioning for partition sizes

Taking these results into account, the IT department decides to consider hash partitioning for all tables with a high number of records.

In addition to this decision, the IT department checks round robin storage and performance although they decide that this approach is not applicable for them (the IT department intends to use primary keys for all of their tables). Interestingly enough, the size of each of the four round robin-based partitions is approximately 333 kilobytes (KB) and the join performance results in a server processing time of 5.1 seconds. Hence, for this scenario, round robin delivers even better storage and performance figures than the hash-based approach.

> **SAP HANA partitioning**
>
> A good introduction to SAP HANA partitioning approaches and their differences is provided in this document: *http://scn.sap.com/docs/DOC-59822*.

3.5.4 A high versus a low number of unique values

SAP HANA uses various compression algorithms to store data efficiently. The impact of the diversity of the values within a specific column is the focus of this test scenario.

High versus low number of unique values

> **eg** The IT department is interested in how well SAP HANA can actually compress data. They are particularly interested in learning about the differences between columns with only a few unique values and columns with almost exclusively unique values.

Therefore, the IT department defines the test scenario outlined in Table 3.12.

Test category:	3 – The physical data model
Test focus:	Physical data modeling — storage
Scenario description:	Analysis of the effect on the compression factor and, therefore, also on storage of columns with a low or high number of unique values
Expected result:	A comparison of the compression factor and storage consumption between columns with a low number of unique values and columns with many unique values
Architecture elements:	Column tables

Table 3.12: Test scenario 3.4: unique values

Figure 3.10 outlines the steps for performing this test.

1. Create two identical tables
2. Add PK to one of the tables
3. Compare memory usage and performance

Figure 3.10: Steps for test scenario 3.4

Step 1 covers the creation of a table with two identical columns. Then, two different datasets with the same number of records are loaded into each column (step 2). Dataset 1 has only 10 unique values and dataset 2 has 10,000 unique values. Completing this test involves comparing the compression factor, column size in memory, and behavior in terms of partitioning the data.

For this test, the IT department copies values for the column FULL_NAME_CREDIT (table MD_CUSTOMER) to a separate table. The column has data type VARCHAR(42) and contains alphanumeric values. For dataset 1, only 10 values were selected and duplicated to 100 million rows. The same procedure was performed for dataset 2 with 10,000 unique values. The result is again collected via the view "SYS"."M_CS_ALL_COLUMNS" and summarized in Table 3.18.

COLUMN_NAME	TOTAL_MEM_KB	AVG_COMPR_%
LOW_UNIQUE_V	178 KB	0.01%
HIGH_UNIQUE_V	410 KB	0.01%

Table 3.13: Test scenario 3.4 result: memory consumption for high vs. low unique values

Taking this result into account, the IT department has confirmation that more unique values require more space in memory. In this scenario, the factor for memory space used is approximately 2.3 relating to a factor of 1,000 for unique values between datasets 1 and 2.

For the dictionary compression algorithm in particular, a high number of unique values is a kind of worst case scenario. Thus, ID columns consume a lot of memory space.

3.5.5 Primary keys

Primary keys (PK) are used to identify each record in a table. They consist either of a single attribute or a combination of multiple table attributes. As with all databases, only one primary key can be defined per table. Similarly to other databases, SAP HANA automatically creates indexes for primary key columns. In the next test scenario, the IT department is interested in exploring the performance effect of primary keys.

Primary keys

> The IT department uses primary keys in their existing reporting solution for database tables. Textbooks and their experience tell them that each table should have an identifier for its records. The department is generally interested in the effect on performance and storage of defining primary keys in SAP HANA.

On this basis, the IT department prepares the test scenario outlined in Table 3.14.

Test category:	3 – The physical data model
Test focus:	Physical data modeling — storage and performance
Scenario description:	Analysis of the impact on storage and performance of using primary keys
Expected result:	A clear overview of storage consumption and read performance impact of defining and using primary keys
Architecture elements:	Column tables

Table 3.14: Test scenario 3.5: primary keys

The IT department executes the test as outlined in Figure 3.11:

1. Create two identical tables → 2. Add PK to one of the tables → 3. Compare memory usage and performance

Figure 3.11: Steps for test scenario 3.5

In the first step, create two identical tables. Add a primary key (step 2) to one of these tables and load the same amount of data to both tables. Finally, select data from these tables to compare storage size and runtime.

As the basis for this test, the IT department creates two copies of the master data table MD_CUSTOMER (65,000 records). After adding the primary key definition to field CUSTOMER_ID in one of the copied tables, the system view `"SYS"."M_CS_ALL_COLUMNS"` is queried again to pinpoint the change in memory consumption. Both tables show exactly the same figures for each column in terms of memory usage and compression factor. The differences noted in Table 3.15 are only visible for the CUSTOMER_ID.

COLUMN_NAME	TOTAL_MEM_KB	AVG_COMPR_%
CUSTOMER_ID (PK)	789 KB	153.27%
CUSTOMER_ID	661 KB	126.99%

Table 3.15: Test scenario 3.5 result: memory consumption for a primary key

The definition of an attribute as primary key increases the memory consumption. The query against the view `"SYS"."M_CS_ALL_COLUMNS"` also shows that no additional internal columns are created for the primary key attribute. An interesting fact is that the compression rate for a column with the primary key constraint is higher. Let us take a closer look at this. The compression rate is calculated as follows: `MEMORY_SIZE_IN_TOTAL / UNCOMPRESSED_SIZE = COMPRESSION RATIO`. Thus, the uncompressed size of the column has to be the same in both cases (with and without the primary key). Checking table M_CS_ALL_COLUMNS again confirms that the uncompressed size is identical for both tables (column UNCOMPRESSED_SIZE shows 520 KB).

Selecting all values for the CUSTOMER_ID column shows almost the same runtime for both tables—an average of 2.7 milliseconds (ms) in this test scenario (server processing time). The same applies to a query accessing all attributes of each table. The server processing runtime determined is 23.5 ms on average.

> **Primary key details**
>
> Retrieve the primary key details from table `"SYS"."CONSTRAINTS"` by filtering on the column `"IS_PRIMARY_KEY" = 'TRUE'`.

> **Improve primary key memory consumption**
>
> When you are using more than one column in the definition of a primary key, the inverted hash option can lead to reduced memory consumption compared to the default definition. To enable this option, add the following statement when you are creating/altering the table:
> `PRIMARY KEY INVERTED HASH ('<column_name>').`

3.5.6 Foreign key constraints

Foreign keys (FK) define a unique connection between the records of two tables. The foreign key is created in a second (foreign) table and refers to the primary key of the first table. There are also rules in the form of referential integrity constraints to ensure that the foreign key is equal to an entry of the primary key in the first table. This concept of relational databases is also applicable in SAP HANA.

> **Foreign key constraints**
>
> To design and implement a sound data schema, the IT department plans to use foreign key constraints. The concept itself is clearly understood, but the department wants to find out more about the impact of the implementation of this concept in SAP HANA with regard to storage and performance.

To better understand the advantages of using foreign keys, the IT department prepares another test scenario (see Table 3.16).

Test category:	3 – The physical data model
Test focus:	Physical data modeling — storage and performance
Scenario description:	Analysis of the impact on storage and performance of using foreign key constraints
Expected result:	A clear overview of the impact on storage consumption and read performance of defining and using foreign key constraints
Architecture elements:	Column tables

Table 3.16: Test scenario 3.6: foreign keys

The test for foreign key constraints encompasses the steps noted in Figure 3.12.

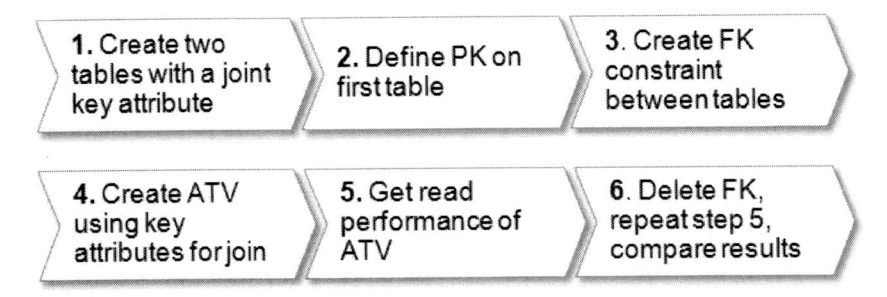

1. Create two tables with a joint key attribute
2. Define PK on first table
3. Create FK constraint between tables
4. Create ATV using key attributes for join
5. Get read performance of ATV
6. Delete FK, repeat step 5, compare results

Figure 3.12: Steps for test scenario 3.6

In the first step, create two column tables with a set of attributes (one or multiple) in common. Secondly, define a primary key in one table and a foreign key constraint between the two tables (steps 2 and 3). Next, as per the test scenario, implement an attribute view joining the tables by using the attributes of the key constraints. Step 5 focuses on obtaining the performance figures for reading data from this view. Then, delete the foreign key constraint and repeat step 5. Finally, compare the performance figures with and without the foreign key constraint.

For this test, the IT department uses a copy of the customer master data table MD_CUSTOMER (TEST_3_6_PK) representing the leading table with the primary key of this scenario. For the second table, they refer to a subset of our fact table FACT_TRANSACTIONS (TEST_3_6_FK). A foreign key constraint is created between these two tables on `Customer ID`.

```
ALTER TABLE "AM_SCENARIOS"."TEST_3_5_FK"
ADD FOREIGN KEY ( "CUSTOMER_ID" ) REFERENCES
"AM_SCENARIOS"."TEST_3_5_PK" ("CUSTOMER_ID")
ON UPDATE RESTRICT ON DELETE RESTRICT
```

The customer table contains approximately 65,000 records and the selected subset of the fact table has around 20 million records.

The analysis indicates that adding a foreign key constraint does not have any impact on memory consumption. The result of `"SYS"."M_CS_ALL_COLUMNS"` proves that the memory consumption for each row remains unchanged before and after adding the foreign key constraint. Also, no additional internal columns are created for the foreign key constraint.

The same findings apply to the read performance. The server processing time for executing a select statement on the attribute view is comparable for both scenarios (with and without foreign key constraints). Variances in the performance figures are within the range of tolerance and are therefore negligible.

Foreign key scenario	Server processing time
With foreign key	2.320 s
Without foreign key	2.529 s

Table 3.17: Test scenario 3.6 result: read processing time for a foreign key

Thus, the IT department notes that foreign key constraints help to ensure data consistency and do not impact memory consumption or read performance in SAP HANA. But what about insert and update statements? The test scenario in Section 3.5.7 explores the impact of foreign key constraints on data loading processes.

CREATE THE DATA MODEL

> **Foreign keys**
>
> There is currently no option for disabling and re-enabling foreign keys in SAP HANA. Thus they are either active or simply do not exist. You can retrieve details on foreign key definitions from table `"SYS"."REFERENTIAL_CONSTRAINTS"`. If no specific referential action for updates and deletes is provided at the time of creation, both are set to RESTRICT by default.

3.5.7 Load performance

In the previous test scenarios, we analyzed the impact on storage and read performance of using primary keys, foreign key constraints, and additional indices. Now, the IT department plans a series of tests around the load performance using these concepts.

> **Load performance**
>
> In addition to optimizing a reporting solution in terms of read performance, the time for updating the data in the database also needs to be considered. To understand the impact of primary key, foreign key constraints, and indices on insert and update statements in SAP HANA, the IT department creates additional database tables to perform its runtime analysis.

An overview of the test is provided in Table 3.18.

CREATE THE DATA MODEL

Test category:	3 – The physical data model
Test focus:	Physical data modeling — performance
Scenario description:	Analysis of the impact on load performance of using primary keys, foreign key constraints, and additional indices
Expected result:	A clear overview of the insert and update performance impact of using primary keys, foreign key constraints, and additional indices
Architecture elements:	Column tables

Table 3.18: Test scenario 3.7: load performance

The steps to be executed in this test scenario are:

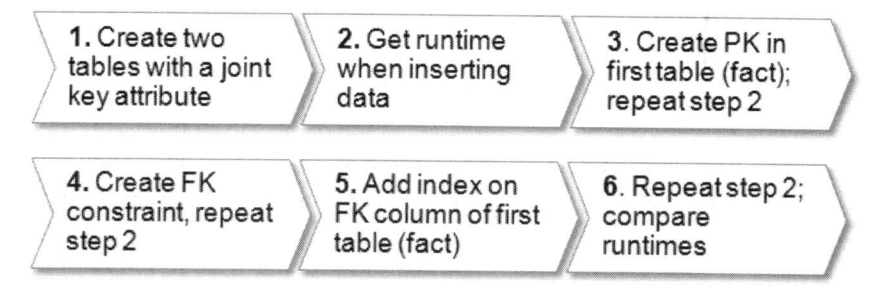

1. Create two tables with a joint key attribute
2. Get runtime when inserting data
3. Create PK in first table (fact); repeat step 2
4. Create FK constraint, repeat step 2
5. Add index on FK column of first table (fact)
6. Repeat step 2; compare runtimes

Figure 3.13: Steps for test scenario 3.7

To begin the test scenario, create two column tables with at least one attribute in common (fact and master data tables). The first performance test focuses on the runtime when you insert a set of data in the fact table (step 2). The next iteration requires the definition of a primary key in the fact table and repetition of the second step (step 3). Next, add a foreign key constraint between the fact and master data table and measure the performance figures when you insert data in the fact table (step 4). In the fifth step, build an index for the foreign key column of the fact table. To conclude this test scenario, obtain the runtime figures (step 6).

83

CREATE THE DATA MODEL

To complete this performance test, the IT department creates a new table with the same structure as the fact table TRANSACTIONS. For the foreign constraint, they use a copy of the MD_CUSTOMER master data table.

Table 3.19 shows the results of the various test steps. Every statement affects 10 million records. The server processing time listed represents the average value gathered from several iterations of the test.

Test step	Server processing time
Insert without primary key in the fact table	33.487 s
Insert with primary key in the fact table but without the foreign key constraint	47.448 s
Insert with primary key in the fact table with a foreign key constraint	54.232 s
Insert with primary key in the fact table with a foreign key constraint and an index column	58.250 s

Table 3.19: Test scenario 3.7 result: insert processing time for a foreign key

The results document that each additional key or index information for a table claims further server processing time. For this reason, the IT department performs one more subtest: drop all key constraints before inserting data into a table.

The runtime for dropping a primary key of the fact table with 10 million records was on average approximately two seconds of server processing time. Recreating the primary key (for the same table and same data volume) took on average approximately 2.5 seconds. Dropping the foreign key constraint took approximately 0.05 seconds, and adding the foreign key constraint again took 0.35 seconds (average values of server processing time).

Thus, taking the runtimes for insert statements as listed above into consideration, it is useful to drop and later recreate the key constraints before inserting mass data. However, you should consider getting approval for this approach from a governance perspective as it temporarily allows you to insert invalid records (until the key constraints are recreated).

The IT department also executed the same tests for update statements. The results indicated similar behavior and insights to those obtained from the test on insert statements.

> **Indexes**
>
> SAP HANA supports different types of indexes. You can find a high-level overview of indexes and instructions on how to handle them here: *https://help.sap.com/saphelp_hanaone/helpdata/en/20/d44b4175191014a940afff4b47c7ea/content.htm.* ⇨ 9

3.5.8 Synopsis of test scenarios

The first set of test scenarios confirms to the IT department that in many ways, SAP HANA behaves like a traditional, relational database. Nevertheless, the tests also clearly highlight the impact of each modeling constraint on performance and memory consumption when working on the database table level. Thus, the impact and benefit of any kind of optimization to the physical model must be analyzed in advance and implemented with due consideration.

For the IT department, the key takeaways are:

- A star schema is a good compromise for situations involving only technical KPIs such as memory consumption and read performance.
- Integer data types are still faster than character types and also help to increase specific database operations.
- Columns with low unique values consume significantly less memory than columns with many unique values.
- Primary keys allocate additional memory space and do not influence server processing time.
- Foreign key constraints help only in regard to data consistency and do not influence read performance.
- Load performance (insert, update) operations are heavily impacted by primary key and foreign key constraints.

Taking these points into account, the next chapter focuses on the information view level and also considers various join scenarios.

4 High-performing information views

In this chapter, we evaluate various implementation variants for the different information views in SAP HANA Studio. We create further test cases as the basis for the evaluation. You can leverage the results of the tests as guidelines and recommendations for using design elements in SAP HANA Studio, as well as for the general use of different view types. We conclude each section with SAP HANA implementation recommendations and best practices.

Now that the IT Director understands the fundamentals of creating a data model, the IT department is concentrating on the question of how to best model the required reporting solution. For this reason, the IT Director analyzes the different information view types: attribute, analytical, and calculation views. His analysis concentrates first on the performance impact of the design variants for each view type individually. This means that he does not compare the same operation across the view types (see Chapter 6 for this analysis). In most IT projects, one of the main factors for determining success is the performance of a reporting solution. Frequently, the performance is not identified as a requirement but is presumed as a given for each solution. In order to avoid complaints by the business, a well-designed SAP HANA data model is necessary. This is the reason why the IT department focuses primarily on recommendations for performance optimization. For further information on information models, please refer to the detailed descriptions in Chapter 3.

One of your first considerations in developing a native SAP HANA application will be how to best implement the business requirements. Furthermore, you should consider the performance as the key driver.

To ensure high-quality information views, the IT department defines numerous test scenarios for the respective view types. Based on the test results, they will define guidelines for future development. We will follow the test procedure introduced in Chapter 2.

4.1 Attribute view

As described in Chapter 3, attribute views represent the fundamental basis for all subsequent views, in addition to transactional tables.

Figure 4.1 provides an overview of the test areas for attribute views.

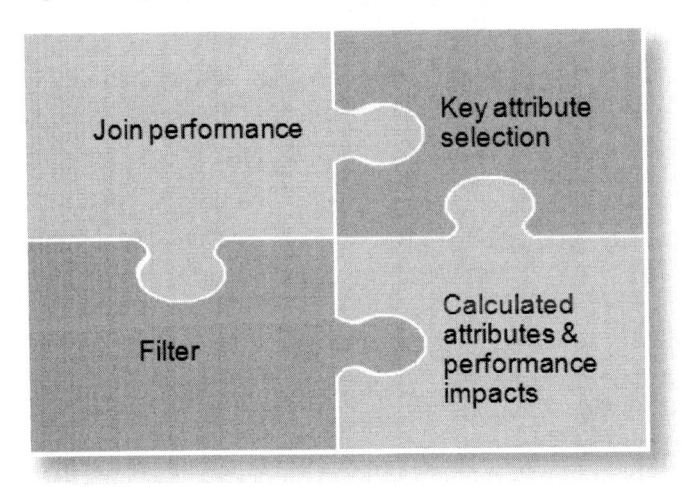

Figure 4.1: Attribute view – test areas

The business department would like to see the transactional data alongside the customer master data in one single report. The idea is to build the fundamental data as early as possible. Therefore, the IT department analyzes the join performance in attribute views. The results of this analysis will provide practical information on the behavior of joins in connection with performance. We will cover these key queries in the following test scenario.

4.1.1 Join performance of attribute views

We will introduce our test scenario 4A.1 by providing you with some general information as noted in Table 4.1.

Test focus:	Join performance
Scenario description:	Analysis of the impact of joins on performance in attribute views
Expected result:	1. Performance overview of different join columns 2. Join performance of different data types 3. Compare the join types during runtime
Architectural elements:	Join on different data and join types, cardinalities and table sizes

Table 4.1: Test scenario 4A.1: join performance of attribute views

The test procedure is divided into five steps (see Figure 4.2).

1. Create an attribute view → 2. Add further join types → 3. Enable cardinalities → 4. Execute joins for various data types → 5. Compare runtime

Figure 4.2: Steps for test scenario 4A.1

We will now look at each step in more detail.

In the first step, the customer master data is joined with the fact table transactions as depicted in Figure 4.3.

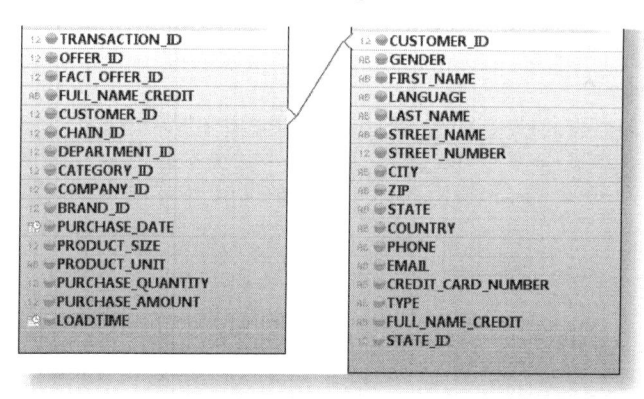

```
TRANSACTION_ID          CUSTOMER_ID
OFFER_ID                GENDER
FACT_OFFER_ID           FIRST_NAME
FULL_NAME_CREDIT        LANGUAGE
CUSTOMER_ID             LAST_NAME
CHAIN_ID                STREET_NAME
DEPARTMENT_ID           STREET_NUMBER
CATEGORY_ID             CITY
COMPANY_ID              ZIP
BRAND_ID                STATE
PURCHASE_DATE           COUNTRY
PRODUCT_SIZE            PHONE
PRODUCT_UNIT            EMAIL
PURCHASE_QUANTITY       CREDIT_CARD_NUMBER
PURCHASE_AMOUNT         TYPE
LOADTIME                FULL_NAME_CREDIT
                        STATE_ID
```

Figure 4.3: Attribute view join

As shown in Figure 4.4, this view accesses almost 50 million rows of data in total.

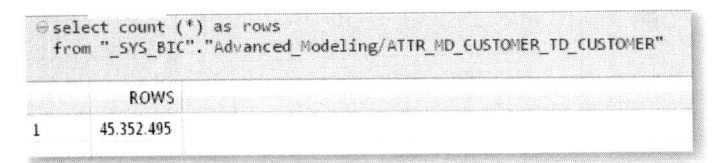

```
select count (*) as rows
  from "_SYS_BIC"."Advanced_Modeling/ATTR_MD_CUSTOMER_TD_CUSTOMER"
```

	ROWS
1	45.352.495

Figure 4.4: Attribute view — total number of rows

The attribute view illustrated will be used as a template in the test scenarios that follow. We will implement the following joins based on the template. Each join is modeled in a separate view:

- Inner join
- Referential join
- Left and right outer join
- Text join

All joins are based on a cardinality of 1:n, except for the text join, which can only be performed with a 1:1 cardinality. In addition to testing the join types noted above, we want to test these joins with and without a cardinality assignment in SAP HANA.

In order to get an overall picture, we need to compare the individual runtime results. Therefore, let's look at Table 4.2.

Test step	Server processing time with cardinality n:1	Server processing time without cardinality
Inner join	943 ms	743 ms
Referential join	941 ms	750 ms
Left outer join	1.014 s	1.014 s
Right outer join	1.042 s	1.035 s
Text join	1.076 s (only 1:1)	Not possible

Table 4.2: Test scenario 4A.1 result (A): join performance of attribute views for join types

As you can see in Table 4.2, the text join and right and left outer joins are the slowest. The inner join and referential join show very similar results. You will also observe that without applying a cardinality, or with the cardinality n:1, there is no impact on the performance.

> **Join types and cardinality**
>
> ▶ We recommend that you use referential or inner joins to ensure high-performing joins if they meet your requirements.
>
> ▶ If you would like to use a text join for language-dependent master data, be aware of the slow performance in attribute views.
>
> ▶ Changing the cardinality does not have a positive or negative performance impact.

Observing the join performance for different data types, we obtained similar results for each alternative (see Table 4.3).

Test step	Server processing time without cardinality
BIGINT	1.405 s
VARCHAR	1.418 s
NVARCHAR	1.406 s
INTEGER	1.402 s

Table 4.3: Test scenario 4A.1 result (B): join performance of attribute views for data types

The processing times do not differ enough for us to provide a clear recommendation based on this test case. However, we will be able to provide a clear recommendation when we get to analytic views (see Section 4.2).

> **Data type**
>
> ▶ Based on our findings at this point, we are unable to provide a clear recommendation.
>
> ▶ However, we recommend using IDs to execute the joins because the data type itself does not have any significant impact (see also Section 4.2.5).

Based on our findings, we decided to use the referential join as a reference. It showed the fastest runtime of 941 ms. This allows us to establish a baseline for the next test scenarios to measure the performance impact of each implementation.

After these tests, all questions regarding join performance are clarified for the IT Director. He is now interested in analyzing calculated columns, as well as key attributes and their effect on the runtime.

First, we will test the calculated columns.

4.1.2 Calculated columns in attribute views

We will now execute test scenario 4A.2. For this test, refer to the content and goals shown in Table 4.4.

Test focus:	Calculated columns
Scenario description:	Analysis of the impact of calculated columns on the performance of attribute views
Expected result:	1. An overview of the performance impact of a calculated column by data type
	2. The impact of several calculated columns on the attribute view performance, also combining data types in correlation to the findings of (1)
Architectural elements:	Calculated columns in attribute views

Table 4.4: Test scenario 4A.2: calculated columns in attribute views

As you can see from Figure 4.5, the test procedure is divided into three steps.

1. Create an attribute view → 2. Implement different calculated columns → 3. Runtime comparison

Figure 4.5: Steps for test scenario 4A.2

We begin the test by creating two attribute views based on an enhanced template of test scenario 4A.1. In the second step, we add a column with a calculation to the first view. The second view is enhanced with a sample currency conversion. Finally, we compare all of the attribute views created to analyze the performance behavior.

Test step	Server processing time
Calculation	940 ms
Conversion	941 ms
Reference	**941 ms**

Table 4.5: Test scenario 4A.2 result: calculated columns in attribute views

Bearing in mind that the runtime of the template attribute view amounts to approximately 941 ms, the calculated column has a negligible impact on the runtime. Thus, we can give the following recommendations.

> **Calculated columns**
> - The calculated columns do not have a performance impact in our scenario.
> - It makes sense to implement calculated columns in an attribute view if the calculated column is to be used throughout all of the analytic views.

After analyzing the performance impact on calculated columns, the IT department dedicates itself to looking at key attributes within attribute views.

93

4.1.3 Key attributes in attribute views

With regard to testing key attributes in attribute views, the IT department currently makes the following assumptions:

- Increasing the key attributes improves the performance significantly.
- Every attribute can be reused/defined as a key attribute.

Table 4.6 provides an overview of test scenario 4A.3.

Test focus:	Key attributes
Scenario description:	Analysis of the impact of selecting one key attribute versus several key attributes
Expected result:	The performance impact of increasing the number of key attributes from one attribute to the actual number of key attributes defining a single record uniquely
Architectural elements:	Attribute views, with selection of key attributes

Table 4.6: Test scenario 4A.3: key attributes in attribute views

Figure 4.6 shows the steps in test scenario 4A.3.

1. Create an attribute view → 2. Increase the number of key attributes used → 3. Compare the performance

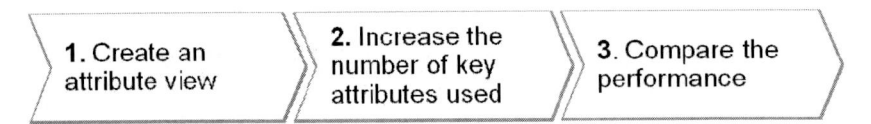

Figure 4.6: Steps for test scenario 4A.3

As shown in Figure 4.6, we first create an attribute view to test the relevance of several primary and random keys. In this context, random keys reflect attributes defined as keys without fulfilling the actual purpose of identifying each dataset uniquely. The idea is to test whether additional key columns lead to new indexes and a better query performance when querying these columns. In the second step, we increase the number of key attributes. In our master data example, the key attributes are the customer ID, company ID, and transaction ID. For this test scenario, the random keys ZIP CODE, COUNTRY, and GENDER are selected for the performance analysis. Finally, we compare the performance results of each prior step.

Based on the execution, the picture noted in Table 4.7 emerges.

Test step	Read key attributes: server processing time	Read random key attributes: server processing time
1 object as key	940 ms	946 ms
2 objects as key	940 ms	951 ms
3 objects as key	947 ms	967 ms
Reference	**941 ms**	**941 ms**

Table 4.7: Test scenario 4A.3: result of key attributes in attribute views

As you can see in Table 4.7, it makes sense to use key attributes. However, selecting additional keys does not lead to an improvement in query performance. The most efficient scenario is to use only one key attribute in your view.

Key attributes

- ▶ Only define attributes as key attributes with a given purpose. Adding key attributes does not result in additional indexes and faster query performance.
- ▶ In general, use key attributes for joining data.
- ▶ Use artificial key columns and implement them as a key attribute.
- ▶ If you want to use several key columns, check the performance impact.

4.1.4 Filters in attribute views

One key to making information models faster is to use filters. Therefore, the IT Director wants to explore filters in the next step.

- ▶ Where should filters be applied?
- ▶ What types of filters are best?
- ▶ Does it make sense to use filters in general?

We will look at the following options in terms of filtering SAP HANA information views:

- Constraint filters/direct filter on object
- Within an SQL statement
- Input parameter
- Semantic layer - variable

In the case of attribute views, filters can only be applied directly on the object or within an SQL statement.

This test scenario here focuses on the topics above. Table 4.8 outlines general information and the expected results for test scenario 4A.4.

Test focus:	Filters
Scenario description:	Analysis of the impact of filters on the performance of attribute views
Expected result:	Performance improvement
Architectural elements:	Filter — attribute views

Table 4.8: Test scenario 4A.4: filters in attribute views

The test procedure is divided into three steps (see Figure 4.7):

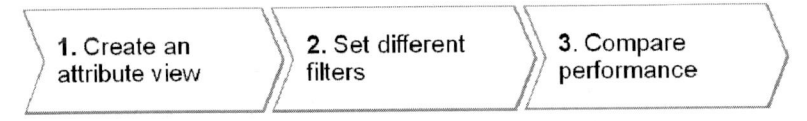

1. Create an attribute view → 2. Set different filters → 3. Compare performance

Figure 4.7: Steps for test scenario 4A.4

We begin the test by creating an attribute view as we did for the previous test cases. Next, we apply the aforementioned filters in order to determine the view's behavior. In the final step, we compare the runtimes between the data foundation and SQL filter and also distinguish between a filter on the master data table and on the fact table.

Test step	Fact table: server processing time	Master data: server processing time
Data foundation: constraint/direct filter	50 ms	57 ms
Data foundation: SQL statement	52 ms	61 ms
Reference	**941 ms**	**941 ms**

Table 4.9: Test scenario 4A.4 result: filters in attribute view

Table 4.9 makes a clear case for using filters on this level. It noticeably reduces the runtime, which leads us to the following conclusions.

> **Filters in attribute views**
>
> We recommend using filters on this level where possible from an implementation and technical point of view.

> **Dynamic filtering in attribute views**
>
> It is not possible to use input parameters or variables in attribute views directly, nor is it possible in the corresponding analytic views.

4.1.5 Result and review of the attribute view

This chapter emphasizes the importance of carefully planning the implementation on the attribute level and taking performance best practices into account. End user satisfaction would probably be influenced by poor performance losses at an early stage.

4.2 Analytic view

The department understands the test results and provides recommendations on how to model attribute views. In the new test series, they investigate the performance behavior of analytic views based on using specific design elements.

We covered detailed information on analytic views in Chapter 3. The analytic view represents a star schema approach that is modeled using the fact table as a starting point in the data foundation. Attribute views are joined to the data foundation as they reflect reusable master data in our data model.

The primary areas of testing are highlighted in Figure 4.8.

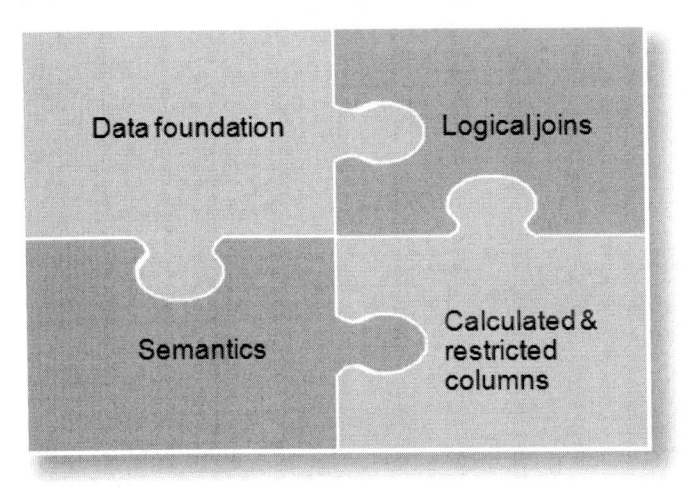

Figure 4.8: Analytic view – test areas

As a starting point, the IT department analyzes the fundamental design principles, disregarding the standard approaches available. To begin analyzing the subjects noted above, the IT department implements test scenario 4B.1.

4.2.1 Join with tables versus join with attribute views

Scenario 4B.1 focuses on the objectives described in Table 4.10.

Test focus:	Table join versus a fact table and attribute view join
Scenario description:	Runtime comparison of analytic views with joins on table level versus joins with attribute views
Expected result:	Performance overview of joining with tables versus joining with attribute views
Architectural elements:	Table columns, joins, and attribute views.

Table 4.10: Test scenario 4B.1: table joins vs. join with attribute views

As shown in Figure 4.9, the steps for this test scenario are as follows:

1. Create analytic view based on master data → 2. Create analytic view based on attribute view → 3. Create analytic view based on tables → 4. Compare steps 2 and 3

Figure 4.9: Steps for test scenario 4B.1

Before the IT department develops the first analytic view, they want to understand the basic design options. Therefore, they implement the first of two design variants (see Figure 4.10).

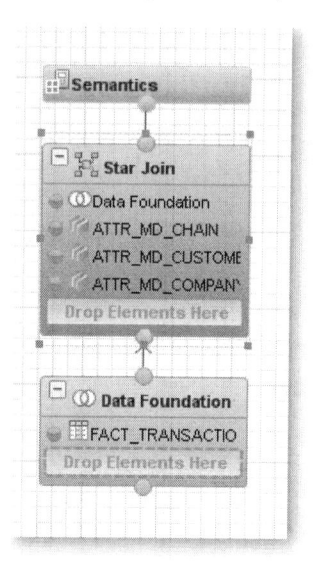

Figure 4.10: Analytic view based on attribute views

99

As you can see in Figure 4.11, the analytic view is built on attribute views and a fact table. The view accesses 50 million rows of data in total.-

```
select count (*) as rows
from "_SYS_BIC"."Advanced_Modeling/ANLV_TRANSACTIONAL"
```

	ROWS
1	50.000.000

Figure 4.11: Number of rows — standard analytic view

The second view (see Figure 4.12) is built on joined tables only and comprises the same amount of data as the first view shown in Figure 4.10.

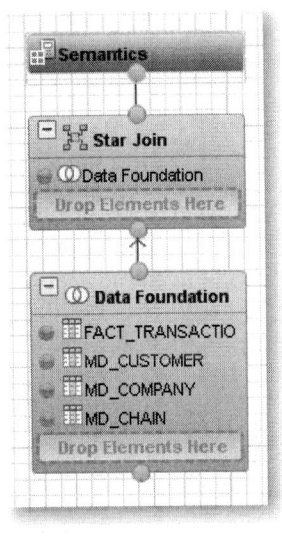

Figure 4.12: Analytic view built on joined tables

```
SQL   Result
select count (*) as rows
from "_SYS_BIC"."Advanced_Modeling/ANLV_04B_1_JOINS_ATTR_TBLE"
```

	ROWS
1	50.000.000

Figure 4.13: Number of rows — table-based analytic view

In the third step, the IT department maps the numeric fields, including the measure in the data models, to investigate whether fact tables only offer performance advantages with key figures and fields (see Figure 4.14).

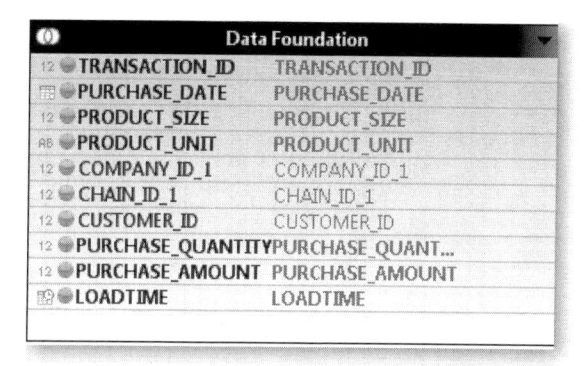

Figure 4.14: Attribute view with numeric fields only

In order to be independent of the requirement for referential integrity, the IT department commonly uses the left outer join for the test scenarios. However, to have the comparison available and to build up knowledge about performance improvement with joins, in some cases the referential join is also tested. This will be stated explicitly in each applicable case.

To understand the impact of using the referential join or the left outer join, the IT department investigates both types in the first test scenario.

The final step in the test is to compare results (see Table 4.11).

Test step	Left outer join: server processing time	Referential join: server processing time
Analytic view based on attribute views and fact table	11.598 s	4.768 s
Analytic view based only on tables	11.342 s	5.068 s
Analytic view based on tables Fact tables: contain numeric fields only	10.310 s	4.712 s
Analytic view based on attribute view Fact tables: contain numeric fields only	10.124 s	4.664 s

Table 4.11: Test scenario 4B.1 result: table join vs. join with attribute views

As you can see in Table 4.11, the result is more or less as expected. A join using tables in the data foundation and a join of the fact table with attribute views are equally fast. This proves that using attribute views does not decrease your performance.

Furthermore, the referential join delivers much faster response times than the left outer join. However, this requires that referential integrity is ensured in your data. In our case study example, this is not the case, which is why the department will use a left outer join going forward.

Finally, there is a slight performance improvement when only selecting integer values from the central fact table. That difference in response time probably arises from the lower number of queried fields as there are now fewer fields supplied from the fact table.

> **Join tables and attribute views**
>
> - Use analytic views with joins based on attribute views due to the reusability of master data across various schemas and views.
> - You should not use analytic views based on tables because there is no real performance gain.
> - Revert to using the referential join when possible.

The analytic view noted above, made up of attribute views and a central fact table, will serve as a reference point for the upcoming test scenarios. Moreover, the server processing time of 11.598 seconds is used as a reference for further scenario runtimes. We have already covered filters in the subsection on attribute views (see Section 4.1.4). Now that we are looking at analytic views, we will look at filter opportunities again. The test procedure is explained in the next section.

4.2.2 Filters in analytic views

Table 4.12 outlines test scenario 4B.2.

Test focus:	Filter
Scenario description:	Analysis of the impact of using different filter types
Expected result:	Pros and cons of using the filter in the data foundation, in the WHERE statement, or in the semantic layer
Architectural elements:	Different approaches to filtering data

Table 4.12: Test scenario 4B.2: filters in analytic views

Figure 4.15 shows the steps for executing this test:

1. Create three identical analytic views → 2. Filter data within the data foundation → 3. Filter data within the SQL statement → 4. Filter data within the semantics → 5. Compare results

Figure 4.15: Steps for test scenario 4B.2

First of all, we create three identical analytic views. In the next steps, we implement several filter variants and select one company number as the filter criterion when executing the query. This means that the second step of the test approach described introduces the filter in the data foundation, whereas in the third step, we filter the data through an SQL statement as shown below:

```
SELECT "CHAIN_ID", "CHAIN_NAME", "STREET", "STREET_NUMBER",
"CITY", "COUNTRY", "STATE", "CUSTOMER_ID", "GENDER",
"FIRST_NAME", "LANGUAGE", "LAST_NAME", "STREET_NAME",
"ATTR_MD_CUSTOMER_STREET_NUMBER", "ATTR_MD_CUSTOMER_CITY",
"ZIP", "ATTR_MD_CUSTOMER_STATE", "ATTR_MD_CUSTOMER_COUNTRY",
"PHONE", "EMAIL", "CREDIT_CARD_NUMBER", "TYPE",
"FULL_NAME_CREDIT", "STATE_REGION", "STATE_ABB",
"COMPANY_ID", "COMPANY_NAME", "ATTR_MD_COMPANY_STREET_NAME",
"ATTR_MD_COMPANY_STREET_NUMBER", "ATTR_MD_COMPANY_CITY",
"ATTR_MD_COMPANY_COUNTRY", "ATTR_MD_COMPANY_STATE",
"TRANSACTION_ID", "OFFER_ID", "FACT_OFFER_ID",
"DEPARTMENT_ID", "CATEGORY_ID", "BRAND_ID", "PURCHASE_DATE",
"PRODUCT_SIZE", "PRODUCT_UNIT", "LOADTIME",
sum("PURCHASE_QUANTITY") AS "PURCHASE_QUANTITY",
sum("PURCHASE_AMOUNT") AS "PURCHASE_AMOUNT" FROM
"_SYS_BIC"."Advanced_Modeling/ANLV_04B_2_FILTER_SQL" where
```

```
COMPANY_id = '102113020'   GROUP BY "CHAIN_ID", GROUP BY
"CHAIN_ID", "CHAIN_NAME", "STREET", "STREET_NUMBER", "CITY",
"COUNTRY", "STATE", "CUSTOMER_ID", "GENDER", "FIRST_NAME",
"LANGUAGE", "LAST_NAME", "STREET_NAME",
"ATTR_MD_CUSTOMER_STREET_NUMBER", "ATTR_MD_CUSTOMER_CITY",
"ZIP", "ATTR_MD_CUSTOMER_STATE", "ATTR_MD_CUSTOMER_COUNTRY",
"PHONE", "EMAIL", "CREDIT_CARD_NUMBER", "TYPE",
"FULL_NAME_CREDIT", "STATE_REGION", "STATE_ABB",
"COMPANY_ID", "COMPANY_NAME", "ATTR_MD_COMPANY_STREET_NAME",
"ATTR_MD_COMPANY_STREET_NUMBER", "ATTR_MD_COMPANY_CITY",
"ATTR_MD_COMPANY_COUNTRY", "ATTR_MD_COMPANY_STATE",
"TRANSACTION_ID", "OFFER_ID", "FACT_OFFER_ID",
"DEPARTMENT_ID", "CATEGORY_ID", "BRAND_ID", "PURCHASE_DATE",
"PRODUCT_SIZE", "PRODUCT_UNIT", "LOADTIME"
```

Listing 4.1: SQL statement

The fourth step encompasses filtering through variables in the semantics node. At the end, we summarize and compare the results as shown in Table 4.13.

Test step	Server processing time
Constraint filter	1.991 s
Data foundation – input parameter	2.363 s
Data foundation – SQL statement	2.183 s
Semantic layer – variable	1.951 s
Reference	**11.598 s**

Table 4.13: Test scenario 4B.2 result: filters in analytic views

As you can see in Figure 4.16, the view accesses 9,378,292 rows of data in total.

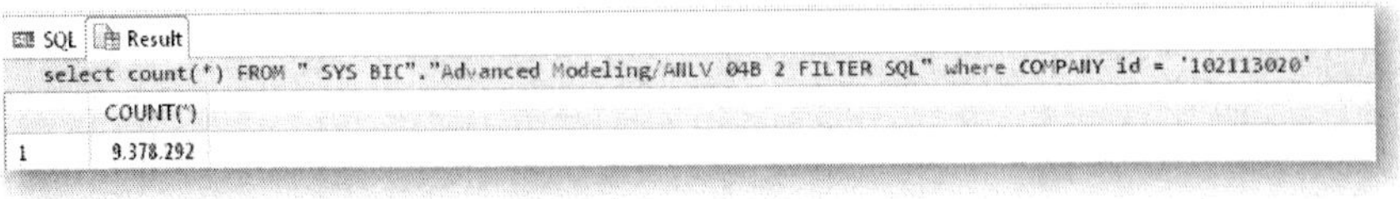

Figure 4.16: Row count filter selection

You can achieve the best performance by using a variable in the semantic layer. In comparison, the performance decreases with an input parameter. The constraint filter and the filter on the data foundation are positioned between the two extremes in terms of performance.

> **Filter**
>
> - Use variables for filtering.
> - You can revert to constraint filters in the data foundation if the value is fixed and no flexibility is required, e. g., for key figures > 0.
> - We recommend using variables in general to restrict the data being queried and improve performance.

In the next step, we want to find out more about the performance impact of using several filters. The following test scenario, 4B.3, realizes the evaluation.

4.2.3 Variable filter performance on several columns versus one column

Table 4.14 provides general information about test scenario 4B.3 as well as the expected result.

Test focus:	Filters
Scenario description:	Comparison of the runtime of filter operations on several columns in parallel versus the runtime of filter operations on only one column
Expected result:	Overview of runtime statistics comparing SQL execution time of an analytic view with filters on several columns versus a one-column filter
Architectural elements:	Analytic view, filters

Table 4.14: Test scenario 4B.3: performance of filters on several columns vs. filter on one column

The test scenario, as shown in Figure 4.17, consists of four major steps.

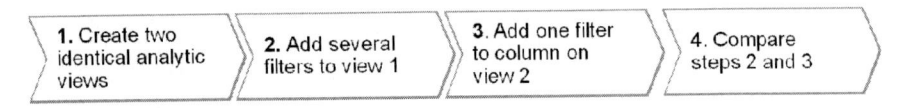

1. Create two identical analytic views → 2. Add several filters to view 1 → 3. Add one filter to column on view 2 → 4. Compare steps 2 and 3

Figure 4.17: Steps for test scenario 4B.3

We initiate the test by implementing two identical analytic views. In one of the views, we apply several filters based on input parameters, whereas in the second view, we select a filter for only one column.

The test cases are grouped into three iterations:

- **Single value:** Set filters with single values. As with the previous filter test scenario, select one customer number.
- **Wide interval:** Set insignificant interval filters, e. g., all customers, or all chains.
- **Reduced interval:** Set significant interval filters, e. g., selected customers in a specific region, or specific time intervals.

What exactly is the purpose of this test? If we set a filter on a certain product and also filter on the product category, does this lead to a decrease in performance? This question should be answered by setting obviously irrelevant filters that do not decrease the result set. Again, the behaviors of the different filters are reflected to understand the performance consequences.

Figure 4.18 provides you with an idea of how the filters are selected for the intervals.

Name	Label
VRBL_DATE	VRBL_DATE
VRBL_CUSTOMER	VRBL_CUSTOMER
VRBL_CHAIN	VRBL_CHAIN

Figure 4.18: Variables used

To ensure the comparability of each test, the filters will be added per execution.

Based on our approach, the following image emerges:

Iteration 1: random value

Test step	Variable: server processing time
Filter: one column	1.951 s
Filter: two columns	829 ms
Filter: three columns	481 ms
Filter: four columns	473 ms

Table 4.15: Test scenario 4B.3 result (iteration 1): filter performance on several columns vs. one column

The results shown in Table 4.15 indicate that by selecting specific filters, i.e., to restrict the data at a high level of granularity, significant performance improvement is achieved. However, it is also clear that adding an additional useless filter does not have a negative impact on the performance.

Let us now look at the interval testing results.

Iteration 2: wide interval

Test step	Mandatory value: server processing time	Optional value: server processing time
Filter 1: Calendar day interval (2 years)	11.598 s	13.503 s
Filter: 2: Customer interval (all customers)	11.598 s	13.454 s
Filter: 3: Chain interval (all chains)	11.598 s	13.469 s
Reference	**11.598 s**	**11.598 s**

Table 4.16: Test scenario 4B.3 result (iteration 2): filter performance on several columns vs. one column

Table 4.16 also shows the same result as before. Applying additional filters does not impact performance negatively. However, it is interesting that when you add an optional input parameter, the performance decreases.

Iteration 3: reduced interval

Test step	Server processing time
Filter 1: Calendar day interval (one year)	7.587 s
Filter 2: Customer interval	1.371 s
Filter 3: Chain interval	1.198 s
Reference	**11.598 s**

Table 4.17: Test scenario 4B.3 result (iteration 3): filter performance on several columns vs. one column

Once again, Table 4.17 confirms that using filters improves your performance.

Based on the test results, we recommend the following approach:

Filter on one or several columns

- ▶ When you introduce filters, decide on a filter concept.
- ▶ Introducing additional filters that do not reduce the amount of data does not result in a performance loss.

▶ If you apply mandatory prompts, you must ensure that you do not have too many filters which would confuse the end user.

The IT department knows the importance of cardinalities from previous experiences with relational data models. They would now like to understand how this topic is handled in SAP HANA native in order to deliver a high-performing data model.

The next scenario will focus on this topic.

4.2.4 High cardinality joins versus low cardinality joins

In scenario 4B.5 we turn our attention to cardinalities. See Table 4.18 for further information.

Test focus:	Join types
Scenario description:	Compare the join performance by considering different cardinalities in joins
Expected result:	Performance improvement
Architectural elements:	Joins

Table 4.18: Test scenario 4B.4: high cardinality vs. low cardinality

The cardinality test includes the steps outlined in Figure 4.19:

1. Create analytic view with high cardinality
2. Create analytic view with low cardinality
3. Compare views

Figure 4.19: Steps for test scenario 4B.4

We will use this test to analyze and understand low and high cardinalities in an analytic view. Therefore, we implement two views, both fulfilling one of the criteria.

As an example of high cardinality, we chose the **customer** attribute, as you can see in Figure 4.20.

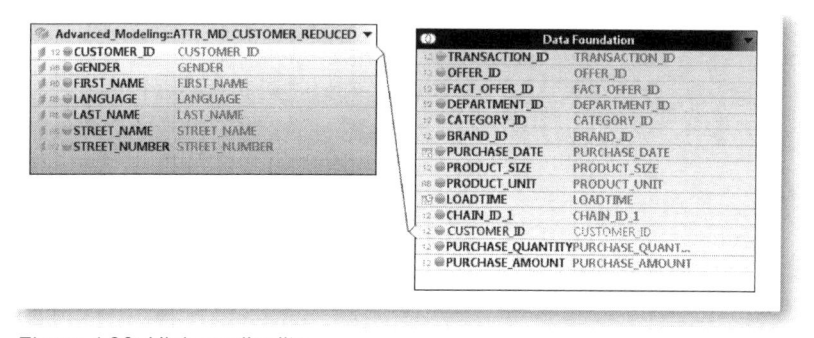

Figure 4.20: High cardinality

The customer table contains 65,863 rows of data in total.

109

Figure 4.21 illustrates the low cardinality of the attribute view **chain**.

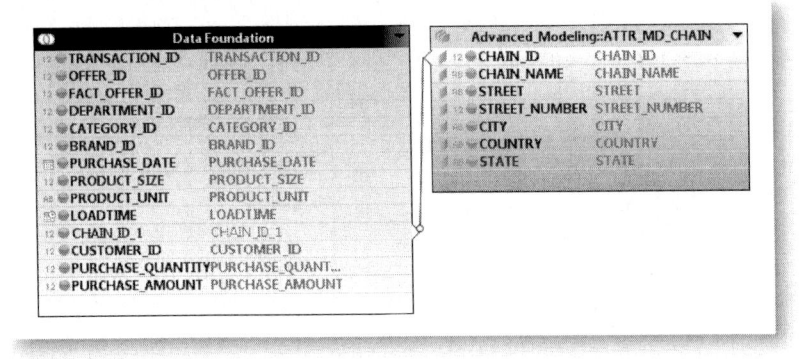

Figure 4.21: Low cardinality

The chain master data table contains only 30 rows of data in total.

To complete the picture, the team analyzes the join types referential join and left outer join.

Test step	Referential join: server processing time	Left outer join: server processing time
High cardinality	4.670 s	5.176 s
Low cardinality	7.496 s	7.715 s
Reference	**11.598 s**	**11.598 s**

Table 4.19: Test scenario 4B.4 result: high cardinality vs. low cardinality

As you can see in Table 4.19, even in the case of SAP HANA dimensions with high cardinality, performance is impacted significantly.

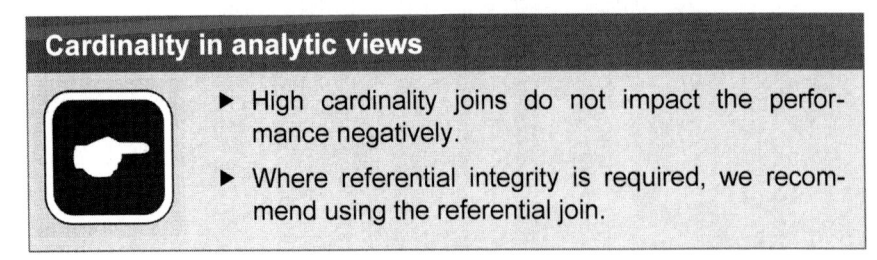

Cardinality in analytic views

▶ High cardinality joins do not impact the performance negatively.

▶ Where referential integrity is required, we recommend using the referential join.

When we looked at attribute views, we analyzed the different joins and impact on runtime. Thus, we will now focus on joins in analytic views. Based on this information, we determined the following test scenario.

4.2.5 Joins in analytic views

Information on scenario 4B.5 is provided in Table 4.20.

Test focus:	Join performance of different data types
Scenario description:	Analysis of the impact of using the different data types for joining data
Expected result:	A ranking of data types by performance when used for joins
Architectural Elements:	Joins based on data types

Table 4.20: Test scenario 4B.5: joins in analytic views

The test on the joins comprises three steps (see Figure 4.22):

1. Create four analytic views
2. Change data type of the column
3. Compare the results

Figure 4.22: Steps for test scenario 4B.5

We initially create four analytic views on different sources. We then analyze the join behavior for the following data types:

- VARCHAR
- NVARCHAR
- INTEGER
- BIGINT

In order to compare the results later on, the *CUSTOMER_ID* is stored in different data types. The fact table contains the *TRANSACTION_ID* to ensure a high data volume. For this test scenario, we use a referential join. To have comparable and informative output, both views access 50 million rows in total.

The data model itself comprises one attribute view and the fields from the data foundation in the star join as shown in Figure 4.23.

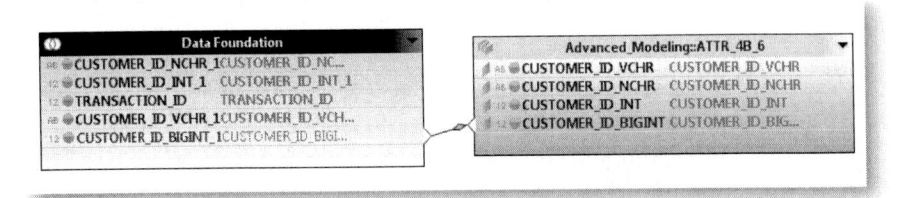

Figure 4.23: Standard analytic view – data model

In contrast, the other data model (Figure 4.24) is built so that all joins are modeled on the data foundation level.

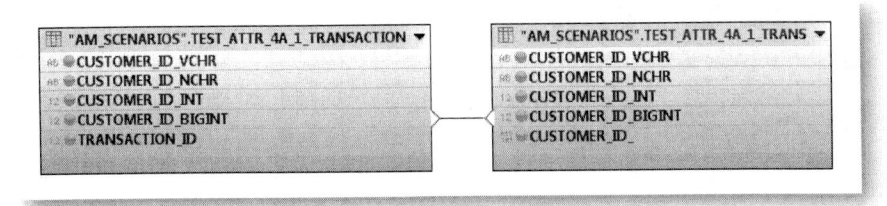

Figure 4.24: Table-based analytic view – data model

In the second step, we analyze the impact of changing the data types in the joins and additionally switching between no cardinality and 1:n cardinality. In the last step, we summarize the results and compare them for future developments.

Table 4.21 evaluates analytic views based on an attribute view and a fact table.

Test step	Server processing time (no cardinality)	Server processing time (n:1 cardinality)
INTEGER	6.346 s	3.782 s
BIGINT	6.305 s	3.808 s
VARCHAR	6.305 s	3.786 s
NVARCHAR	6.365 s	3.775 s

Table 4.21: Test scenario 4B.5 result (A): joins in analytic views – standard analytic view

In the second test, we compare execution times when the join is based completely on tables.

Test step	Server processing time (no cardinality)	Server processing time (n:1 cardinality)
INTEGER	6.393 s	3.801 s
BIGINT	6.318 s	3.820 s
VARCHAR	6.333 s	3.833 s
NVARCHAR	6.342 s	3.843 s

Table 4.22: Test scenario 4B.5 result (B): joins in analytic views – fact table

The first finding when comparing the results in Table 4.21 with the results in Table 4.22 is that there are no significant differences. This means that both analytic views, one based on a join of tables in the data foundation and the other one based on an attribute view and a fact table, deliver similar performance. A comparison of the performance for the different data types shows no significant difference between INTEGER, BIGINT, VARCHAR, and NVARCHAR. It must be noted here that the columns contained the same IDs and we changed only the data type. Therefore, the only reason to use numeric field types instead of character types is the lower memory consumption for numeric types as discussed in Section 3.5.2. Finally, all of the approaches resulted in better performance when the cardinality was set to n:1. In a further test for the different join types, it became clear that setting cardinality only improves performance for inner and referential joins.

> **Joins in analytic views: table-based**
> - The data type itself has no impact on the join performance when you are using numeric IDs.
> - Use INTEGER or BIGINT fields to reduce the memory consumption.
> - Set cardinalities for referential and inner joins.

4.2.6 Calculated columns and calculation before aggregation

Business departments have company-specific key figures they want to report on and introduce with new reporting solutions. In some cases, the calculation can be complex. Therefore, the IT department would like to test the impact of implementing calculated key figures in HANA. For this evaluation, the next test demonstrates different levels of complexity in the calculation.

We will now look at test scenario 4B.6 to explore calculated columns with various levels of complexity. Further information for the test scenario is provided in Table 4.23.

Test focus:	Complex calculated columns
Scenario description:	Runtime comparison for columns with various levels of calculation complexity and calculation before aggregation
Expected result:	Overview of changes in runtime when using calculated columns, including calculation before aggregation with different levels of complexity
Architectural elements:	Analytic view, calculated columns

Table 4.23: Test scenario 4B.6: calculated columns with different levels of complexity

We will proceed as outlined in Figure 4.25; however, we will perform these steps with different variants:

1. Create three analytic views → 2. Add different calculated columns → 3. Increase complexity of the calculation → 4. Retest with calculation before aggregation → 5. Compare runtimes

Figure 4.25: Steps for test scenario 4B.6

Here is an example of a calculated column with low complexity:

```
if("GENDER"='Female',if("ATTR_MD_CUSTOMER_STATE"='New York',1,3),2)
```

In the third step, we increase the complexity by adding an `IF` statement accessing an additional column.

```
if ("GENDER"= 'Female', 1, if("GENDER" = 'Male',2,0))
```

Listing 4.2: Calculated column with medium complexity

We then create a column with high complexity in the third analytic view.

```
if("GENDER"='Female',if("ATTR_MD_CUSTOMER_STATE"='New
York',1,3),2)
```

Listing 4.3: Calculated column with high complexity

In the fourth step, we perform all the tests once again with calculation before aggregation.

The aforementioned variants include:

- Variant 1: Selection of all fields in the view
- Variant 2: Selection of a subset of the fields in the view
- Variant 3: Calculation before aggregation with the same subset as in Variant 2

As a result, we have the runtimes outlined in Table 4.24:

Test step	Server processing time (Variant 1)	Server processing time (Variant 2)	Server processing time (Variant 3)
Low complexity	12.346 s	7.107 s	7.680 s
Medium complexity	12.858 s	7.315 s	8.626 s
High complexity	13.247 s	7.630 s	9.311 s
Reference	**11.598 s**	-	-

Table 4.24: Test scenario 4B.6 result: calculated columns with different levels of complexity

The results show that as soon as we increase the complexity of a calculation, the runtime decreases slightly.

Moreover, any calculation before aggregation impacts the performance, especially for more complex calculations.

> **Calculated columns with different levels of complexity**
>
> ▶ Keep your calculation as simple as possible, otherwise the performance declines with each added complexity.
>
> ▶ The same rule applies for calculations before aggregation.

4.2.7 Calculated columns on calculated columns

Since the results of the last test scenario were based on single calculated columns, we will now try to separate the calculations. In doing so, the IT department hopes to reduce the complexity and simultaneously improve the performance. This means that we will implement more calculated columns so that the actual calculation is divided into separate columns. The following test scenario investigates this topic.

We will now look at test scenario 4B.7. See Table 4.25 for the content and target of this test.

Test focus:	Calculated columns
Scenario description:	Analysis of the behavior of a calculated column based on a calculated column
Expected result:	Performance-related restrictions in the further use of calculated columns
Architectural elements:	Calculated columns

Table 4.25: Test scenario 4B.7: calculated columns on calculated columns

1. Create two analytic views → 2. Add calculated column → 3. Add calculated column on calculated column → 4. Compare steps 2 and 3

Figure 4.26: Steps for test scenario 4B.7

As shown in Figure 4.26, two congruent analytic views are implemented in the first step. We then add one calculated column in the second step, performing two calculations. In our case, the business department intends to analyze the price per quantity. Additionally, they want to perform currency conversion. In contrast to the previous approach, we now split the calculation into two calculated columns. The first one includes the price per quantity and the second one performs the currency conversion. The outcome is shown in Table 4.26.

Test step	Server processing time
Calculated column (currency conversion)	25.541 s
Calculated column on calculated column (currency conversion)	24.395 s
Calculated column with high complexity	13.247 s
Calculated column on calculated column with high complexity	14.703 s
Reference	**11.598 s**

Table 4.26: Test scenario 4B.7 result: calculated columns on calculated columns

Overall, calculated columns have a significant impact on performance. If we split consecutive calculations into separate calculated columns, the performance decreases. However, as Table 4.26 shows, if we split a calculated column and currency conversion into separate calculated columns, the performance improves.

Calculated columns on calculated columns

- Try to avoid splitting complex calculations into several columns.
- In the case of currency conversions, the split may have a positive effect.

4.2.8 Metrics with semantics

The business needs unit conversions for their daily analysis. Currently, the data delivered contains different units, which complicates a cross-comparison of products. Therefore, the business would like flexible reporting in which they can choose the units themselves.

The IT Director knows that there are different options for solving that requirement and would like an answer to the following questions:

- In which information model (i.e., analytic or calculation view) should we implement the unit conversion?
- Which approach would be the best with regard to performance?

Table 4.27 outlines scenario 4B.8, which covers functionality and performance.

Test focus:	Functionality and performance
Scenario description:	Analysis of the functionality and performance of metrics with the currency code or unit of measure
Expected result:	Demonstration of functionality and runtime performance when joining metrics with type currency code or unit of measure, date, or geographic location
Architectural elements:	Analytic view, calculated columns

Table 4.27: Test scenario 4B.8: metrics with semantics

The unit conversion test is executed in the order outlined in Figure 4.27:

1. Create an analytic view
2. Add calculated columns with semantic types
3. Compare runtimes

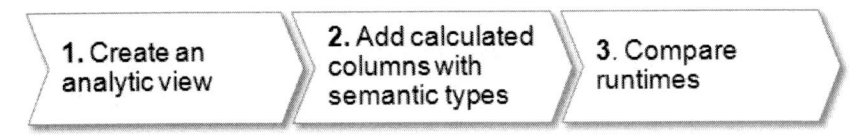

Figure 4.27: Steps for test scenario 4B.8

Based on the aforementioned approach, we first implement three analytic views and then create the conversion options below in the second step:

- Input parameter
- Fixed conversion
- From a column

Finally, we evaluate the results and draw conclusions (see Table 4.28).

Test step	Server processing time
With input parameter	24.629 s
Fixed conversion	24.166 s
From a column	24.321 s
Reference	**11.598 s**

Table 4.28: Test Scenario 4B.8 result: metrics with semantics

Based on Table 4.28, we can conclude that implementing the unit conversion leads to a performance decrease in the server processing time by a factor of approximately 2 to 2.5. If the conversion has to be realized on the level of the analytic views due to IT or business requirements, then input parameters are the preferred method of implementation. We recommend this type of filter because it gives you flexibility, which business users generally require.

> **Metrics in semantics**
>
> ▶ If a conversion is mandatory, you can use input parameters to supply the target unit used in the conversion.

4.2.9 Currency conversion in analytic views

An additional requirement from the business is the reporting of key figures in different currencies, especially with regard to flexible currency conversion. Of course, flexibility should not have a negative impact on performance. The use of currency conversion adds great value for the business, as the business department plans to roll out the reporting solution to the subsidiaries spread around the world.

The following methods are available for currency conversion in SAP HANA and will therefore be analyzed:

- ▶ Currency selection via an input parameter
- ▶ Fixed conversion currency (e.g., always convert to euro)
- ▶ Determination via a column containing the target currency

Table 4.29 gives you an overview of scenario 4B.9 and its content.

Test focus:	Currency conversion of key figures
Scenario description:	Analysis of the performance impact of currency conversion
Expected result:	A performance comparison of the analytic view before and after the implementation of the currency conversion
Architectural elements:	Key figures with semantic type

Table 4.29: Test scenario 4B.9: currency conversion in analytic views

We will execute the currency conversion test in accordance with the steps depicted in Figure 4.28.

1. Create three analytic views → 2. Add a key figure for currency conversion → 3. Set three different types of conversions → 4. Compare the analytic views

Figure 4.28: Steps for test scenario 4B.9

Figure 4.28 shows the test approach for the currency conversion. Again, we create three similar analytic views with a conversion-enabled key figure. In the second step, we perform the currency conversion. The conversion uses the previously mentioned conversion methods.

Finally, we compare the three runtime results.

Test step	Server processing time
Input parameter	24.063 s
Fixed currency	23.850 s
Selected column	23.842 s
Reference	**11.598 s**

Table 4.30: Test scenario 4B.9 result: currency conversion in analytic views

Table 4.30 clearly demonstrates the effect of currency conversion. The runtime increased by a factor of 2 to 2.5 compared to the reference time.

> **Currency conversion**
>
> ▶ As the execution times for the different conversion types do not differ significantly, select the method best suited to your requirements.

4.2.10 Data type conversions

You will face the issue that the data format delivered by the source system does not fit the required output format, or that it needs to be converted to another format for a calculation. Using this test, the IT department addresses this issue and determines how best to solve it.

Table 4.31 provides an overview of scenario 4B.10.

Test focus:	Functionality and performance
Scenario description:	Analysis of the functionality and performance of calculated columns using data type conversions
Expected result:	Functionality and runtime performance using calculated columns with data type conversions
Architectural elements:	Analytic view, calculated columns

Table 4.31: Test scenario 4B.10: data types/type conversions

The test comprises the following steps:

1. Create analytic views → 2. Add different data type conversions → 3. Compare performance before and after

Figure 4.29: Steps for test scenario 4B.10

As depicted in Figure 4.29, our first task is to create four identical analytic views. Next, we add one data type conversion to each view. In this scenario, we focus on the conversions listed below.

Based on our experience, the most common target data types are:

- DOUBLE
- INTEGER
- DECIMAL
- NVARCHAR
- VARCHAR

Once we have completed the test, we compare the runtime results (see Table 4.32).

Test step	Server processing time
Cast to DOUBLE	11.912 s
Cast to INTEGER	12.560 s
Cast to DECIMAL	12.219 s
Cast to NVARCHAR	17.082 s
Cast to VARCHAR	16.462 s

Table 4.32: Test scenario 4B.10 result: calculation before aggregation, also with different data types/type conversions

As evident in the test results shown in Table 4.32, the conversion to INTEGER, DOUBLE, and DECIMAL is much faster than the conversion to NVARCHAR or VARCHAR. An interesting finding is that the cast to INTEGER is slower than the conversion to DOUBLE. However, this conversion still has a less significant impact on performance than character type conversions.

Data type conversion

- If possible, cast to double rather than to integer.
- Avoid casting to character types on the fly; instead, store already casted values in the database table directly.

4.2.11 Restricted columns

In many cases, the business department analyzes the same data with the same or similar restrictions applied (e.g., net sales, but only for one product category). Therefore, the IT Director wants to try the restricted columns feature. This test investigates whether restricted columns impact the performance. General information and an overview of the expected results of scenario 4B.11 are provided in Table 4.33.

Test focus:	Restricted columns
Scenario description:	Test of the performance impact of restricted columns in analytic views
Expected result:	Before/after comparison of the performance using restricted columns
Architectural elements:	Restricted columns, analytic views

Table 4.33: Test scenario 4B.11: restricted columns

We split the test into the steps shown in Figure 4.30.

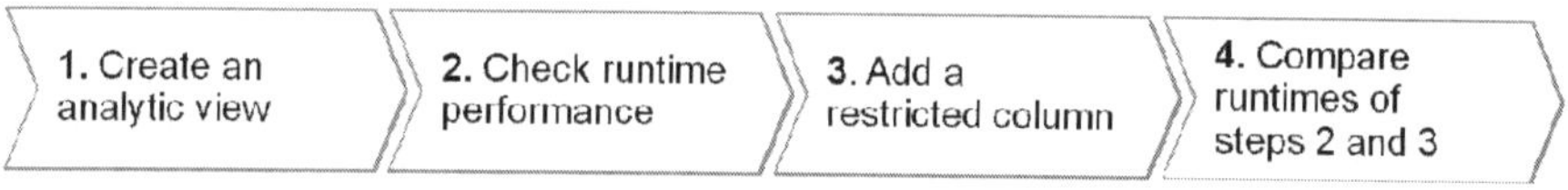

1. Create an analytic view → 2. Check runtime performance → 3. Add a restricted column → 4. Compare runtimes of steps 2 and 3

Figure 4.30: Steps for test scenario 4B.11

For this approach, we create one analytic view and measure its performance as part of the first and second step. In the third step, we add a restricted column. In our case, the attribute **state** is restricted to the value New York.

Test step	Server processing time
Analytic view with restricted column	18.082 s
Reference	11.598 s

Table 4.34: Test scenario 4B.11 result: restricted columns

Looking at the results in Table 4.34, it is clear that the runtime of an analytic view with a restricted column and the runtime of an analytic view without a restricted column differ significantly. From a performance point of view, it is better not to use restricted columns to deliver data relevant for reporting at this point in time.

> **Restricted columns**
>
> ▶ Avoid using restricted columns.
>
> ▶ We recommend that you implement the restriction in the frontend where possible instead.
>
> ▶ In our experience, a good alternative approach consists of using calculated columns with `IF` statements.

4.2.12 Counters

The IT Director wants to perform further evaluations and explores the SAP HANA *counter* functionality which counts the number of unique values for a certain attribute or attribute group. His idea to test the counter is further reinforced by the business department's request. For instance, the business might be interested in finding out how many customers shop in a specific region.

Table 4.35 provides general information about test scenario 4B.12.

Test focus:	Counters
Scenario description:	Creation of a counter in an analytic view
Expected result:	Performance improvement using the advantage of the SAP HANA database
Architectural elements:	Counter in analytic view

Table 4.35: Test scenario 4B.12: counter

Our test includes the steps shown in Figure 4.31.

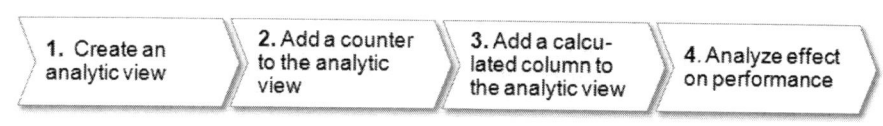

```
1. Create an      2. Add a counter    3. Add a calcu-     4. Analyze effect
   analytic view     to the analytic     lated column to     on performance
                     view                the analytic view
```

Figure 4.31: Steps for test scenario 4B.12

Similarly to the other test scenarios, we first create the analytic view. In the next step, we implement the counter and execute the view. In the third step, we add a calculated column and execute the view again.

As shown in Figure 4.32, the place of residence (customer's city) is selected as the attribute for the counter.

```
Name:*                      CUSTOMER_CITY_COUNTER
Label:                      Counter Customer City

Column Type:                Measure
Exception Aggregation Type: COUNT_DISTINCT
☐ Hidden

Counter
   Column
      ATTR_MD_CUSTOMER.CITY
```

Figure 4.32: Counter – customer city

Finally, we investigate the results.

Test step	City: server processing time	Customer: server processing time
Analytic view with counter	30.686 s	30.979 s
Analytic view with counter and calculated column	33.059 s	34.179 s
Reference	**11.598 s**	**11.598 s**

Table 4.36: Test scenario 4B.12 result: counters

The test results in Table 4.36 clearly show the effect of counters on the view's performance: introducing the counter almost triples the runtime. However, an additional calculated column does not result in a proportional increase in the server processing time.

125

When viewing the result in PlanViz, it becomes clear that SAP HANA executed the entire join and aggregation operations twice. From our perspective, this would appear to be a bug which might be corrected in a later revision of SAP HANA. Were we to take only the slower join and aggregation function, the whole operation would take between 17 and 20 seconds instead of 30 seconds.

> **Counter**
>
> ▶ From a backend performance perspective, avoid using a counter in analytic views.
>
> ▶ Either revert to the calculation view or implement the counter in the frontend.

4.2.13 Calculated columns (attributes)

The IT Director has collected requirements from previous projects in which the business requested key figures as attributes. Therefore, in test scenario 4B.13, we will focus on the feature of calculated columns. An overview of this test scenario is given in Table 4.37.

Test focus:	Calculated columns
Scenario description:	Analysis of the performance impact of calculated columns (attributes)
Expected result:	The performance impact of a calculated column of type attribute
Architectural elements:	Calculated columns of type attribute

Table 4.37: Test scenario 4B.13: calculated columns in analytic views

The steps for the test are outlined in Figure 4.33:

1. Create two identical analytic views → 2. Add a simple calculated column → 3. Add a complex calculated column → 4. Compare the results

Figure 4.33: Steps for test scenario 4B.13

First of all, we create two identical analytic views. For the first view, we add a simple calculated column with a data type conversion of the type attribute. In the other view, we also implement a calculated column of type attribute with a complex calculation. After doing so, we compare the test results.

The executions of both views return the following results (see Table 4.38):

Test step	Server processing time
Calculated column with simple calculation	14.156 s
Complex calculation	17.444 s
Reference	**11.598 s**

Table 4.38: Test scenario 4B.13 result: calculated columns in analytic views

The results show that implementing a calculated column of the type attribute has a negative impact on the performance. Depending on the number of rows selected by the user, a calculation in the backend may be faster than a calculation in the frontend.

> **Calculated columns of type attribute**
>
> Depending on the complexity of a calculated column of type attribute, the performance can decrease significantly.

4.2.14 Temporal join

One further requirement from the business department consists of implementing time-dependent master data in relation to transactional data. The master data itself contains a validity interval based on a valid from and valid to column. To fulfill this request, in the next test we will use the unique SAP HANA temporal join functionality to see whether this meets the requirements.

Table 4.39 provides the overview of information for test scenario 4B.14.

Test focus:	Temporal join
Scenario description:	Analysis of the performance impact of using a temporal join condition
Expected result:	A comparison of the performance of a temporal join
Architectural elements:	Temporal join, physical table, filters

Table 4.39: Test scenario 4B.14: temporal join

Here we proceed as follows:

1. Create an analytic view → 2. Apply different temporal conditions → 3. Compare condition runtimes

Figure 4.34: Steps for test scenario 4B.14

The first step involves the creation of the analytic view. In the following step, the temporal join conditions are executed:

- Include both
- Exclude both
- Exclude to include from
- Include to exclude from

> **Temporal join**
>
> For further information, please refer to the following link: http://scn.sap.com/community/hana-in-memory/blog/2014/09/28/using-temporal-join-to-fetch-the-result-set-within-the-time-interval. ⇨10

> **Available join types**
>
> The temporal join works only with an inner join or referential join.

For the runtime performance, refer to the reference runtime of 8.165 seconds (see Section 4.2.1).

The final step is the runtime comparison illustrated in Table 4.40.

Test step	Server processing time
Include both	8.394 s
Exclude both	8.168 s
Exclude to include from	8.243 s
Include to exclude from	8.336 s
Reference	**8.165 s**

Table 4.40: Test scenario 4B.14 result: temporal join

As the runtime results in Table 4.40 indicate, it is clear that the temporal join has a negligible effect on performance.

> **Temporal join**
>
> ▶ Temporal joins are very well suited for time-dependent master data.
>
> ▶ There is hardly any impact on the performance from using temporal joins.

4.2.15 Hidden columns

In some of the previous test scenarios we have dealt with calculated measures. We now want to go into further detail and enhance the calculation with supplementary columns. *Supplementary columns* simplify calculations either by delivering intermediate results or by delivering data that is not needed for reporting. This test focuses on hidden columns and their impact on the view's performance.

To get an understanding of scenario 4B.15, see Table 4.41.

Test focus:	Hidden columns
Scenario description:	Analysis of the impact on performance of using hidden columns
Expected result:	Demonstration of the performance impact of using hidden columns
Architectural elements:	Analytic view, calculated columns

Table 4.41: Test scenario 4B.15: do hidden columns impact performance?

The hidden columns test is performed as shown below:

1. Create an analytic view → 2. Add calculated columns → 3. Hide columns → 4. Compare steps 2 and 3

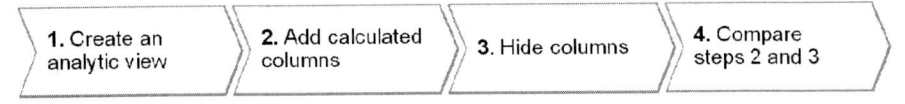

Figure 4.35: Steps for test scenario 4B.15

As in all of the previous test scenarios, we begin by implementing an analytic view. We then add calculated columns and execute the view without selecting the calculated column itself. After doing so, we set the columns to hidden and execute the view again. Our scenario is completed by comparing the different runtimes.

Based on the execution the following picture emerges (see Table 4.42):

Test step	Server processing time
Hidden column with calculated column not hidden	10.395 s
Hidden column with hidden calculated column	10.448 s
Reference view for reduced columns via SQL	**10.380 s**

Table 4.42: Test scenario 4B.15 result: do hidden columns impact performance?

As illustrated in Table 4.42, hidden columns do not affect the performance behavior as long as they are not included in further calculations.

> **Hidden columns**
>
> ▶ Apply this function for better transparency for the end user, for example to hide columns that the end user should not/does not need to see.
>
> ▶ Use this feature if you have reporting-relevant key figures based on supplementary columns that are not relevant for reporting and should therefore not be visible to end users.

4.2.16 Result and review of the analytic view

This chapter unequivocally demonstrated that the way you implement your analytic view strongly influences the performance. The chapter provided some interesting and unexpected insights into the inner workings of analytic views. The highlights are:

- ▶ Filtering works efficiently to reduce the amount of data and is best achieved through using variables.
- ▶ High cardinality can lead to better performance than low cardinality.
- ▶ Splitting consecutive calculations into separate calculated columns results in a performance decrease.
- ▶ Currency conversion impacts performance heavily.
- ▶ Restricted columns and counter operations decrease performance considerably.
- ▶ Temporal joins in analytic views have little or no influence on performance.
- ▶ Hidden columns do not affect the overall view processing time when excluded from further calculations.

Keep these recommendations in mind for your future developments.

4.3 Calculation views

This subsection focuses on the performance behavior of calculation views. As calculation views become increasingly important in the SAP HANA modeling world, it is essential for the IT department to learn how to best leverage the various components of a calculation view. The following test scenarios evaluate filtering, join operations, calculated columns, semantic types, hierarchies, and special operations such as exception aggregation, counters, and calls of procedures.

For most of the subsequent test scenarios, the IT department refers to a standard calculation view (aggregation as top node) including the reference analytic view ANLV_TRANSACTIONAL via a projection node. In the analytic view, the fact table is joined with customer, company, and chain master data. This basic calculation view requires 12.752 seconds server processing time on average for the top 20,000 records. This value is used as a reference point throughout the following tests.

4.3.1 Filter in projection nodes

First, the IT department is interested in the performance effects and handling of filters in projection nodes. They have heard a lot about SAP HANA capabilities for increasing performance when applying appropriate data filtering. The test scenario is summarized in Table 4.43.

Test category:	4C – Calculation views
Test focus:	Projection nodes, performance
Scenario description:	Analysis of the handling of filters in projection nodes
Expected result:	An overview of the execution and handling of filters in projection nodes and their impact on runtime performance
Architecture elements	Calculation views, projection nodes

Table 4.43: Test scenario 4C.1: filter in projection nodes

This test has the following steps (see Figure 4.36).

1. Create calc. view on top of reference ANV → 2. Add filter to projection nodes → 3. Compare runtime

Figure 4.36: Steps for test scenario 4C.1

The IT department creates a new graphical calculation view (type CUBE). They add the reference analytic view ANLV_TRANSACTIONAL via a projection node (step 1). In the second step, they start adding filters on selected attributes. With each additional filter, the runtime is captured and analyzed (step 3).

The results of this test are compiled in Table 4.43. All of the filters use an AND operator. The values shown for the server processing time are based on the selection of the top 20,000 records per statement. The column **Overall result rows** shows the maximum number of records matching the filter setting.

Filter settings	Server processing time	Overall result rows
Without filters	12.752 s	50 m
With one filter	6.701 s	22.2 m
With two filters	1.736 s	1.8 m
With three filters	238 ms	2.300

Table 4.44: Test scenario 4C.1 result: filter in projection nodes

The results show that with each filter criterion, the server processing time improves. The rate of improvement also depends on **how** strongly the filter reduces the number of result records. In this way, the IT department determines that only one very restrictive filter helps to reduce the server processing time considerably. The tests with just one single filter returning only 4,560 rows in total have a runtime of approximately 1.3 seconds. Adding a second filter, which further reduces the number of result rows compared to the first filter, does not improve the processing time. In this example, adding a second filter again resulted in a runtime of approximately 1.3 seconds to receive 580 records (smaller result set than just one filter).

> **Filter**
>
> - Filters help to significantly reduce the server processing time.
> - Combining filters does not have any negative impact on server processing time.
> - The effect of filters on server processing time correlates with the number of retrieved records.

> **A reference calculation view is slower than an analytic view**
>
> In preparing this test and retrieving the reference value of the server processing time for the basis calculation view, the IT department learned the following: directly executing the reference analytic view results in a response time of 11.598 seconds. Including the same analytic view directly via a projection node in a calculation view increases the runtime by more than one second to 12.752 seconds.

4.3.2 Calculated columns

Calculated columns are a key feature in enabling the IT department to develop their reporting use cases (e.g., to calculate the average purchase price per item by dividing the purchase amount by the purchase quantity). For those kinds of scenarios, which require the on-the-fly calculation of additional columns, the impact on runtime and the execution plan needs to be understood. Calculated columns can be defined in projection nodes and aggregation nodes. In addition to finding out more about the general behavior of calculated columns, the IT department wants to determine whether there is a performance difference between using calculated columns for projection nodes and using them for aggregation nodes. Therefore, the test scenario in Table 4.45 is defined:

Test category:	4C – Calculation views
Test focus:	Projection nodes, aggregation nodes, calculated columns, performance
Scenario description:	Analysis of the handling of calculated columns in projection nodes and aggregation nodes
Expected result:	An overview of the execution and handling of calculated columns in projection nodes and aggregation nodes and their impact on the runtime performance
Architecture elements:	Calculation views, projection nodes, aggregation nodes

Table 4.45: Test scenario 4C.2: calculated columns in projection nodes and aggregation nodes

To implement this test scenario, the IT department performs the steps outlined in Figure 4.37:

1. Create two calc. views on top of reference ANV → 2. Add calculated columns to projection node → 3. Add calculated columns to aggregation node → 4. Compare runtime

Figure 4.37: Steps for test scenario 4C.2

First of all, create two identical calculation views on top of the reference analytic view (step 1). Next, create calculated columns of various types (measure or attributes) in a projection node of the first calculation view. In the third step, add calculated columns of various types iteratively to the aggregation node of the second view. In the last step, compare the runtime results.

For the calculated columns in the projection nodes, implement the following scenarios:

- Execution of a string concatenation of two attributes (column type attribute).
- A mathematical operation (sum, product, division) for two key figures (column type measure).
- Use of an if ... then... formula to return a specific result (column types both attribute and measure).

The if...then case scenario uses the same formula as the one we created in the similar test scenario for analytic views (see Section 4.2.6).

```
if("GENDER"='Female',if("STATE"='New York',1,3),2)
```

The test results for this test scenario are shown in Table 4.46 (**Bottom node** column). The test views consist of two nodes, a bottom and a top node, in which the calculations are implemented.

Test step	Node	Server processing time	
		Bottom node	Top node
String concatenation	Projection	14.988 s	14.983 s
	Aggregation	15.220 s	15.604 s
Mathematical operation	Projection	14.568 s	14.402 s
	Aggregation	14.443 s	15.427 s
If...then operation (attribute)	Projection	15.367 s	15.401 s
	Aggregation	15.402 s	15.439 s
If...then operation (measure)	Projection	12.777 s	12.766 s
	Aggregation	12.765 s	12.933 s
All four calculated columns	Projection	19.306 s	19.437 s
	Aggregation	19.336 s	38.954 s
Reference		**12.752 s**	

Table 4.46: Test scenario 4C.2 result: calculated columns

The overview of the results indicates that calculations with result type attribute have larger negative impacts on the overall runtime than the type measure (assuming similar complexity). Similarly to the results of the tests on analytic views, the runtime increases logically with each additional calculation (either due to additional calculated columns or more complex operations).

As the IT department more or less expected this result, they decide spontaneously to execute these tests again in a slightly different setup. Instead of defining the calculated columns on the lowest level of the view, they add them to the top node. They perform this test setup for both the projection node and aggregation node using exactly the same definitions for calculated columns. The values in the far right column of Table 4.46 show the runtime of the same calculated key figures in the top nodes of the calculation view.

You can see that the server processing time for projection nodes is approximately the same on both levels. For aggregation nodes, the processing time is a little slower on the top level compared to the lowest level. This effect may increase if the complexity of the model is increased. In contrast, however, the runtime for the test step using all calculated columns at once in the highest level of the type aggregation node is approximately twice the runtime for the comparison value for the lowest node.

Calculated columns

The result shows that calculated columns of the type attribute do impact the runtime of a view significantly (especially when compared to implementing the same scenario as a measure). This applies to both the projection node and aggregation node regardless of the level at which the calculated column is defined. For aggregation nodes in particular, the calculated columns should be defined on the lowest view level.

Calculated columns not queried

Calculated columns that are not processed further within the calculation view are not considered during execution and therefore do not impact the runtime of the view.

4.3.3 Projection nodes versus variables

The IT department knows from SAP BW and other databases that there are scenarios such as 0INFOPROVIDER that influence the execution of a query in the correct direction to the correct table or view respectively. The IT department certainly wants to explore whether a similar scenario can be rebuilt in SAP HANA. See Table 4.47 for the next test scenario.

Test category:	4C – Calculation views
Test focus:	Projection nodes, functionality, performance
Scenario description:	Analysis of the handling and options for directing the query execution to the correct database table via projection nodes. In contrast, the standard behavior of a variable on the top node is analyzed.
Expected result:	An overview of the runtime behavior when rules are implemented to influence the query execution towards predetermined datasets versus the standard behavior of a variable
Architecture elements:	Calculation views, projection nodes, union node, variables

Table 4.47: Test scenario 4C.3: projection nodes vs. variables

The following steps form the framework for this test (see Figure 4.38):

1. Create two calc. views on top of reference ANV → 2. Use projection nodes with static filter on source → 3. Add union node with constant column → 4. Implement variable in second Calc View → 5. Compare runtime

Figure 4.38: Steps for test scenario 4C.3

The IT department starts this test with two identical calculation views on top of the reference analytic view (step 1). For the first calculation view, they add two more projection nodes also referencing the respective analytic view. For the attribute **purchase_date**, they define distinct constraint filters, each filtering on a specific year. In this case, a purchase date is chosen with a "between" filter from 01/01 to 12/31 per year (step 2). In the union node, a constant column containing the mapping of the technical projection node names and a constant value (in this case the year) is added to the target. The constant column is propagated to the semantics node. The query for a specific year can then be directed to the respective projection node via filtering on the constant column. This scenario can be optimized by physically splitting the data over various tables which are individually selected in the respective projection nodes (step 3).

> **Table distribution in an SAP HANA scale-out scenario**
>
> ❗ Please consider when running an SAP HANA scale-out scenario that you also have to define a sophisticated distribution of your tables within your server farm. This has to be prepared from an application point of view, especially for very large tables, and should be revised regularly.

The associated data model and definition of the CONSTANT VALUE column in the mapping settings of the union node are highlighted in Figure 4.39 and Figure 4.40.

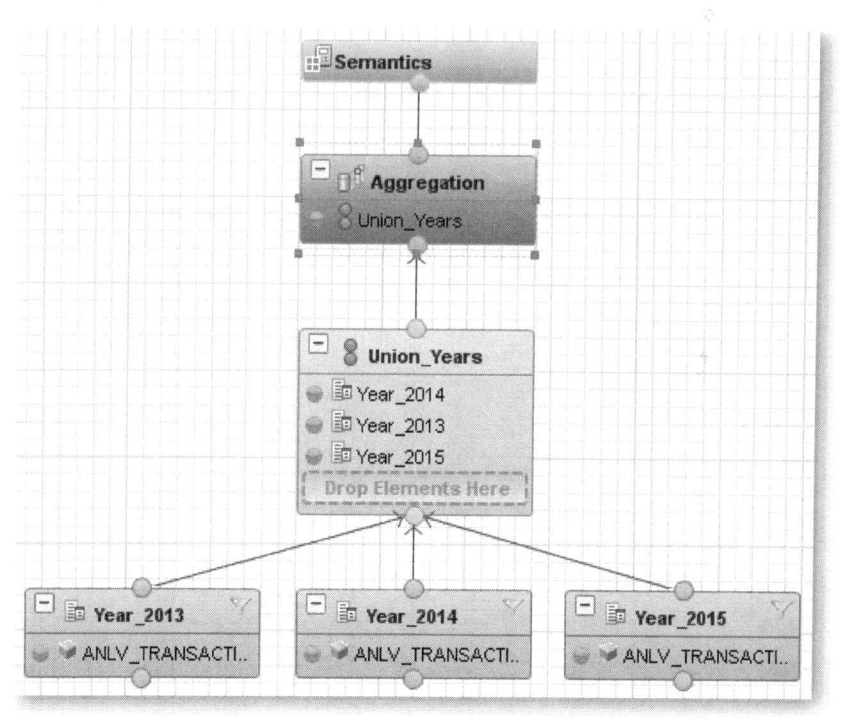

Figure 4.39: Test scenario 4C.3: data model

139

HIGH-PERFORMING INFORMATION VIEWS

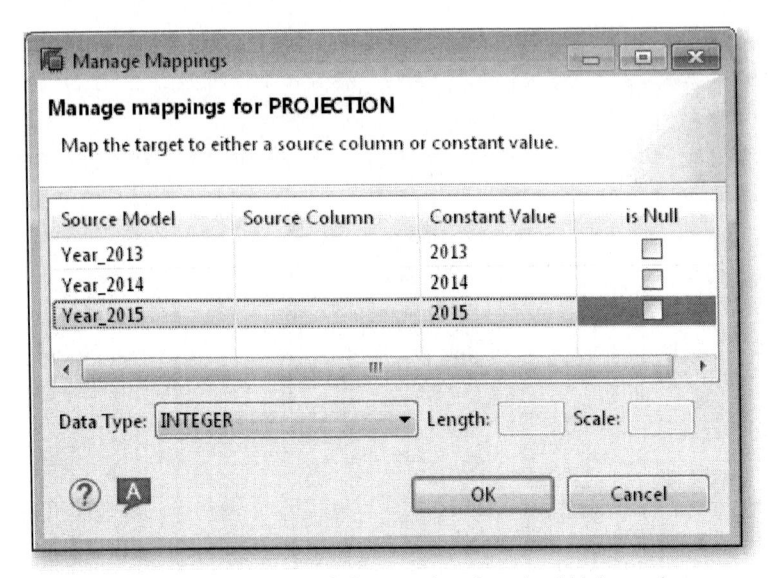

Figure 4.40: Test scenario 4C.3: mapping Constant Value column

Step 4 uses the standard calculation view described in Section 4.3.1 and simply adds a variable to the attribute **purchase_date** in the semantics node. Executing both scenarios results in the following server processing time figures.

Scenario	Server processing time
Multiple projection nodes with union node and constant value column	4.671 s
Single variable in semantics node	4.610 s

Table 4.48: Test scenario 4C.3 result: projection nodes vs. variables

This scenario demonstrates that SAP HANA is very different to BW and that SAP BW designs cannot simply be applied 1:1 in the SAP HANA world.

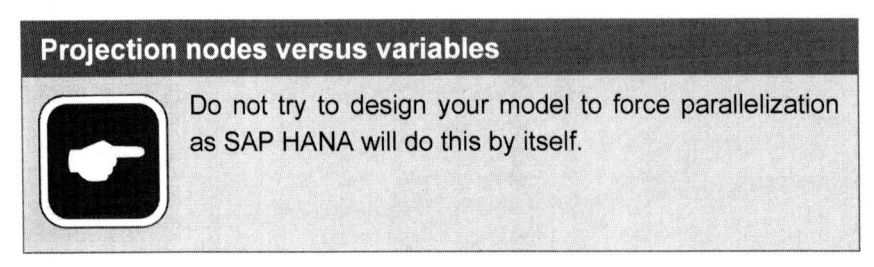

> **Projection nodes versus variables**
>
> Do not try to design your model to force parallelization as SAP HANA will do this by itself.

4.3.4 Query with a single projection node versus tailored projection nodes

Following up on the previous test scenario, the IT department is interested in obtaining a better understanding of the performance behavior of SAP HANA using projection nodes. The focus of this scenario is the difference between the following: firstly, querying a single view providing exactly the required attributes for a specific query; secondly, obtaining the data of all attributes supplied in a projection node. The details of this test scenario are summarized in Table 4.49.

Test category:	4C – Calculation views
Test focus:	Projection nodes, performance
Scenario description:	Performance comparison of a query selecting attributes over the full width of a projection node versus using a single node covering only the required attributes (without projection nodes)
Expected result:	Transparency on the differences in runtime performance when selecting attributes across the complete set of a projection node versus executing attributes via a single, specifically designed view
Architecture elements	Calculation views, projection nodes

Table 4.49: Test scenario 4C.4: number of projection nodes

The IT department uses the approach outlined in Figure 4.41 to execute the test scenario:

1. Create two calc. views on top of reference ANV
2. Activate only attributes needed in view 1
3. Query both views with same set of attributes
4. Compare runtime

Figure 4.41: Steps for test scenario 4C.4

The IT department starts by creating two calculation views that reference the same basic analytic view as in the previous tests. Within the first calculation view, they select and activate, on the lowest node level, exactly those attributes that are needed for a specific query. Both views are queried with the same set of attributes (which is equal to the maximum number of attributes for the first view). After running both views, the IT department compares the results (see Table 4.50).

Scenario	Server processing time
Tailored projection node according to query	9.137 s
Select specific attributes in query only	9.050 s
Reference	**12.752 s**

Table 4.50: Test scenario 4C.4 result: query over all projection nodes vs. single view

The results indicate that there is no real difference between providing an exactly tailored top node to the tool consuming the data and selecting and querying only the attributes needed in the tool. For the IT department, the differences identified are within the accepted inaccuracy of durable measurement. Thus, they will not create additional, specifically tailored nodes for similar reporting scenarios.

> **Query over all projection nodes**
>
> There is no measurable difference between querying selected attributes of a view with a high number of fields and providing the exact attributes needed for a specific query.

4.3.5 Filters in calculation views

One of the standard operations in querying data is filtering the data. SAP HANA offers various options for filtering data (constraint filter, input parameter, variable) which are analyzed later in this chapter (for variables see Section 4.3.15 and for input parameters Section 4.3.16). Here, the IT department would like to determine how well filtering works on calculation views. The background for this test is an increasing database table size. To investigate this, the IT department designs a specific test scenario using the constraint filter approach (see Table 4.51).

HIGH-PERFORMING INFORMATION VIEWS

Test category:	4C – Calculation views
Test focus:	Filters, performance
Scenario description:	Analysis of the performance of filters in calculation views
Expected result:	An overview of the performance of a calculation view when using filters to restrict the result to a constant number of rows but increasing the source dataset
Architecture elements:	Calculation views, filters

Table 4.51: Test scenario 4C.5: filters in calculation views

This test scenario involves the following steps (see Figure 4.42):

1. Create calc. views on top of reference ANV
2. Apply constraint filter in projection node
3. Execute view after each data loading iteration
4. Compare runtime

Figure 4.42: Steps for test scenario 4C.5

The basis for this test scenario is the implementation of calculation views built on the reference analytic view. To filter the data, a filter on the attribute **state** is added to the projection node (step 2). Starting with a relatively low number of values in the basis table, the volume of data is increased gradually and the processing times measured. To complete this test series, the IT department generates an overview comparing the server processing time of each result set (see Table 4.52).

Scenario	Server processing time
10 million records in source	2.553 s
20 million records in source	2.665 s
50 million records in source	2.864 s
Reference (without filter)	**12.752 s**

Table 4.52: Test scenario 4C.5 result: filters in calculation views

The results show that applying suitable filters also helps significantly in increasing the number of records in the database. In the scenario conducted by the IT Department, the number of records in the source table is increased by a factor of five and the overall runtime only decreases by 0.3 seconds (around a 12% loss in performance compared to 500% more records).

> **Filter in calculation views**
>
> It is not really surprising that filters in calculation views do help in terms of performance gain. However, the outcome of this test scenario also shows that even with an increasing data volume, the filter functionality works very efficiently.

4.3.6 Input parameter versus constraint filter

To deepen the insight from the previous test, the IT department considers an additional test for filtering. In this scenario, they compare input parameters and direct filters (constraint filters). This test scenario is outlined in Table 4.53.

Test category:	4C – Calculation views
Test focus:	Input parameters, filters, performance
Scenario description:	Analysis of performance when using input parameters compared to using direct filters in calculation views
Expected result:	Transparency about the performance of a calculation view using either input parameters or direct filters for the same scenario
Architecture elements	Calculation views, input parameters, filters

Table 4.53: Test scenario 4C.6: input parameter vs. constraint filter

For this scenario, the IT department develops the test scenario outlined in Figure 4.43.

1. Create two calc. views on top of reference ANV → 2. Add input parameter as filter in first view → 3. Add direct/constraint filter in second view → 4. Execute view again and compare runtime

Figure 4.43: Steps for test scenario 4C.6

To realize this test case, the IT department builds two identical calculation views on top of the reference analytic view (step 1). In the first view, the team implements an input parameter to filter the data, and in the second view, they add a direct filter (steps 2 and 3). Both calculation views are filtered using the same attribute with the same restrictions. The comparison of the server processing time is the last step in this test. The results of this test are summarized in Table 4.54.

Scenario	Server processing time
Constraint filter	2.855 s
Input parameter	2.839 s
Reference	**12.752 s**

Table 4.54: Test scenario 4C.6 result: input parameter vs. direct filter

The results show that both approaches for reducing the number of requested records are equally fast. The slight advantage for the input parameter is seen as a measurement inaccuracy.

> **Input parameters versus filters**
>
> Both approaches result in the same runtime and query output. Direct filters are good if you have a stable requirement (e.g., company code). In contrast, input parameters offer a more flexible filtering approach, especially when it comes to end user reporting.

4.3.7 Constant column in union node

Using constant columns in union nodes is a powerful feature for supporting various kinds of data operations. An example often quoted is an alternative approach to implementing join operations (see also Section 4.3.9). Going back one step, the IT department is interested in the impact of using a constant column in a union node. To find the answer, they execute the following test scenario (see Table 4.55).

Test category:	4C – Calculation views
Test focus:	Union node, performance
Scenario description:	Analysis of the performance impact of using constant columns in a union node
Expected result:	Transparency about the performance impact of using constant columns on a union node
Architecture elements	Calculation views, union node

Table 4.55: Test scenario 4C.7: constant columns in union node

The test for this scenario encompasses the steps outlined in Figure 4.44.

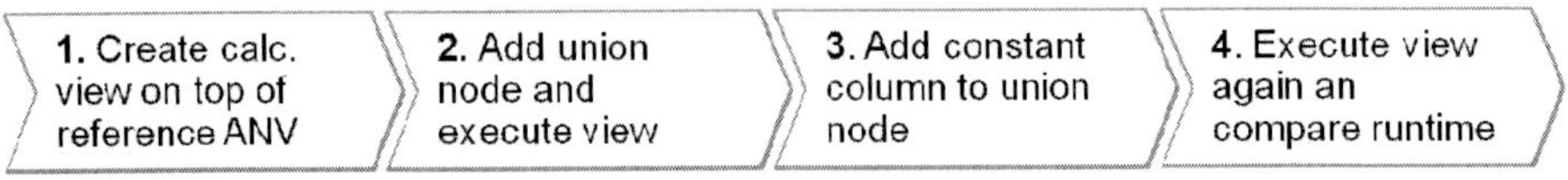

1. Create calc. view on top of reference ANV → 2. Add union node and execute view → 3. Add constant column to union node → 4. Execute view again an compare runtime

Figure 4.44: Steps for test scenario 4C.7

Leveraging the reference analytic view again (step 1), the IT department creates a calculation view scenario with several projection nodes combined with a union node (step 2). This calculation view is executed to obtain the reference value for the server processing time. Next, the IT department adds a constant column to each of the projection nodes and forwards them to the union node (step 3). After executing the view again, the IT department obtains the following comparison of the corresponding server processing times (see Table 4.56). The server processing time again reflects the selection of the top 20,000 records.

Scenario	Server processing time
Without constant column	19.705 s
Constant columns mapped to one common field in union node	19.615 s
Constant columns mapped to individual fields in union node (with usage of constant values)	19.775 s

Table 4.56: Test scenario 4C.7 result: constant column in union node

Table 4.56 shows that the server processing times are more or less identical. However, as the IT department runs each scenario several times, the end result is always an average value to mitigate the inaccuracy of the measurement. Looking at the server processing times, there is even a slight hint that adding a constant column to a union node improves the runtime. Nevertheless, the key takeaway is that constant columns have no measurable impact on the performance.

> **Constant columns**
>
> Constant columns do not measurably influence performance.

4.3.8 Joins in calculation views

The IT department has heard a lot about the differing experiences of joining data in calculation views. In Chapter 3 and Section 4.1, we learned a lot about the runtime behavior when joining data with respect to the underlying data type. Assuming that the previous results are also valid for calculation views, in this test scenario the IT department concentrates on the number of join operations and their type of execution in calculation views. The volume of data processed is also considered.

Test category:	4C – Calculation views
Test focus:	Join node, performance
Scenario description:	Analysis of the performance when joining data in calculation views
Expected result:	A chart depicting the performance of the join execution in correlation to the way the join is realized and executed as well as the data volume which is processed
Architecture elements:	Calculation views, join node

Table 4.57: Test scenario 4C.8: joins in calculation views

This test requires the execution of the following steps (see Figure 4.45):

| 1. Create calc. view joining tables only | 2. Add additional join nodes on table level | 3. Execute the views in the calc. - and SQL engine | 4. Define the same scenario as for star join | 5. Compare runtime |

Figure 4.45: Steps for test scenario 4C.8

This comprehensive test series on join operations starts with defining the table joins using the join node of a calculation view (step 1). After gathering the first results for server processing time, the IT department continues to enhance the view with additional table joins using the left outer join option and N:1 cardinality (step 2). As calculation views can be processed in the calculation engine as well as in the SQL engine, the IT department checks the processing time of each execution type in the third step. They then build the same join scenario using the star join function, encapsulating each master data table as a dimensional calculation view (calculation view type: dimension). A projection node is used to include the fact table in the star join node (left outer join with cardinality N:1).

> **Star join functionality specifics**
>
> ❗ Star join functionality has been available since SPS 7. Attribute views, analytic views, and base tables are not allowed in the star join node. Instead, model your master as a dimensional calculation view and use projection nodes to include tables or analytic views. The details are described in the SAP HANA modeling guide: http://help.sap.com/hana/SAP_HANA_Modeling_Guide_en.pdf.

The implemented scenario is shown in Figure 4.46. The left-hand side shows the star join scenario, and the right-hand side shows the three sequentially arranged join operations of the database tables.

The different test results are summarized in Table 4.58 (top 20,000 records selected).

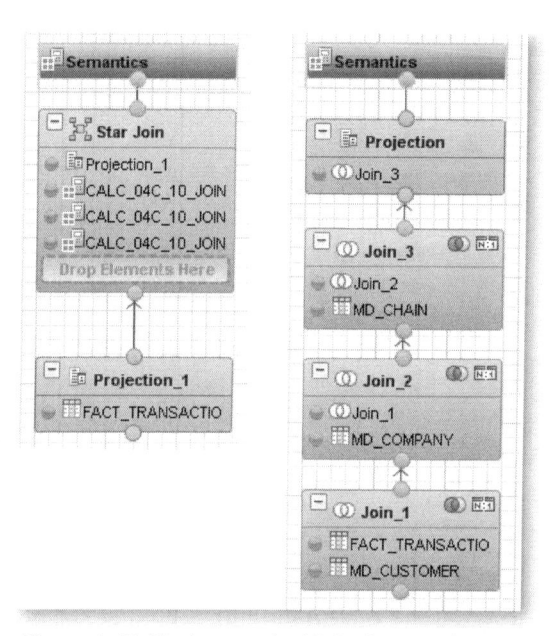

Figure 4.46: Test scenario 4C.8: data model showing join operations

Number of Joins	Engine	Server processing time
1 table join (top 20,000)	Calculation engine	1.198 s
1 table join (top 20,000)	SQL engine	1.048 s
1 table join (all records)	SQL engine	5.062 s
2 table joins (top 20,000)	Calculation engine	11.817 s
2 table joins (top 20,000)	SQL engine	11.882 s
2 table joins (all records)	SQL engine	15.936 s
3 table joins (top 20,000)	Calculation engine	13.437 s
3 table joins (top 20,000)	SQL engine	13.291 s
3 table joins (all records)	SQL engine	18.620 s
3 table joins (star join and top 20,000)	Calculation engine	13.552 s
3 table joins (star join and top 20,000)	SQL engine	13.609 s
3 table joins (star join and all records)	SQL engine	18.537 s

Table 4.58: Test scenario 4C.8 result: join in calculation views

For this scenario, executing joins directly on a database table level, the IT department could not ascertain any reliable advantage or disadvantage in terms of the execution engine. Clearly, increasing the number of join operations as well as the number of data records involved increases the server processing time. The IT department also observed that only selecting the top 20,000 records consistently improves the runtime by four to five seconds regardless of how complex the scenario is. This means that the first and simplest scenario shows the best proportional improvement when this filter restriction is applied. An even more interesting fact for the IT department is that in the selected scenario, the newly introduced star join slightly increases the time for providing the requested result. In this scenario, switching the execution engine does not produce any considerable difference in the server processing time.

> **Joins in calculation views**
>
> Join operations on a database level can quickly become expensive when you increase the number of joins as well as the number of records processed within a calculation view. The star join feature provides a reasonable alternative for defining joins as the modeling does not need to be done at the table level and the performance loss is not significant.

> **Execute in SQL engine**
>
> There is an SAP Note for the execution of calculation views in the SQL engine (SAP Note: 1857202 - SQL execution of calculation views). The Note also gives a valuable explanation of the calculation of the result set when using the SQL engine. Thus, we strongly recommend that you check this Note and the attached PDF document.

HIGH-PERFORMING INFORMATION VIEWS

> **Optimize join operation**
>
> For join operations, there is an additional property that influences the performance. In the property of a join definition, you can set the **Optimize Join** column to true. This option is available only for the left outer join or text join (with cardinality 1:1 or N:1) and right outer join (with cardinality 1:1 or 1:N). This setting leads to the exclusion of join columns that are not required when retrieving data from the database. This does not work in the constraint filters that are defined on join columns. Further information can be found in the SAP Help at http://help.sap.com/saphelp_hanaplatform/helpdata/en/05/0f14f7a6d94d2da905b0a4072ba546/content.htm. ⇨11

4.3.9 Join with analytic view and attribute view

The IT department knows that the way they choose to set up join operations is crucial for the performance of the entire data model. Thus, they prepare another test scenario. This time the focus is on the join behavior when using different types of objects in the join node. The high-level description of the test scenario is provided in Table 4.59.

Test category:	4C – Calculation views
Test focus:	Join node, performance
Scenario description:	Analysis of the performance behavior when joining different types of views
Expected result:	Transparency about the behavior when joining attribute views and analytic views within calculation views; overview of performance results
Architecture elements:	Calculation views, attribute view, analytic view, join node

Table 4.59: Test scenario 4C.9: joins in calculation views

The IT department uses the following procedure to obtain the requested results:

151

```
1. Create calc.     2. Create calc.      3. Create calc.
   view joining        view joining table    view joining table
   tables              and ATV               and ANV

4. Create calc.     5. Create calc.      6. Compare
   view joining ATV    view joining ANV      runtime
   and ANV             and ANV
```

Figure 4.47: Steps for test scenario 4C.9

This test scenario encompasses several steps in order to provide a clear understanding of the join behavior in this regard. The IT department starts with a calculation view joining just database tables using the left outer join option. They use the FACT_TRANSACTIONS and MD _CUSTOMER tables. They also maintain the cardinality setting of the join property as N:1 (step 1). The next enhancement is the join between a database table (FACT_TRANSACTIONS) and an attribute view based on MD_CUSTOMER (step 2). This is accomplished by joining a database table (MD_CUSTOMER) with an analytic view based on FACT _TRANSACTIONS (step 3). The next steps cover the combination of an attribute view with an analytic view (step 4) and lastly the join of two analytic views (step 5). For steps 4 and 5, the team reuses views from the earlier steps in this scenario. The comparison and summary of the runtimes is the obligatory final step in this test series. To ensure a comparable result, the number and width of data records is identical for each join scenario, see also Table 4.60. The runtime is based on the selection of the top 20,000 records.

Scenario	Server processing time
Join of two tables (via SQL)	1.037 s
Join of a table and an ATV	11.050 s
Join of a table and an ANV	8.153 s
Join of an ATV and an ANV	15.335 s
Join of an ANV and an ANV	16.608 s
Star join of ANV and dimensional calculation view	10.661 s
Star join of fact table and dimensional calculation view	1.035 s

Table 4.60: Test scenario 4C.9 result: join with analytical and attribute view

This scenario proves to the IT department that joining analytical and attribute views significantly reduces the runtime in calculation views. Again, as in the previous test, switching the execution engine to SQL did not affect the runtime considerably and is therefore not explicitly stated. The obvious finding in this scenario is that joining a table with an analytic view is faster than joining it with an attribute view. In any case, as working on the database table level is not an option for the IT department, they decide to perform an additional test run, this time building the same query requirement using the star join option. As no attribute views or analytic views can be used in this concept, they replace the attribute view of MD_CUSTOMER with a corresponding dimensional calculation view. The analytic view encapsulating the fact table is included using a projection node as the data foundation in this case. The result obtained shows that in this constellation, the star join performs just as well as the join of two tables via SQL.

> **Join with analytic view and attribute view**
>
> The test confirms that the join performance of analytic views and attribute views can be poor inside the calculation view. The star join of two tables can compete with the SQL statement.

4.3.10 Metrics with semantics

Building on the previous test scenario, the IT department now concentrates on metrics with semantics. The comprehensiveness of metrics with semantics steadily increases with every new SPS. In this section, the IT department focuses on date functions (column type attribute) and key figures with units and the conversion of these units (column type measure). Currency conversion will be handled separately in Section 4.3.11. The geospatial semantic type is not relevant for the business and IT departments and is therefore not covered.

Test category:	4C – Calculation views
Test focus:	Calculated columns, performance
Scenario description:	Analysis of the performance behavior when using calculated columns with various semantic types in calculation views
Expected result:	An overview of the performance impact when using various semantic types and conversion logics in calculated columns
Architecture elements	Calculation views, calculated column

Table 4.61: Test scenario 4C.10: semantic types of metrics in calculation views

This test scenario is based on the approach outlined in Figure 4.48:

1. Create calc. view on top of reference ANV	2. Add calculated column of semantic type date	3. Add calculated column of semantic type unit	4. Compare runtime

Figure 4.48: Steps for test scenario 4C.10

The IT department uses their standard calculation view as the starting point and adds a calculated column for semantic type date (steps 1 and 2). To obtain a proper understanding of the effect on performance, they create variants of this calculated column considering also date functions. As the basis for these tests, they use **purchase_date** as a semantic attribute. Step 3 of this test scenario is comparable to the second step but works with semantic type unit and the conversion of units. The IT department uses **purchase_quantity** as the measure and **product_unit** as the column providing the respective units. For conversion functions, the column type measure generally has to be chosen. Comparing and summing up the various runtime results is the concluding step of this test scenario. The results of the individual steps are shown in Table 4.62. The processing time figures are based on the selection of the top 20,000 records.

Scenario	Server processing time
Date (additional date as cc)	12.812 s
Date functions (adddays)	13.723 s
Unit (additional unit as cc)	14.450 s
Unit conversions (measure)	34.160 s
Reference	**12.752 s**

Table 4.62: Test scenario 4C.10 result: metrics with semantics

Summarizing the results, the IT department recognizes that working with date measures or data functions has a slight impact on the overall performance. The same is true for unit measures. However, when it comes to conversion functions, the processing time more than doubles (this result is even worse than for analytic views – see Section 4.2.8). The IT department adds a note to check the necessity of unit conversions and find ways to precalculate as much as possible in advance of the actual query execution. See also the discussion of virtualization versus persistency in Chapter 3.

Date functions

SAP HANA functions for date operations are relatively limited. If you want to execute operations on attributes of data type date, revert to SQL operations as documented in: *https://help.sap.com/saphelp_hanaone/helpdata/en/20/9f228975191014baed94f1b69693ae/content.htm.* ⇨12

Prerequisite for unit conversion

To enable unit conversion, the following prerequisite has to be fulfilled: tables T006, T006D, and T006A have to be provided in the respective schema nominated for unit conversion. For further details, please refer to:

http://help.sap.com/saphelp_hanaplatform/helpdata/en/36/d87a0a5f53412b9efec8b3fe228681/frameset.htm. ⇨13

> **Metrics with semantics and conversion functionality**
>
> Plain metrics with semantics only have a minimal impact on the performance. However, enabling conversion for those metrics decreases the overall runtime significantly. Thus, try to precalculate converted measures as much as possible. In the case of flexible conversions, use input parameters to realize this requirement.

4.3.11 Currency conversion

The last step in the series for analyzing calculated columns covers currency key figures and the conversion of these key figures. Similar to the tests in analytic views, the IT department sets up scenarios in calculation views. Table 4.63 provides an overview of this test scenario.

Test category:	4C – Calculation views
Test focus:	Calculated columns, performance
Scenario description:	Analysis of the performance impact of using calculated columns with currency conversion in calculation views
Expected result:	Transparency on the performance impact of various types of currency conversion in calculated columns
Architecture elements	Calculation views, calculated column

Table 4.63: Test scenario 4C.11: currency conversion in calculation views

Figure 4.49 outlines the steps in this test scenario.

1. Create calc. view on top of reference ANV → 2. Add calculated column of semantic type currency → 3. Compare runtime

Figure 4.49: Steps for test scenario 4C.11

The reference calculation view for the IT department is copied to perform the test on currencies (step 1). Calculated columns are defined to implement the various currency conversion options (step 2):

- Input parameter
- Fixed conversion
- From a column

Currency conversion does not work for projection nodes. Hence, the IT department prudently implements the scenarios mentioned above in the top aggregation node, knowing that calculations in an aggregation node may be slow in terms of performance (see Section 4.3.2). The resulting server processing times are shown in Table 4.64 (step 3).

Scenario	Server processing time
Input parameter	32.367 s
Fixed	31.723 s
Selected column	32.016 s
Reference	**12.752 s**

Table 4.64: Test scenario 4C.13 result: currency conversion in calculation views

This result clearly highlights that running currency conversion on calculation views is even worse in terms of performance than the runtime for the same operation in analytic views (around eight seconds slower than the same scenario in an analytic view, see Section 4.2.9). We can also see that the difference between the various scenarios is quite small and almost negligible in this scale. This statement is especially valid when considering that the choice of conversion option primarily depends on the requirement you have to implement.

> **Prerequisite for currency conversion**
>
> To enable currency conversion, the following tables have to be imported into the intended schema for conversion: TCURC, TCURF, TCURN, TCURR, TCURT, TCURV, TCURW, and TCURX. You can find more details on this prerequisite and the date conversion at:
> http://help.sap.com/saphelp_hanaplatform/helpdata/en/a8/2e57d651414e f5a0ad7f10aaf2edfe/frameset.htm. ⇨14

> **Using currency conversion**
>
> Flexible currency conversion is a very common requirement in reporting. Use input parameters to provide full flexibility for your users, but also consider that currency conversions increase the runtime of your view significantly. For that reason, also take precalculation options into account (e.g., precalculate the most commonly used target currencies). See also Section 6.5.

4.3.12 Hierarchies

Handling hierarchies is a special feature in SAP HANA. Level and parent-child hierarchies are the two types of hierarchies available. As many business entities are organized in hierarchies, they are interested in the functionality and performance behavior of SAP HANA in this regard. Table 4.65 provides an overview of this test scenario.

Test category:	4C – Calculation views
Test focus:	Hierarchies, functionality, performance
Scenario description:	Analysis of the functionality of hierarchies and the impact on performance of using hierarchies in calculation views
Expected result:	Clarity on the functionality and performance of using hierarchies in calculation views
Architecture elements	Calculation views, hierarchies

Table 4.65: Test scenario 4C.12: hierarchies in calculation views

The IT department uses the procedure outlined in Figure 4.50 to execute this test.

> 1. Create calc. view on top of reference ANV → 2. Add level-based hierarchy → 3. Add parent-child hierarchy → 4. Compare runtime

Figure 4.50: Steps for test scenario 4C.12

This test scenario follows the same pattern as the previous section and in step 1 a calculation view based on the reference analytic view is built. A level-based hierarchy is then added and corresponding performance tests are performed. The hierarchy is reciprocally activated or deactivated (step 2). The third step repeats the same test steps for a parent-child hierarchy. To define the hierarchy, the IT department uses the attributes country/state/city from the company master data table. The parent-child hierarchy also uses an input parameter to enable a flexible selection of the hierarchy root value for the analysis. The last step in this scenario is the comparison of the functionality and runtime.

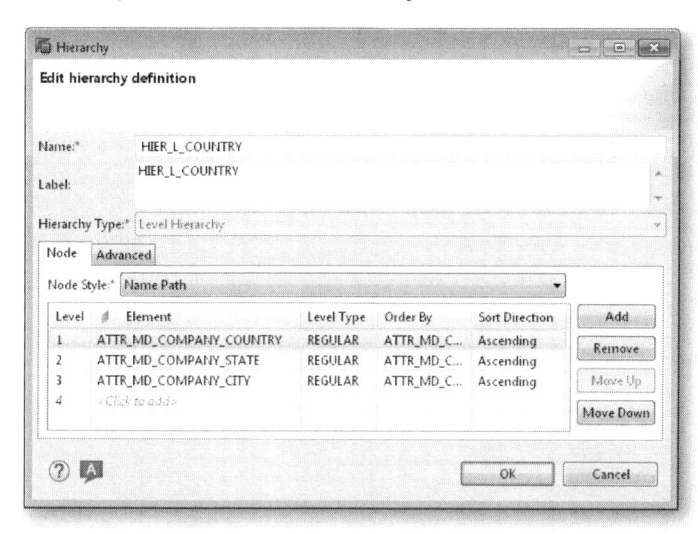

Figure 4.51: Test scenario 4C.12: definition of level hierarchy

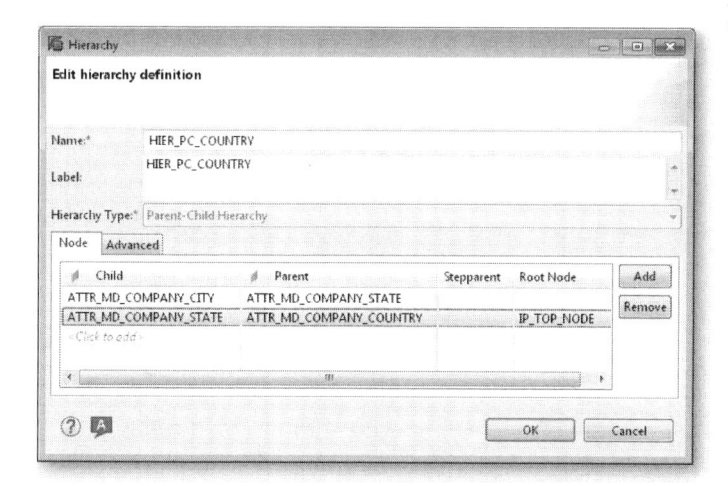

Figure 4.52: Test scenario 4C.12: definition of parent-child hierarchy

159

HIGH-PERFORMING INFORMATION VIEWS

> **Data preview for hierarchies**
>
> SAP HANA Studio does not provide a hierarchical data preview at the moment. To view and test the hierarchy, a MDX-based frontend tool has to consume the corresponding HANA view.

As hierarchies cannot be displayed in all frontend tools, the IT department conducted some trials with frontends such as SAP Lumira, Analysis for Office, and Microsoft Excel. For all tools, they used the same direct ODBC connection to SAP HANA. For SAP Lumira, only level-based hierarchies can be consumed at the moment. A screenshot with an example of how a hierarchy is represented is shown in Figure 4.53. The example shows the level hierarchy defined above in SAP Lumira.

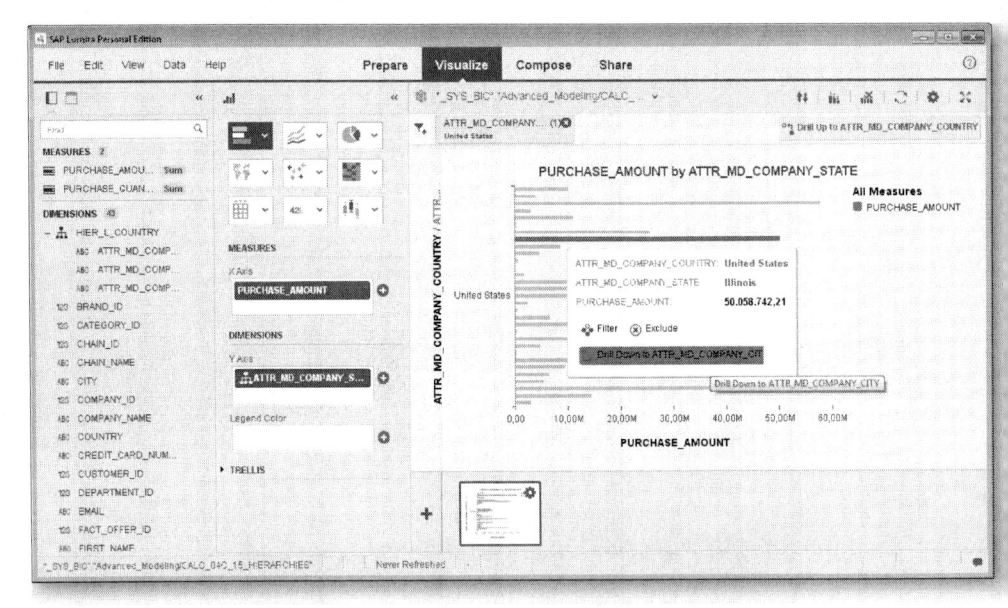

Figure 4.53: Test scenario 4C.12: screenshot level hierarchy in SAP Lumira

With regard to the runtime, the IT department conducted some field testing with Analysis for Office and a direct Microsoft Excel connection. Comparing level and parent-child hierarchy to each other did not really make sense for them as the decision about which hierarchy type is applicable for your scenario depends on your data and business requirement. Nevertheless, the tests showed very good response times for navigation through the hierarchies in SAP Lumira and Analysis for Office. The Microsoft Excel direct connection was considerably slower and therefore definitely not to be recommended (connection using SAP HANA MDX Provider).

> **Further information on SAP HANA hierarchies**
>
> Details about the various settings and options for creating hierarchies in SAP HANA are described in the SAP HANA modeling guide: *http://help.sap.com/hana/SAP_HANA_Modeling_Guide_en.pdf*.

> **Analysis of queries executed by frontend tools**
>
> Query tools sometimes do not provide helpful support in analyzing query runtime or elapsed time when executing navigation steps. Therefore, SAP HANA provides trace files to give a clear picture of the actual operations and steps performed on the machine in the overview of the instance via the DIAGNOSIS FILES tab. Search for the latest file in your index server with type trace.

> **Hierarchies**
>
> Hierarchies generally work fine in SAP HANA. Depending on the frontend tool, you will still experience one or other restriction or (major) limitation. As SAP continuously enhances its tools, check the latest release information for your intended frontend tool regarding the support for SAP HANA hierarchies. Compared to SAP BW, the definition of hierarchies in SAP HANA does not yet provide the same functionality and capability (e.g., you have to build your own time-dependency or version-dependency for hierarchies).

4.3.13 Counters

As already tested for analytic views, the IT department would also like to use the counter functionality for calculation views. Counters are helpful

161

for meeting business requirements such as counting, sorting, or ABC analysis. The test scenario is summarized in Table 4.66.

Test category:	4C – Calculation views
Test focus:	Counter, performance
Scenario description:	Analysis of the impact on performance of using counter functionality in calculation views
Expected result:	Transparency on the performance impact of using the counter functionality in calculation views
Architecture elements:	Calculation views, counter

Table 4.66: Test scenario 4C.13: counter in calculation views

This test scenario comprises three clear steps (see Figure 4.54):

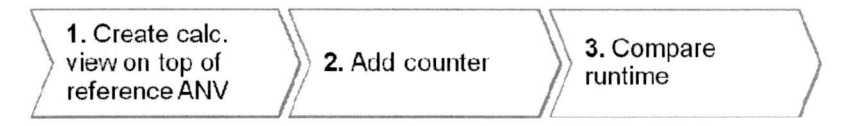

1. Create calc. view on top of reference ANV → 2. Add counter → 3. Compare runtime

Figure 4.54: Steps for test scenario 4C.13

Based on a copy of the basic calculation view, a counter is added to the view definition (step 1 and 2). In step 3, the view is executed and the result presented as shown in Table 4.67.

Scenario	City: server processing time	Customer: server processing time
Counter	31.934 s	32.359 s
Reference	**12.752 s**	**12.752 s**

Table 4.67: Test scenario 4C.13 result: counter performance

Similarly to the results from the same test scenario in the section on analytic views, the runtime significantly increases when the counter functionality is used. In this scenario, the server processing time more than doubles. The data type and number of distinct values of the selected attribute only influence the runtime marginally compared to the overall performance loss.

As noted in Chapter 4.2.12, the aggregation and join are executed twice, resulting in a performance loss of a factor greater than 2.

> **Counter**
>
> ☞ Realizing the counter functionality in SAP HANA leads to a significant reduction in the runtime. As common frontend tools also provide counter operations, try to implement this functionality in the frontend. Alternatively, and of course dependent on the business scenario, you may also use the aggregation type **count** with columns in aggregation node to fulfill specific requirements in terms of counting records or specific values respectively.

4.3.14 Exception aggregation

The business department has several analytical requirements which require a calculation at a specific low level of granularity. In the reporting itself, a higher level of granularity is required. Hence, the calculation must not be aggregated at the level of granularity chosen in the query. Realizing this requirement calls for the implementation of an exception aggregation.

The IT Director has heard that the SAP HANA *keep flag* option enables this functionality. To familiarize himself with this option, he sets up a separate test scenario (see Table 4.68).

Test category:	4C – Calculation views
Test focus:	Aggregation node, projection node, functionality, performance
Scenario description:	Activation of keep flag for a selected attribute in the projection node to implement exception aggregation; understanding the performance impact
Expected result:	Transparency about the performance impact of using the keep flag functionality in calculation views
Architecture elements:	Calculation views, aggregation node, projection node

Table 4.68: Test scenario 4C.14: keep flag option in calculation views

For this test, the steps listed in Figure 4.55 are executed:

1. Create calc. view on top of reference ANV
2. Activate keep flag option for selected attribute
3. Compare runtime

Figure 4.55: Steps for test scenario 4C.14

This test scenario is based on the initial calculation view (step 1). For the identifying attributes **company** and **category**, the keep flag property is set to true in the semantics node (step 2). The view is executed and the runtime compared to the reference value. The results are provided in Table 4.69.

Scenario	Server processing time
Keep flag	17.075 s
Without keep flag	15.952 s

Table 4.69: Test scenario 4C.165 result: exception aggregation

The results show that calculating an exception aggregation has an acceptable impact on the performance of the execution of your view (especially when you come from early SAP BW releases). The reason for this is that all columns with the keep flag property set have to be included in the SQL statement in order to calculate the result at the correct level of granularity.

> **Keep flag property**
>
> Since SAP HANA SPS 9, the keep flag property has been available for aggregation as well as projection nodes. An attribute with this option set as true has to be retrieved from the database even if it is not requested by the query statement. Thus, this attribute is included in the group by clause even if it is not selected. More details are provided in the SAP HANA modeling guide:
>
> help.sap.com/hana/sap_hana_modeling_guide_en.pdf

> **Performance improvement for exception aggregation**
>
> An alternative approach for realizing exception aggregation and improving performance in parallel is to precalculate the respective values and store them physically in an SAP HANA table. This decision has to be made on a case-by-case basis dependent on object usage and number of dependent records.

4.3.15 Variables

Variables enable flexible filtering of data. The IT department wants to take closer at the functionality and performance behavior of variables. The corresponding test scenario is shown in Table 4.70.

Test category:	4C – Calculation views
Test focus:	Variables, functionality, performance
Scenario description:	Demonstration of the functionality and performance impact of variables in calculation views
Expected result:	Understanding of the functionality and impact on the execution plan as well as performance of using variables in calculation views
Architecture elements:	Calculation views, variables

Table 4.70: Test scenario 4C.15: variables in calculation views

This test scenario uses the approach outlined in Figure 4.56:

1. Create calc. view on top of reference ANV → 2. Add variables of different types → 3. Compare runtime

Figure 4.56: Steps for test scenario 4C.15

Leveraging the reference calculation view in this chapter (step 1), the IT department starts to create and add variables to analyze the effect on the server processing time and the records returned by the query. Variables are defined in the semantics node of a calculation view only. The IT department also executes this test in several variants using different types of variables (single value, multiple single value, range, and interval). Finally, the team compares the results (step 3).

Scenario	Server processing time	Overall result rows
One variable, single entry (attribute 'language')	1.609 s	1,233,554
One variable, single entry as interval (attribute 'language')	1.678 s	1,233,554
One variable, multiple entries (attribute 'language')	1.742 s	1,752,816
Two variables, single entry (attributes 'language' + 'gender')	1.538 s	1,084,928
Reference	**12.752 s**	**50,000,000**

Table 4.71: Test scenario 4C.15 result: variables

Variables work very well and are efficient for reducing the number of records down to those required but also to significantly reduce the server processing time. Variables work like a `where clause` in the SQL statement. The different variable type settings demonstrate the expected behavior and performance runtime.

> **Variables**
>
> Variables can be considered a reasonable option for flexible data filtering without any further options to influence the data processing logic.

> **A note on generated SQL statements**
>
> If you are using a single value variable type, or a single value allowing multiple entries, when you execute the calculation view with assigned variables via the generated SQL statement in SAP HANA Studio, the where clause will always be built using the IN operator. This applies even if only one value was selected. For example, two single entries in the attribute **language** and one single entry in the attribute **gender** leads to the following SQL where clause: `WHERE (("LANGUAGE" IN ('English') OR "LANGUAGE" IN ('Italian') )) AND (("GENDER" IN ('Male') )).`

> **Complex filter selections**
>
> If you need to support a comprehensive filtering (e.g., by combining include and exclude filtering within the same variable), use the range option along with the multiple entries option. On the prompt screen, you can change the operator from not equal to equal and the various greater or less operators on a case-by-case basis. In contrast, the single value option allows only the equal operator (in addition to the null validation). The interval is restricted to the between operator.

4.3.16 Input parameters

Input parameters are an alternative and powerful approach for dealing with user-specific entries. To an end user, an input parameter has the same behavior as a variable. For this reason, the IT department is interested in the features, use, and impact on the performance of using input parameters. They design the following test scenario (see Table 4.72).

Test category:	4C – Calculation views
Test focus:	Input parameters, functionality, execution plan, performance
Scenario description:	Demonstration of the functionality and performance impact of various input parameters in calculation views
Expected result:	Understanding of the functionality and impact on the execution plan as well as performance of using various input parameters in calculation views
Architecture elements:	Calculation views, input parameters

Table 4.72: Test scenario 4C.16: input parameters in calculation views

The steps in Figure 4.57 outline the test approach:

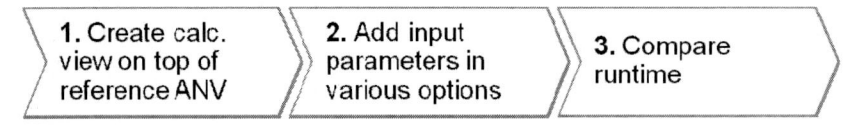

1. Create calc. view on top of reference ANV → 2. Add input parameters in various options → 3. Compare runtime

Figure 4.57: Steps for test scenario 4C.16

The starting point is the reference calculation view, which is enriched by input parameters of various types and complexities (step 2). On one hand, input parameters are used as a filter in a projection node (attribute: **state**) and on the other, as a value for influencing the calculation of a calculated column. The IT department decides to implement one calculated column with a simple calculation scenario, and a second calculation scenario with a more complex column using three input parameters to calculate the variance in purchase quantity based on a given, external parameter for a specific region. The formula is:

```
if(((leftstr("ZIP",1) = $$IP_ZIP$$) and ("COUNTRY"
='$$IP_COUNTRY$$')),
$$IP_VALUE$$*"PURCHASE_QUANTITY","PURCHASE_QUANTITY")
```

The results (step 3) are shown in Table 4.73.

Scenario	Server processing time
Input parameter as filter	2.904 s
Input parameter in calculated column (simple scenario)	13.594 s
Input parameter in calculated column (complex scenario)	14.487 s
Reference	**12.752 s**

Table 4.73: Test scenario 4C.16 result: input parameters

In terms of data filtering and the query result, input parameters provide the same result from a functional perspective as variables. Moreover, input parameters can also be used to influence the query structure and the result itself. Thus, there are more powerful uses of input parameters, as this test scenario demonstrates. We have already learned in Section 4.3.6 that when looking at performance aspects, there are no concerns with using input parameters. As far as calculated columns are concerned, the server processing time strongly depends on the scenario you build. For that reason, the IT department does not overly emphasize the runtime results of this test. Furthermore, the key learning for the IT department is the high variety and richness of options for leveraging input parameters. The following options are available for defining an input parameter: direct input, values from a column or a static list, or values derived from a table or even a procedure. Nevertheless, there is also a downside to input parameters as there is currently no option for interval or range selection: only single and multiple single entries are permitted in the current SAP HANA version (SPS 9). For interval or range selections, you have to implement a workaround.

Input parameters

Input parameters can be used in a multifunctional manner. They work well as filters, but also as a powerful feature for influencing the query output or the processing of the query. The disadvantage of input parameters is that there are currently no selection options for intervals and ranges.

> **Processing input parameters**
>
> Input parameters are handled as PLACEHOLDERS in the `FROM` clause of an SQL statement. In contrast, variables are treated within the `WHERE` clause. For the end user, there is no transparency about whether a prompt is variable or an input parameter.

> **Using input parameters with third party tools**
>
> Please consider that there are still third party frontend tools that cannot consume input parameters. You must therefore check your specific tool and version individually. Hierarchies or a combination of hierarchies with calculated key figures may therefore be a challenge for the frontend tool, including some SAP-owned tools.

4.3.17 Hidden columns

SAP HANA offers functionality for hiding columns. Defining attributes or key figures as hidden allows you to use the objects for calculations within the view without them being visible to the end user. The IT department wants to understand this feature and especially its impact on view runtime. Table 4.74 highlights the objective of this test.

Test category:	4C – Calculation views
Test focus:	Hidden columns, performance
Scenario description:	Analysis of the performance impact for hidden columns in calculation views
Expected result:	Understanding of the performance impact of hidden columns in calculation views
Architecture elements:	Calculation views, hidden columns

Table 4.74: Test scenario 4C.17: hidden columns in calculation views

The steps in Figure 4.58 show the test approach:

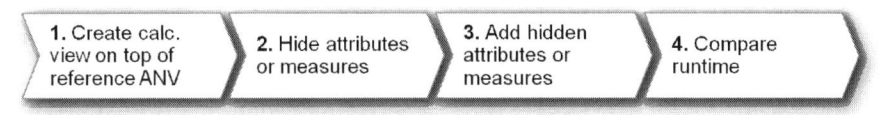

1. Create calc. view on top of reference ANV → 2. Hide attributes or measures → 3. Add hidden attributes or measures → 4. Compare runtime

Figure 4.58: Steps for test scenario 4C.17

The IT department refers to the reference calculation view which is used throughout the entire test series (step 1) and starts hiding both attributes and measures step by step (step 2). Afterwards, they reverse the test and add hidden columns to the reference calculation view. In this context, they also include a hidden column in the calculation of a visible column (step 3). An overview of the results is given in Table 4.75.

Scenario	Server processing time
Hiding 5 attributes/measures	12.123 s
Hiding 10 attributes/measures	10.882 s
Hiding 15 attributes/measures	10.375 s
Adding 5 hidden attributes/measures	12.780 s
Adding 10 hidden attributes/measures	12.799 s
Using hidden columns in a visible column (e. g., currency conversion)	32.019 s
Reference	**12.752 s**

Table 4.75: Test scenario 4C.17 result: hidden columns

The results clearly show that hiding an attribute or measure reduces the server processing time. The higher the number of attributes that are hidden, the more the runtime decreases, as the attributes are no longer included in the select statement. The IT department established that the behavior of this feature is like not querying the specific attribute. Thus, for a reporting scenario in which the source provides some fields that are not needed, this feature is good for defining a tailored interface. In addition, columns should be hidden at the lowest possible level within the view. Furthermore, the IT department learned that adding hidden fields does not impact the performance. However, when using hidden fields in a visible column, the hidden field is part of the view execution and therefore impacts performance.

> **Hidden columns**
>
> Hidden columns help shrink the width of the result set and therefore reduce the runtime. The behavior is similar to only selecting the desired fields in an SQL statement. Hiding all fields provided by a secondary table/view via a join operation can also lead to the join operation being omitted depending on the join type and the property settings of the join. Adding hidden columns does not impact the performance. Hidden columns can be used in any other column within the view normally.

> **Access hidden columns using SQL**
>
> The tests indicated to the IT department that a hidden attribute or measure is not visible for the end user or the next view level (e.g., on the DATA PREVIEW tab of SAP HANA studio); however, the hidden attribute or measure can still be queried with the resulting values displayed via standard SQL.

4.3.18 SQL versus CE functions

When SAP HANA was introduced, SAP recommended using CE functions in scripted calculation views instead of standard SQL. Another clear statement from SAP is not to mix up both scenarios (SQL and CE). However, the IT department has some concerns about the capabilities of CE functions in terms of richness and performance. To get a better insight on this, they define another test to compare SQL and CE functions (see Table 4.76).

HIGH-PERFORMING INFORMATION VIEWS

Test category:	4C – Calculation views
Test focus:	SQL and CE functions
Scenario description:	Comparison of the performance using CE functions versus standard SQL operators for the same scenario
Expected result:	A structured performance comparison of each CE function with its equivalent SQL function within a scripted calculation view
Architecture elements:	Scripted calculation views, CE functions, standard SQL operators

Table 4.76: Test scenario 4C.18: SQL vs. CE functions

For this test scenario, the IT department performs the steps shown in Figure 4.59.

1. Create two scripted calc. views → 2. Implement a scenario using CE functions in view 1 → 3. Implement same scenario with SQL in view 2 → 4. Compare runtime

Figure 4.59: Steps for test scenario 4C.18

This test starts from scratch and defines two empty skeletons of scripted SAP HANA views in the first step. Next, the same scenario is built twice: once using CE functions and once using standard SQL (steps 2 and 3). The IT department divides this test further into a simple scenario (selecting data directly from the fact table), a medium complexity scenario (selecting and joining data from two tables), and a complex scenario (selecting and joining data from tables and attribute views). The test scenario ends with a comparison of the runtimes for each view. The results are summarized in Table 4.77.

Scenario	Script	Server processing time
Simple	SQL	9.464 s
	CE function	16.800 s
Medium	SQL	13.412 s
	CE function	13.032 s
Complex	SQL	12.911 s
	CE function	14.468 s

Table 4.77: Test scenario 4C.18 result: SQL vs. CE functions

173

The results clearly demonstrate that the SQL engine has improved significantly compared to earlier SAP HANA revisions. In almost all disciplines of this test scenario, SQL is superior to the CE functions. The IT department is confused by the high runtime of the CE function in the simple scenario (even after running the test several times). The optimizer for CE functions apparently has some deficiencies. It appears that the CE functions are not the preferred scripting approach, not only in terms of functionality (there has been little to no recent news on updates or enhancements of CE functions), but also with regards to performance.

> **SQL versus CE functions**
>
> This test underscores that scripted views based on standard SQLScript are the preferred solution compared to CE functions. In particular, when taking into account that for CE functions, a new syntax has to be learned and the vocabulary is still limited, SQL becomes a real option.

> **SAP's early best recommendations**
>
> There is an often quoted but also outdated slide deck available with best practices for SAP HANA modeling which provides a good comparison of SQL versus CE functions in terms of functionality
> (see *http://scn.sap.com/docs/DOC-13267*).
>
> In addition, there is a very interesting SCN blog which explains why CE functions are no longer state of the art: *http://scn.sap.com/community/hana-in-memory/blog/2014/12/11/calculation-engine-ce-functions--rest-in-peace.* ⇨15

4.3.19 Input parameters in scripted views

Continuing the investigation into scripted calculation views, the IT department is looking for answers on how to leverage input parameters. In parallel, they are again strongly interested in the performance behavior. Thus, they execute the test scenario described in Table 4.78.

Test category:	4C – Calculation views
Test focus:	Input parameters, functionality, performance
Scenario description:	Examination of the functionality and performance of input parameters in scripted functions
Expected result:	Demonstration of the functionality and performance impact of using input parameters in scripted functions
Architecture elements:	Scripted calculation views, input parameters, CE functions, SQL operators

Table 4.78: Test scenario 4C.19: input parameters in scripted functions

This test is set up as outlined in Figure 4.60.

1. Create two scripted calc. views (SQL+CE) → 2. Add same kind of input parameter to both views → 3. Compare runtime

Figure 4.60: Steps for test scenario 4C.19

For this test, the IT department creates copies of the scripted views from the previous test (step 1) and implements an input parameter on column **brand_id** (step 2) for each view. For CE functions, the syntax for applying the input parameter (IP_BRAND) is given below.

```
sl_1 = CE_COLUMN_TABLE ("AM_DML"."FACT_TRANSACTIONS",
[CUSTOMER_ID,BRAND_ID,PURCHASE_DATE,PURCHASE_AMOUNT,
COMPANY_ID]);
pr_1 = CE_PROJECTION(:sl_1,[CUSTOMER_ID,BRAND_ID,PURCHASE_
DATE,PURCHASE_AMOUNT,COMPANY_ID], ' "BRAND_ID" = :IP_BRAND ');
```

The impact on the server processing time is compared (step 3) and the results are shown in Table 4.79.

Scenario	Server processing time
SQL	0.347 s
CE functions	2.393 s

Table 4.79: Test scenario 4C.19 result: input parameters in scripted views

The IT department determines that input parameters work as expected from a functional perspective and as known from a graphical modeling approach. However, in terms of performance, the IT department recognizes a large difference between SQL and CE functions in favor of SQL.

> **Input parameters in scripted views**
>
> Input parameters work well in scripted views. SQL-based views using input parameters are significantly faster than those implemented on CE functions.

4.3.20 Scripted calculation view in graphical calculation view

This test scenario is very important to the IT department. They assume that not all business requirements can be realized using graphical modeling. Leveraging the richness of scripted implementation for some of the selected complex calculations or transformations and combining it at the end with a governed, graphically supported data model seems to be a reasonable approach. See Table 4.80 for an overview of the test scenario.

Test category:	4C – Calculation views
Test focus:	Scripted calculation views, graphical calculation views, performance
Scenario description:	Analysis of performance using a scripted calculation view in a graphical calculation view
Expected result:	Understanding of the performance impact of a scripted calculation view in the context of a graphical calculation view
Architecture elements	Scripted calculation view, graphical calculation view, join node

Table 4.80: Test scenario 4C.20: scripted calculation views in graphical calculation views

This test is set up as outlined in Figure 4.61.

| 1. Create calc. view on top of reference ANV | 2. Create scripted calc. view and get runtime | 3. Include scripted View in graphical calc. view | 4. Compare runtime |

Figure 4.61: Steps for test scenario 4C.20

Reusing the basic calculation view (step 1), the IT department additionally generates a scripted calculation view. They execute the scripted view in stand-alone mode and record the runtime (step 2). In the third step, the team incorporates the scripted view into the graphical view. Therefore, the IT department starts with a single projection node carrying the scripted calculation view. Using a union node, the projection node with the scripted view is then combined with another projection based on the reference analytic view. Finally, the team analyzes the overall runtime of the graphical view and compares the reference times (stand-alone graphical view and stand-alone scripted view). The server processing times are given in Table 4.81.

Scenario	Server processing time
Scripted view stand-alone	12.911 s
Scripted view in projection node only	13.099 s
Scripted view in projection node and union within graphical view	45.920 s
Analytic view in calculation view with the same fields and logic	2.701 s
Reference	**12.752 s**

Table 4.81: Test scenario 4C.20 result: scripted calculation view in graphical view

Including scripted views in a graphical view is easy from a functional perspective. Looking at the runtime, solely binding the scripted view to a projection node does not really impact the server processing time. However, including the scripted view in an existing graphical calculation view using a union node increases the runtime of the test scenario significantly. This applies to both engines (calculation engine and SQL engine). The IT department checks for the root cause of this and, in the PlanViz execution overview, establishes that just like with the counters, the join and aggregation are performed twice. We assume that this is not the intended behavior. Merging the result is again an expensive operation in terms of costs.

Finally, the IT department executes the same logic with the same field selection by enhancing the reference calculation view. The outcome shows that the same result is achieved in 2.7 seconds, which indicates to the IT department that scripted calculation views should be avoided.

> **Scripted view in calculation view**
>
> ▶ Try to avoid scripted calculation views whenever possible.
>
> ▶ Scripted views in calculation views are a valid option and work as expected (e.g., for complex calculations).

4.3.21 Call of procedures

This test scenario can be seen as complementary to the previous test. Procedures help to encapsulate the sequence of several transformation or calculation steps. For the IT department, procedures are an acceptable concept for maintaining a good structure and overview of their implementation. Table 4.82 shows the IT department's intended test scenario.

Test category:	4C – Calculation views
Test focus:	Scripted calculation views, performance
Scenario description:	Analysis of functionality and performance when calling procedures within scripted calculation views
Expected result:	Depiction of the performance behavior for procedure calls within scripted calculation views
Architecture elements	Scripted calculation view, procedures

Table 4.82: Test scenario 4C.21: call of procedures

The steps below outline the approach of this test:

| 1. Create a scripted calc. view | 2. Create a procedure and obtain runtime | 3. Include call procedure in scripted calc. view | 4. Compare runtime |

Figure 4.62: Steps for test scenario 4C.21

This scenario starts with the creation of a scripted calculation view. To do this, the IT department copies the initial scripted calculation view from a previous test and obtains its runtime as a reference (step 1). Secondly, they implement a procedure and analyze the runtime when executing the procedure in a stand-alone scenario (step 2). In the third step, the procedure call is included in the scripted view. The impact on the overall runtime and comparison with the stand-alone runtimes are presented in Table 4.83.

Scenario	Server processing time
Scripted view	12.832 s
Procedure	10.182 s
Scripted view with procedure	12.996 s

Table 4.83: Test scenario 4C.21 result: call of procedures

Procedures can be used to encapsulate a certain functionality or sequence of operations. From this test, the IT department learns that their logic from the previous test case can be completely outsourced to a procedure. Thus, the actual view contains only the call procedure statement as shown here:

```
/********* Begin Procedure Script ************/
BEGIN
call "AM_DML"."CALC_04C_PROC" ( var_out );
END /********* End Procedure Script ************/
```

It is very interesting that the execution of the plain procedure is considerably faster than calling the same logic from a scripted view. Thinking about more complex scenarios, the IT department likes this approach as it also has no measurable impact on the runtime.

> **Call of procedures**
>
> Procedures are a helpful feature for encapsulating transformation and calculation logics. They do not have a negative impact on the overall performance.

4.3.22 Projection node versus physical data duplication

The IT department has heard a lot about the challenges of building an overall high-performing data model. Virtualization and data persistency were discussed in general in Chapter 3, and the IT department would now like to build up a test scenario that somehow deals with modeling concepts of calculation views versus a physical data preparation, or even duplication. The test scenario is summarized in Table 4.84.

Test category:	4C – Calculation views
Test focus:	Data duplication via physical table or projection node, performance
Scenario description:	Examination of modeling approaches for data duplication: physical additional data storage versus projection nodes. The scenario covers reporting cases where, e. g., a sum over all attribute values for one dimension should be available.
Expected result:	A performance comparison of a query running on a calculation view with a projection and one running on a table with duplicated master data
Architecture elements	Attribute view, analytic view, calculation view, projection node, SQL query

Table 4.84: Test scenario 4C.22: projection node vs. physical data duplication

This complex test scenario comprises the steps noted in Figure 4.63.

1. Create an enhanced table on customer
2. Insert records and update STATE_PROMPT
3. Duplicate records with All_State value
4. Create ATV and adjust reference ANV
5. Include new ANV in reference calc. view
6. Compare runtime

Figure 4.63: Steps for test scenario 4C.22

First of all, the IT department starts by creating an additional, physical master data table based on the customer. They add an additional column STATE_PROMPT for the subsequent data selection (step 1). After loading the data from the existing MD_CUSTOMER table into the new customer master data table (STATE_PROMPT has the same values as STATE), they also add STATE_PROMPT to the primary key attributes (step 2). In the third step, they duplicate all records in the table one by one and set the corresponding value of column STATE_PROMPT to All States. Next (step 4), they build a separate attribute view for this new master data table and include the new attribute view in the reference analytic view (the existing attribute view on customer master data is replaced). Finally, they add the new analytic view to the reference calculation view (step 5). The IT department compares the results of this scenario based on the execution of several complex queries (see Table 4.85).

Scenario	Server processing time
New calculation view with altered master data table	25.773 s
Calculation view with union based on existing analytic view	44.341 s
Reference	**12.752 s**

Table 4.85: Test scenario 4C.22 result: call of procedures

The results show that data duplication through projection nodes using the same view or table multiple times with the same dataset results in a severe decrease in performance.

> **Projection nodes versus physical data duplication**
>
> Storing additional information physically increases the overall runtime of your data model. You should also avoid duplicating data virtually. However, as discussed in Chapter 3, you have to find the right balance between physical storage of data and virtual, on-the-fly calculation.

4.3.23 Filter pushdown

With this test scenario, the IT department investigates filter pushdown behavior and, therefore, the effect on the performance of SAP HANA. The focal points in the test are input parameters and variables used in multilayer scenarios. The understanding of the IT department is that SAP HANA always tries to push down the filter operation to the lowest possible layer so that only the actual volume of data needed is processed. The IT department wants to prove this for its own scenario. See Table 4.86 for a description of the test scenario.

Test category:	4C – Calculation views
Test focus:	Calculation views, execution plan, performance
Scenario description:	Test of the filter pushdown of variables and input parameters through several layers of calculation views
Expected result:	A performance comparison of the top calculation view with a filter only versus the lowest calculation view using filters and input parameter mapping
Architecture elements	Calculation view, projection node, input parameter, variables

Table 4.86: Test scenario 4C.23: filter pushdown

The IT department performs this test following the steps outlined in Figure 4.64:

| 1. Create two calc. views on top of reference ANV | 2. Define filter restriction in top node of view 1 | 3. Define same filter in lowest layer of view 2 | 4. Compare runtime |

Figure 4.64: Steps for test scenario 4C.23

The IT department creates two identical calculation views for this scenario, leveraging the reference analytic view. For a solid test result they include two projection nodes and a union node in each of the views (step 1). Then, in the first view they add a variable to the top node and then implement the same restriction in the bottom node (steps 2 and 3). Comparing the runtime of these two views provides insights into the behavior and performance results of these two approaches. For the results of this test, see Table 4.87.

Scenario	Server processing time
Variable on top node	42.292 s
Variable on bottom node	42.579 s

Table 4.87: Test scenario 4C.23 result: filter pushdown

This result confirms that filter pushdown works as expected in SAP HANA. Thus, the takeaway for the IT department is that they can easily use the filter definition in the top node of their calculation views. Also, the investigation of the execution plan in PlanViz confirmed that in this test scenario, the chosen filter was applied on the lowest possible level in the database.

Filter pushdown

SAP HANA pushes filter operations (variables, input parameters) to the lowest possible level of execution. The result set is thereby restricted to the essential data as early as possible.

> **Detailed filter analysis**
>
> A useful approach for analyzing the execution plan and the exact point where filter definitions are applied is to use the PlanViz tool. Details are provided in Chapter 3 of this book.

4.3.24 Calculation over several aggregation levels

Next, the IT department wants to research calculation over several aggregation nodes. They would like to understand how the calculation view behaves in terms of performance in comparison to a physical representation of the output. This scenario is consequently related to the case described in Section 4.3.22. An overview of this test scenario is provided in Table 4.88.

Test category:	4C – Calculation views
Test focus:	Calculation views, performance
Scenario description:	Analysis of the performance behavior through calculations performed over different levels of aggregation within a calculation view. The analysis considers either the execution during runtime or the storage of the result as part of an ETL process.
Expected result:	Information about the performance behavior through calculations over several aggregation levels. Measurement of the performance if the calculation is performed in an "ETL-like process" and stored physically.
Architecture elements	Calculation view, calculated column, projection node

Table 4.88: Test scenario 4C.24: calculation over several aggregation levels

The test is executed by the IT department as follows:

1. Create calc. view on top of reference ANV
2. Add union and aggregation nodes in calc. view
3. Get runtime of calc. view
4. Create table with required aggregation level
5. Create corresponding ATV and ANV
6. Copy and extend calc. view; compare runtime

Figure 4.65: Steps for test scenario 4C.24

To start this test scenario, the basic calculation view used by the IT department is enhanced with several aggregation nodes for a specific calculation (e.g., average). Moreover, a union node mapping to the aggregate node with the standard (normal) date is added (steps 1 + 2). The IT department now records the performance behavior with the additional aggregation and union node (step 3). In the fourth step, the aspect of the physical data storage is covered and the IT department creates a table with the required aggregation level. In step five, the corresponding attribute view and analytic view are created. Lastly, the IT department creates a copy of the existing calculation view and adds a union node with the old and new analytic view. The team then compares the runtimes (see Table 4.89 for the results).

Scenario	Server processing time
Projection nodes (variant 1)	0:52.122 min
Physical table (variant 2)	1:06.321 min

Table 4.89: Test scenario 4C.24 result: calculation over several aggregation levels

The results indicate that there are scenarios in SAP HANA that work better with direct access to the full width and size of a source table instead of precalculating specific key figures and storing them in separate tables. This scenario is strongly dependent on the complexity of the calculation logic. As mentioned in Section 3.1, we have learned from many projects that not all calculations can be performed during runtime. Thus, this test demonstrates to the IT department that each data model for a specific scenario has to be tested individually.

HIGH-PERFORMING INFORMATION VIEWS

> **Calculation over several aggregation levels**
>
> SAP HANA optimizes the calculation over several aggregation levels and it works very well. The test shows that precalculating key figures in separate tables might even lead to a performance loss. Nevertheless, this insight has to be proven for each use case individually as it is dependent on the complexity of the calculations and not all calculations can be performed directly in a calculation view.

4.3.25 Rank node

To bring the test series about calculation views to a close, the IT department prepares its final research on the rank node. The *rank node* can be used to find, for example, the top 10 customers for a certain key figure combination. The feature is new as of SPS 9 and was formerly primarily implemented by using window functions in the scripted calculation view.

> **Rank node help**
>
> The documentation on the rank node is still under construction but you can find a preview here:
>
> http://help.sap.com/saphelp_hanaplatform/helpdata/en/05/0f14f7a6d94d2da905b0a4072ba546/content.htm?fullscreen=true ⇨ 16

Test category:	4C – Calculation views
Test focus:	Calculation views, rank nodes
Scenario description:	Analysis of the performance behavior of rank nodes with different parameter settings (partition columns, sort direction, dynamic partition elements, threshold)
Expected result:	Information about the performance behavior of the rank node with different settings
Architecture elements	Calculation view, rank node

Table 4.90: Test scenario 4C.24: calculation over several aggregation levels

The test is executed by the IT department as follows:

1. Create three calculation views with a rank node → 2. Add three different levels of complexity → 3. Execute the views with different settings → 4. Document the results

Figure 4.66: Steps for test scenario 4C.25

To start this test the IT department creates three calculation views, with each containing a rank node (step 1). In the second step, the IT department adds three different levels of complexity/granularity to the calculation views. This means that the calculation view with low granularity only sets the ranking at a very low level of detail (rank by state). The medium and high complexity views then add a ranking at increasing levels of granularity. In step 3, the views are executed with different settings (with input parameters, with varying thresholds, and with or without dynamic partitioning). Finally, step 4 consists of documenting the results as shown in Table 4.91.

Level of granularity	Top X elements	Without dynamic partition elements	With dynamic partition elements	With input parameter
Low granularity	Top 10	59.039 s	58.934 s	59.576 s
Low granularity	Top 1,000	60.390 s	59.754 s	58.384 s
Low granularity	Top 10,000	59.390 s	59.270 s	58.926 s
Medium granularity	Top 10	96.097 s	95.058 s	95.996 s
Medium granularity	Top 1,000	126.928 s	127.633 s	127.033 s
Medium granularity	Top 10,000	177.581 s	178.553 s	180.806 s
High granularity	Top 10	168.726 s	168.646 s	168.894 s
High granularity	Top 1,000	219.881 s	218.911 s	219.882 s
High granularity	Top 10,000	230.414 s	229.874 s	230.996 s

Table 4.91: Test scenario 4C.25 result: rank node

The results shown in Table 4.91 clearly show that the rank node has a high impact on the performance of your calculation view (the reference calculation view executed in 12.752 seconds). As this is the first release with rank nodes, we believe the performance may still improve. For the moment, we suggest you still use scripted calculation views. Secondly, the performance decreases heavily with the level of granularity chosen for the ranking and also with the number of elements chosen for the ranking. A final observation is that there is no key figure or attribute created automatically which contains the ranking number, therefore further usage of the rank is not possible. A positive aspect to the rank node is that dynamic partitioning or the use of input parameters do not affect the server processing time.

> **Rank nodes in calculation views**
>
> ▶ Rank nodes have a significant performance impact and we do not recommend using them with SPS 9, Rev. 91.
>
> ▶ The number of elements chosen for ranking (in our example 10, 1,000, 10,000) impacts the performance.
>
> ▶ The level of granularity also decreases performance further.

4.3.26 Synopsis of calculation views

This comprehensive chapter on calculation views gave us valuable insights into the behavior of calculation views. Based on these results, we can state the following recommendations:

- ▶ Filtering data works efficiently to reduce the amount of processed data as quickly as possible.
- ▶ Filters are pushed down to the lowest level as expected.
- ▶ Input parameters are reasonable for filtering but do not provide interval or range restrictions.
- ▶ Attribute views or analytic view joins are significantly slower than the same scenario on the database table level.
- ▶ A star join is a reasonable alternative with at least comparable or even better runtime compared to the standard join in calculation views.
- ▶ Hierarchies generally work fine, however their functionality is not yet as rich as BW for example; in particular, today's frontend tools cannot leverage hierarchies in their full extent.

- Exception aggregation is possible using the keep flag setting and works well even from a performance perspective.
- Conversion operations (semantic types) decrease the runtime of a view clearly and in this regard are even worse than analytic views.
- Standard SQL is probably better than CE functions.
- Procedures help to structure your scripted views and keep them maintainable; there is no impact on performance when you encapsulate logic in procedures.

5 Advanced modeling techniques

When the IT department transformed the business requirements into SAP HANA views and reports, they discovered the capabilities of SAP HANA and also identified certain limitations that require workarounds. One of these capabilities is the SAP HANA development perspective because it offers unique integration and implementation options. As well as looking at the development perspective, in this chapter we analyze limitations and the corresponding alternatives before wrapping up the chapter with a discussion on development methods.

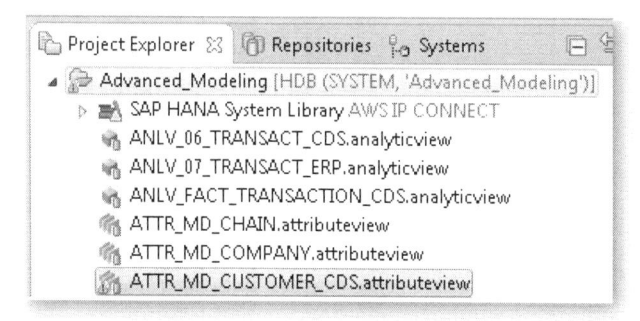

5.1 Development perspective

The *SAP HANA development perspective* provides developers with the option to leverage development technologies in Eclipse-like environments such as Javascript, Java, SAPUI5, R statistics development, SQLScript debugging, and many more. Some of the technologies require an installation in SAP HANA Studio and some even require an installation on the server side. The technologies benefit the company by providing a large number of functionalities in one environment.

In the development perspective, projects can be developed in parallel as SAP HANA Studio/Eclipse offers functionality for synchronizing projects with the server version and for resolving conflicts. In some cases, the conflict resolution can be performed automatically. In other cases, the developer has to resolve the conflicts manually. Figure 5.1 provides an overview of the development perspective for a general development project.

Figure 5.1: Development perspective

5.2 Core Data Services

One of the features available in the SAP HANA development perspective is modeling tables in an environment similar to a programming language called Core Data Services (CDS). *CDS* enables you to model and create tables, column views, data types, and other elements. In this chapter, we will discuss the advantages and disadvantages of CDS-based table design based on our data model in Chapter 3. In Table 5.1, you can see a comparison of CDS and the standard table creation via SQL DDL or a graphical model.

	SQL/graphical	CDS
Field documentation/single point of truth (SPoT)	Additional manual documentation required	Automatically included in CDS document
Table alteration/deletion	Mostly via SQL	Modification of CDS document
Model integrity checks for views	Non-existent	Existing, not enforced
Relationship modeling	Foreign key constraints only via SQL, primary keys also graphically	Possible addition as code to the table
Table naming	Completely user-defined	Only with namespace convention
Data types	SQL and SAP HANA SQL data types	Reduced set of data types
Development effort	Low	Medium

Table 5.1: Comparison of CDS and standard HANA table design

Field documentation

The first advantage of using CDS is the automatic documentation of the table fields. In the CDS document, you work on the definition of the table structure, which is simultaneously documented with the code you write. The document already provides information about the table name, the field name, the data type, and the field length where applicable during the design phase. Normally, when an IT project does not run according to plan, the first measure consists of cutting the time planned for documentation. Therefore, the documentation being offered with coding tables in CDS is a major advantage compared to the table creation in SAP HANA via SQL or the graphical interface. Furthermore, when writing proper design documents in a project, you can use the code for the table creation directly from the design document.

Also, using CDS you automatically keep a document which serves as the single point of truth. Even if you use several documents (e.g., for different domains), you always have a single point of truth of the tables for each domain. This cannot always be guaranteed for all of the tables if you use a central document stored and edited online. By adding comments to the document, you can even explain why a table or field was created. Therefore, this document replaces separate table documentation.

Table alteration

A second advantage of CDS is the ability to alter a table or delete it in a CDS document. Anyone who has designed tables graphically in SAP HANA knows that there are several features missing for altering graphical tables, such as changing the data type, the primary key, or modeling foreign key relationships. This is not the case in CDS, where you can adjust a table easily by changing the table definition. Let's look at the table creation example from Chapter 3. We have the tables FACT_TRANSACTION and MD_CUSTOMER and would like to create these not graphically but using CDS, as shown in Figure 5.2 (noted here with a suffix _CDS).

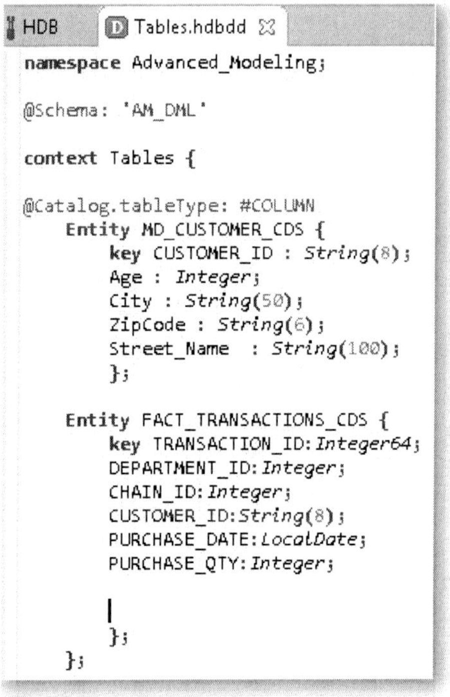

```
 HDB       Tables.hdbdd
namespace Advanced_Modeling;

@Schema: 'AM_DML'

context Tables {

@Catalog.tableType: #COLUMN
    Entity MD_CUSTOMER_CDS {
        key CUSTOMER_ID : String(8);
        Age : Integer;
        City : String(50);
        ZipCode : String(6);
        Street_Name : String(100);
    };

    Entity FACT_TRANSACTIONS_CDS {
        key TRANSACTION_ID: Integer64;
        DEPARTMENT_ID: Integer;
        CHAIN_ID: Integer;
        CUSTOMER_ID: String(8);
        PURCHASE_DATE: LocalDate;
        PURCHASE_QTY: Integer;

        |
    };
};
```

Figure 5.2: CDS development code

When you activate the file, the validity of the syntax is checked and, provided there are no errors, the tables are created automatically. Let us assume that in the first version of the file the field PURCHASE_DATE is not available and has to be added. The only action we have to take is to change the code by adding the field purchase date. The table is recreated automatically and even if data is already available in the table, the field is added with the value NULL (or the defined default value). On the other hand, renaming the tables is not solved as elegantly in CDS as with SQL code. Here, renaming a table leads to the deletion and recreation of the table.

Model integrity check

The model integrity check is a very useful feature. If you alter a table using SQL, SAP HANA does not check the integrity of the dependent objects such as information views. Even after a refresh, manually created views will still show that they are correct even though the structure of the source table has changed. For views created in the development perspective and when you alter the table definition file, SAP HANA automatically checks dependent views and issues an error message. The error message provides the list of views that are affected, albeit in the form of text. You can then either ignore the message by altering the tables anyway, or you can decide to implement the changes.

Relationship modeling

CDS offers the option of modeling a relationship between two tables as a foreign key relationship. This concept can of course be done via SQL as well, but the advantage of CDS is that you have the definition directly visible in the definition file. If you place the relationship in the code next to the table, you have the link attached to the table definition. For standard SQL or graphically created tables, foreign key relationships are not shown in the table itself but only in the public table `SYS.Referential _Constraints`.

Table naming

One of the restrictions of CDS is the naming of tables, as depicted in Figure 5.3.

```
_Modeling [HDB (SYSTEM, 'Advanced_Modeling')]
ANA System Library AWS IP CONNECT
:alog
Public Synonyms
AM_DML
  Column Views
  EPM Models
  EPM Query Sources
  Functions
  Indexes
  Procedures
  Sequences
  Synonyms
  Tables
    Advanced_Modeling::Tables.FACT_TRANSACTIONS_CDS
    Advanced_Modeling::Tables.MD_CUSTOMER_CDS
    FACT_OFFER
    FACT_TRANSACTIONS
    MD_CHAIN
    MD_COMPANY
    MD_CUSTOMER
    MD_OFFER
```

```
namespace Advanced_Modeling;

@Schema: 'AM_DML'

context Tables {

@Catalog.tableType: #COLUMN
  Entity MD_CUSTOMER_CDS {
    key CUSTOMER_ID : String(8);
    Age : Integer;
    City : String(50);
    ZipCode : String(6);
    Street_Name : String(100);
  };

  Entity FACT_TRANSACTIONS_CDS {
    key TRANSACTION_ID: Integer64;
    DEPARTMENT_ID: Integer;
    CHAIN_ID: Integer;
    CUSTOMER_ID: String(8);
    PURCHASE_DATE: LocalDate;
    PURCHASE_QTY: Integer;

  };
};
```

Figure 5.3: Table naming convention using CDS

You can see that the tables created automatically have the namespace as a prefix followed by two colons, the CDS definition file name and finally a

195

period followed by the actual table name (e.g. "FACT_TRANSACTION _CDS"). This results in very long table names on the one hand, but offers the option of implementing governance rules for table creation on the other hand. For example, the namespace could be used to denote the data domain (e.g., accounting) and the file name could refer to whether the table belongs to the staging or data mart layer. If you want to use different naming conventions however, CDS cannot be your tool of choice.

Data types

Another slight disadvantage of CDS is the inability to use all available SAP HANA standard SQL data types. For example, you will not be able to model TINYINT or SMALLINT in CDS. However, as shown in Chapter 3, only BIGINT has an effect on the storage itself and therefore, the fact that the TINYINT and SMALLINT data types are missing are not really a loss at all.

> **Data types**
>
> For a complete list of data types, see the SAP HANA Developer Guide, which is available for download via the SAP Help portal. *http://help.sap.com/hana/SAP_HANA _Developer_Guide_for_SAP_HANA_Studio_en.pdf*

Development effort

If we compare the graphical table modeling and SQL table creation with CDS, you will notice that the development effort for CDS versus SQL, or even graphical table creation, seems to be much higher. You will first have to learn a new programming language. For example, tables are now called entities and have to be enclosed in brackets and followed by semicolons. Activating the content is more cumbersome as it takes longer than just executing an SQL statement. However, the previously discussed advantages such as integrated integrity checks outweigh this disadvantage.

Summary

Overall, CDS offers many advantages compared to the classical DDL approach using SQL or the graphical approach. From our point of view,

CDS is a hidden gem for SAP HANA development. Also, the development perspective has the advantage that several people can work on the CDS definition file, meaning that the number of users creating tables is not limited to one. Some of the advantages of CDS presented in this subsection are:

- The option to document the physical data model directly while creating tables
- The ability to easily alter tables using the CDS document
- The integrity check that is included when you activate the CDS document and thereby, create and change the tables

5.3 Challenges in SAP HANA modeling

In this section, we will take a look at modeling functionalities that are not provided out of the box in SAP HANA. Figure 5.4 provides an overview of the following sections.

Problem area	Problem description
Calculations and aggregations	How are calculations performed in calculation views influenced by aggregation behavior?
Exception aggregation	How can I calculate a KPI on a lower aggregation level than my actual output aggregation level?
Moving averages	How do I calculate moving averages in SAP HANA?
Time-dependent master data	How do I model time-dependent master data most efficiently in SAP HANA?

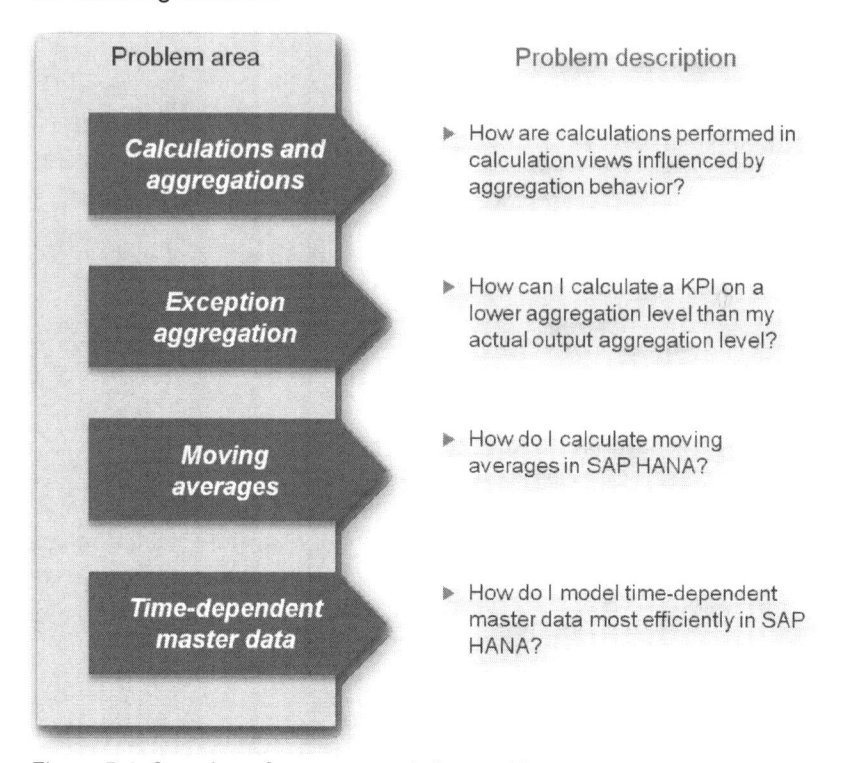

Figure 5.4: Overview of common modeling problems

5.3.1 Calculations and aggregations

Calculations and aggregations in SAP HANA information views are more complex in comparison with other databases where the SQL view directly defines the required aggregation level. The rules for calculations and aggregations defined in SAP HANA are adapted to fit the columnar structure and the advantages of compressing data as such. Table 5.2 depicts the main aspects influencing calculation and aggregation behavior in SAP HANA.

Driver	Explanation
Columns queried in SQL	Only columns selected in a query are read from the table.
No standard average aggregation	The average always has to be calculated by a formula.
Keep flags	Keep flags directly influence the aggregation behavior.
Counters depend on aggregation	Counters might calculate differently on another aggregation level.
Constant values for attributes	Constant values in attributes are only read in combination with a measure.

Table 5.2: Drivers of SAP HANA aggregation behavior

In the following subsections, we analyze these drivers and explain the rules for designing any calculation graphically in SAP HANA.

Columnar SQL querying

Whenever a query is executed on an SAP HANA information view with inherent aggregation, only the columns that are selected in the query are processed. This of course is normal SQL behavior, but what is not standard SQL behavior is the immediate aggregation to the distinct values available in the queried column combination. Whenever a query is run, only distinct values are selected for attributes, or attribute combinations, and only measures are aggregated to the value applying to each row. This has two major impacts:

1. Whenever you convert an attribute to a measure, make sure you do it on the correct aggregation level.
2. Any calculation that does not sum up or subtract measures has to be designed to incorporate this SAP HANA principle.

The advantage of the SAP HANA approach is the exact use of the columnar structure. SAP HANA only stores distinct values and rows that are constructed using indexes. Thus, the fewer the number of columns read, the fewer the number of rows that need to be reconstructed. Therefore, automatic aggregation is only logical. This, of course, leads to a significant improvement in performance.

On the other hand, in contrast to standard SQL, HANA requires a new way of thinking when it comes to designing reports. Let's look at an example in which a multiplication needs to be performed for each row and the result needs to be aggregated. Normally in SQL, a select without the distinct command would have been performed, the measures multiplied, and afterwards the measures aggregated. In the SAP environment, you need to explicitly implement the measures that are calculated before any aggregation. You can do this either by marking the analytic view flag CALCULATE BEFORE AGGREGATION in a calculated column, or for example by using a projection node based on a table directly in a calculation view for calculating a measure. However, as shown in Chapter 4, both result in a loss of performance.

> **Influencing aggregation behavior**
>
> Use projection nodes before any aggregations to calculate key figures on the lowest level. Otherwise, ensure that you calculate measures on the highest possible aggregation level in order to improve performance. We will discuss an example in the following subsection No standard average aggregation on page 198.

This SAP HANA approach has an additional advantage: when you calculate averages, for example in the final aggregation node, they are automatically calculated correctly on the level of aggregation supplied in the query.

No standard average aggregation

SAP HANA does not provide a standard average aggregation in graphical calculation views, which is why it has to be calculated manually. However, averages can be calculated quite easily. The behavior of these averages is closely linked to the aggregation problem discussed in the previous subsection. Whenever an average is calculated on a lower level in a calculation view, it must be ensured that a later aggregation node via sum, min, max, or count does not cause any unwanted behavior. The same applies to averages calculated in analytic views before aggregation, but at least here the aggregation behavior is foreseeable. Let's take a look at an example.

> **Calculate the average price**
>
> [eg] The pricing manager in our case study would like to see the average price on different aggregation levels, such as city, state, or country so that he can compare the average prices of a product to other grocery stores in the region. He also wants a price for all states to be shown with the attribute value `All states` instead of a blank attribute value.

Without further analysis, our IT department designs the first version of a calculation view that comes to mind. For this scenario, they use our reference analytic view with the transactional data joined to master data as a basis. To increase the level of complexity and for testing purposes, a join based on the purchase date is added to the calculation view (see Figure 5.5). It has two streams: one maps the normal states (stream on the right-hand side in Figure 5.5) and a stream on the left-hand side that aggregates without the **state** attribute, instead mapping `All states` as a constant value to the **state** column inside the union node. The IT department decides to include the following measures for testing the average price (purchase amount divided by purchase quantity if purchase quantity is greater than 0):

1. CC_AVG_ PRICE_PROJ as the average price calculated in the two projection nodes (see the two nodes on the lowest level in Figure 5.5)
2. CC_AVG_PRICE as the average price calculated in the aggregation nodes underneath the union node

3. CC_AVG_PRICE_FIN_AGG as the average price calculated in the final aggregation node

Each of the average calculations leads to a different result in the output of the calculation view. However, if you adjust the aggregation level of the output by adding additional attributes to the query, the same results can be achieved. The measures `purchase amount` and `purchase quantity` are added as aggregated columns in the aggregation nodes beneath the union node. They are then aggregated and not treated as attributes.

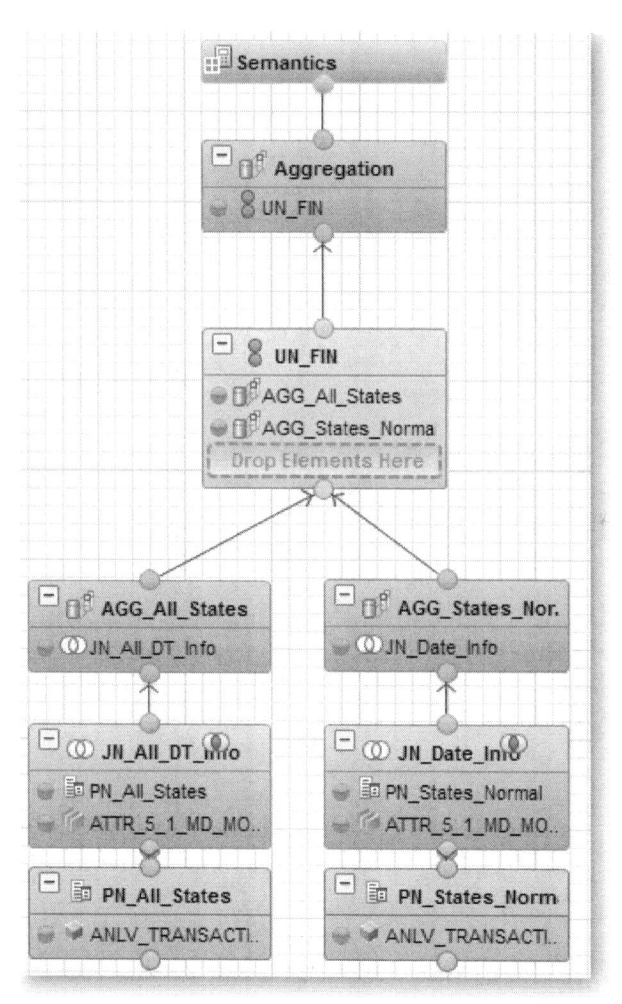

Figure 5.5: Aggregation behavior in views

The IT department runs a query on the view, selecting all three measures as shown in the code example and Table 5.3 (with an excerpt of the result set).

```
SELECT TOP 20000 DISTINCT "MONTH_ID",
SUM("CC_AVG_PRICE_PROJ") AS "CC_AVG_PRICE_PROJ ",
SUM("CC_AVG_PRICE") AS "CC_AVG_PRICE ",
SUM("CC_AVG_PRICE_FIN_AGG") AS "CC_AVG_PRICE_FIN_AGG"
FROM "_SYS_BIC"."Advanced_Modeling/CALC_5_5_HANA_AGG_BEHAV"
GROUP BY "MONTH_ID"
ORDER BY "MONTH_ID" ASC
```

MONTH_ID	CC_AVG_PRICE_PROJ	CC_AVG_PRICE	CC_AVG_PRICE_FIN_AGG
1	€ 166.55	€ 5.54	€ 2.77
2	€ 167.20	€ 5.57	€ 2.79
3	€ 176.00	€ 5.68	€ 2.84
4	€ 172.93	€ 5.77	€ 2.88

Table 5.3: Average comparison per aggregation level

How can these different calculation results be explained?

The CC_AVG_PRICE_PROJ is calculated before the join on the level of the purchase date. As the join happens on the purchase date level, SAP HANA needs to pull the data into the projection on purchase date level. As the measure has the aggregation type **sum** set in the aggregation nodes above, this produces the values of over 100. In essence, the averages calculated on purchase date level are summed up.

The CC_AVG_PRICE equals the CC_AVG_PRICE_FIN_AGG multiplied by two. You might already know the reason: there are two streams being combined in the UN_FIN node (UNION operation). The two resulting rows per MONTH_ID are aggregated in the final aggregation node and the CC_AVG_PRICE is summed up again.

The CC_AVG_PRICE_FIN_AGG shows the actual average as it is calculated on this aggregation level over all rows.

Now, how do we get all three key figures to match? We will find the answer by going down to the aggregation levels of the measures. The CC_AVG_PRICE_PROJ measure is calculated on purchase date level, ergo the attribute **purchase date** needs to be included. The CC_AVG_PRICE stream is based on the state in one stream and the aggregation over all states in the other. Therefore, the **state** attribute needs to be added to the query.

The code example below incorporates these changes and Table 5.4 shows a result excerpt with the expected matching averages.

```
SELECT TOP 20000 DISTINCT "MONTH_ID", "STATE",
"PURCHASE_DATE", SUM("CC_AVG_PRICE_PROJ") AS
"CC_AVG_PRICE_PROJ ", SUM("CC_AVG_PRICE") AS "CC_AVG_PRICE
", SUM("CC_AVG_PRICE_FIN_AGG") AS "CC_AVG_PRICE_FIN_AGG "
FROM "_SYS_BIC"."Advanced_Modeling/CALC_5_5_HANA_AGG_BEHAV"
GROUP BY "MONTH_ID", "STATE", "PURCHASE_DATE"
ORDER BY "MONTH_ID" ASC, "STATE" ASC, "PURCHASE_DATE" ASC
```

MONTH_ID	STATE	PUR-CHASE_DATE	CC_AVG_PRICE_PROJ	CC_AVG_PRICE	CC_AVG_PRICE_FIN_AGG
1	Virginia	02/03/ 2015	€ 2.69	€ 2.69	€ 2.69
1	Virginia	03/03/ 2015	€ 2.50	€ 2.50	€ 2.50
1	Virginia	04/03/ 2015	€ 2.57	€ 2.57	€ 2.57

Table 5.4: Average comparison on the same aggregation level

Using the keep flag

The *keep flag* is used inside calculation views in aggregation nodes and, since SAP HANA Revision 91, also in projection nodes. It ensures that a certain attribute is read through the layers even though it is not explicitly used in the SQL statement. This makes calculations possible on certain lower aggregation levels.

203

ADVANCED MODELING TECHNIQUES

> **Daily price average**
>
> *eg* The price manager would like to ensure that the average is calculated for each state first and only then aggregated via average to the `All states` value.

The solution to this requirement would be to set the keep flag in the aggregation node for the all states stream (AGG_All_States). Then, a count of the states would have to be implemented in this node. In the final aggregation node, the calculated average would have to be divided by this count. In this way, the average over the average is calculated.

Counters and aggregation

The counter function as a calculated column is used to count the distinct values of a certain attribute or attribute combination. In detail, the counter in SAP HANA behaves like a count distinct in standard SQL. Let's take a look at an example.

> **Number of states contributing to the net sales**
>
> *eg* The sales department would like to see the number of states that contributed to the sales of a certain product in a certain month. Therefore, the IT department implements a counter and firstly, tests it only on the month level.

The counter functionality in our example sums up the number of unique states which can be found in the raw data per output row. This means that, for example, if you want to see key figures on a country level and there are 50 different states in the country, the counter would equal 50.

Below you will see an example of the SQL statement and output per month of the counter counting the number of states in the final aggregation node (see Figure 5.5 for the architecture reference):

204

```sql
SELECT TOP 20000 DISTINCT "MONTH_ID",
SUM("CC_AVG_PRICE_FIN_AGG") AS "CC_AVG_PRICE_FIN_AGG",
SUM("CC_AVG_PRICE") AS "CC_AVG_PRICE ",
SUM("CC_COUNT_STATE") AS "CC_COUNT_STATE "
FROM "_SYS_BIC"."Advanced_Modeling/CALC_5_5_HANA_AGG_BEHAV"
GROUP BY "MONTH_ID"
ORDER BY "MONTH_ID" ASC
```

MONTH_ID	CC_AVG_PRICE _FIN_AGG	CC_AVG _PRICE	CC_COUNT _STATE
13	2.82 €	39.45 €	15
14	2.79 €	38.27 €	14
15	2.82 €	36.15 €	13

Table 5.5: Example of counter aggregation

We can also see a pitfall of using counters: SAP HANA implements the counter as if the keep flag were set to true for the **state** attribute. This means that the state is additionally queried through all nodes below the final aggregation. This is also why the measure CC_AVG_PRICE coming from the aggregation nodes beneath the union UN_FIN is summed up to such a high value. The correct way of fulfilling the business requirement of adding All states and calculating the average is to calculate the average in the final node.

Constant values for attributes

When you add a constant value in a union for a certain union participant and only this attribute is queried from the calculation view, the constant value is not in the output. Figure 5.5 serves as a good example. Here, AGG_All_States brings the constant value of All states for the attribute **state** into the union. If you now query only **state**, All states is not shown as an output value. This is planned SAP HANA behavior and whenever you query a second attribute or a measure, All states will automatically appear as a value again.

205

5.3.2 Exception aggregation

Exception aggregation represents an aggregation which can

1. Differ from the way the KPI is aggregated by default (e.g., average instead of sum); or,
2. Be calculated on the level of a certain attribute.

For the first option, simply add a calculated column with a different aggregation type to the original key figure. An example for the second option is to calculate average values on the basis of the **country** attribute. This means the average is calculated for each country. If the aggregation in the query is on a higher level than the country level, the average over the average should be calculated. By setting the keep flag in the first aggregation to true for a certain attribute and adding a count on this attribute, you can calculate the average on this attribute level. In the consecutive aggregation node, you simply divide the calculated average by the count. Thus, you have implemented an exception aggregation on the country level using an average. For details on the keep flag function refer to the previous section Using the keep flag. It is more problematic to calculate key figures with different exception aggregation levels. If you are using different attributes for the exception aggregation of the different key figures, the problem cannot be solved with two aggregation nodes. The solution can also involve using a union node to accomplish the goal. If the exception aggregation of the different key figures is based on attributes that can be modeled as a parent-child hierarchy, then the exception aggregation can be accomplished without a union node. A parent-child hierarchy means that a child node cannot have more than one parent (1:n relationship). In this case, the lowest aggregation node has the highest level of detail for the exception aggregation and the above aggregation nodes each have a higher aggregation level. To provide an example of a time hierarchy:

- ▶ The first aggregation node has a calculation on the day level (keep flag on the calendar day).
- ▶ The next aggregation node calculates the key figure on the month level (keep flag on month).
- ▶ The subsequent aggregation node includes the calculation on year level.
- ▶ The final calculation node includes any final calculations.

The problem becomes more difficult if the key figures for which an exception aggregation should be performed are modeled in an m:n relationship. Then, the only solution in graphical calculation views is to create several aggregation nodes with the same attributes and different keep flag settings for each exception aggregation in each aggregation node. Next, the result sets need to be combined using a union node, and any additional necessary calculations can be executed in the final aggregation node. Of course, this approach leads to a significant loss of performance.

Another option is to perform exception aggregation in the frontend. However, the frontend may have to query a large volume of data in order to be able to perform the exception aggregation.

5.3.3 Moving averages

As different modes of average calculations have already been discussed in the previous subsections, here we will take a look at the more complex problem of *moving averages* in SAP HANA. KPIs formulated as moving averages are a calculation frequently requested by businesses that require specific modeling in any BI environment. Moving averages are calculated by creating a sequence of averages over subsets of the dataset. As an example, a moving three week average would be the average over three weeks, but viewed over several weeks on a weekly level. Let's look at an example of the amount sold per week and the three week moving average (see Table 5.6):

Week	Amount sold	Average formula	Three weeks moving average
1	100	-	Not enough data
2	150	-	Not enough data
3	200	(W1 + W2 + W3)/3	(100 + 150 + 200) / 3 = 150
4	250	(W2 + W3 + W4)/3	(150 + 200 + 250) / 3 = 200
5	300	(W3 + W4 + W5)/3	(200 + 250 + 300) / 3 = 250

Table 5.6: Example of moving average calculation

ADVANCED MODELING TECHNIQUES

In this section, we will discuss how to model the averages while trying to maintain acceptable performance.

As moving averages are generally calculated based on defined time periods, we will take a look at three month and six month moving averages. Furthermore, we will look at how to model moving averages, e.g., on a weekly basis or over a different time span based on a number of sequential days while using different calendars (different holidays/working days).

Data preparation and architecture

To supply the moving averages, an additional table supplying additional information to a date such as the year and month is necessary along with additional columns which will be explained in the course of the next example.

> **Moving average of purchased amount**
>
> **eg** The sales manager would like to have a three month and six month moving average in order to be able to track the business development over longer periods of time. An additional seven day moving average is planned for store level reporting.

The IT department wants to test the design in the backend and comes up with a solution which first needs a new table. The calculation in the frontend may be more efficient here, but for the sake of trying several solutions, the IT department first tries this in SAP HANA. The table has the following columns (see Table 5.7):

Column	Description
CAL_DATE	The date (e. g., 01/01/2015)
DAY_ID	Sequential ID of a date starting with 1 for the lowest date (Date 01/01/2015 = ID 1)
MONTH_ID	Sequential ID of the year and month starting at 1 (e. g. Month 01.2015 = ID 1)
MONTH	Month and year of a date (e. g. 01/2015)
MONTH_PLUS_1	Month and year plus 1 of a date (e. g. 02/2015)
MONTH_PLUS_2	Month and year plus 2 of a date (e. g. 03/2015)
MONTH_PLUS_3	Month and year plus 3 of a date (e. g. 04/2015)
MONTH_PLUS_4	Month and year plus 4 of a date (e. g. 05/2015)
MONTH_PLUS_5	Month and year plus 5 of a date (e. g. 06/2015)

Table 5.7: Additional table for the moving average calculation

The purpose of each of these columns can be explained as follows:

- ▶ The date is necessary to perform a join to the transactional data.
- ▶ The DAY_ID as an integer value makes it easy to define a span of, e. g., 7 days. As the ID is sequential, a seven-day span would be the current ID and all IDs up to current ID – 6.
- ▶ The MONTH_ID as an integer value is the same as the DAY_ID, only on a monthly basis.
- ▶ The MONTH is the year and month combination belonging to CAL_DATE and serves as the value a user can read and select from.
- ▶ MONTH_PLUS_1 – MONTH_PLUS_5 is the MONTH column +1 to 5 month(s). We will explain the use in the example of a calculation view.

This table can also be based on the time attribute view SAP HANA offers as a standard functionality for time-based master data. However, as the ADD_MONTHS function is currently only available for SQL and not for information views, we do not recommend calculating the columns above (MONTH_PLUS_1 – 5) on the fly. The calculation is increasingly complex for each month that is added, so MONTH_PLUS_5 is the most complex calculation. This is due to the change of the year which happens for the months August to December when calculating the current month +5 in the MONTH_PLUS_5 calculation. Finally, the storage of each month can be avoided through an even better solution as will be explained in the test later.

To leverage this table, it will be published as an attribute view and joined to our existing analytic view via the PURCHASE_DATE. For the implementation, you can either choose the graphical way (Variant 1) or the scripted version (Variant 2).

The two solutions will be presented using the three and six month moving averages.

Three month moving average

Figure 5.6 depicts the architecture of **Variant 1a** for the calculation of the three month average.

The problem when creating a moving average is that essentially the data needs to be duplicated, because each month is used three times in the moving average calculation. In line with Table 5.6, the general formula for calculating the moving average of the purchase amount (PA) can be defined as (PA1+PA2+PA3)/3. Here, PA1 is the purchase amount of the first month, PA2 the purchase amount of the second month, and PA3 the purchase amount of the third month. When viewing the average for each month, the value of each month is used in three different three month average calculations. This implies that a solution has to be found for tripling the row for each month. In the calculation view shown in Figure 5.6, each aggregation node below the union node represents one month.

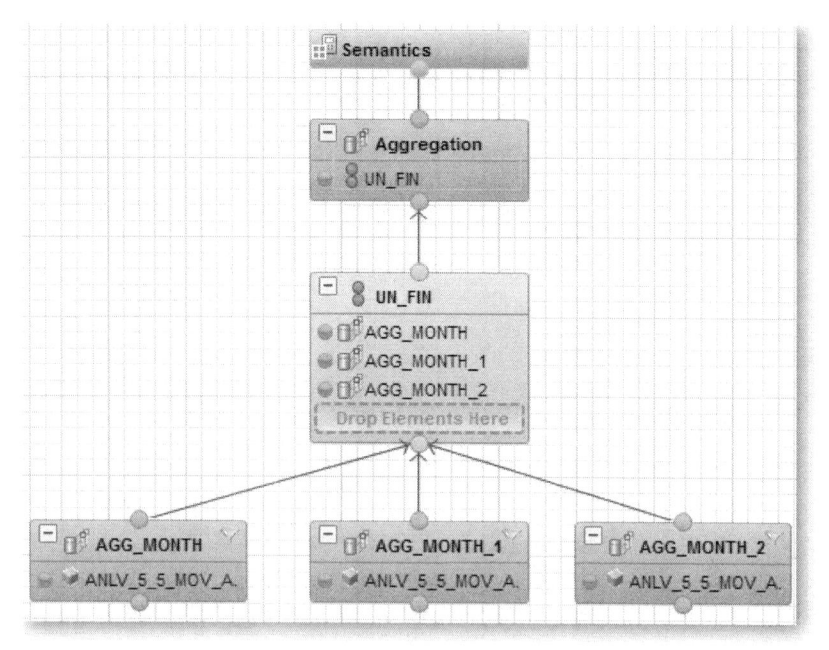

Figure 5.6: Three month moving average with a graphical calculation view

Another design topic is mapping the same month in the union node while combining three different purchase amounts (PA1-3) from three different aggregation nodes. To accomplish this, the structure shown in Table 5.7 is leveraged. Each aggregation node has the same attributes except for the purchase month. The following mappings are applied:

- AGG_MONTH maps the MONTH column
- AGG_MONTH_1 maps the MONTH_PLUS_1 column
- AGG_MONTH_2 maps the MONTH_PLUS_2 column

In the union node, the MONTH column is then added to the output only and the MONTH_PLUS_1 and MONTH_PLUS_2 columns are mapped to the MONTH column. Thus, the same month is mapped from each aggregation node, but with the value of the next month, or respectively the month after the next.

In the final aggregation node, the purchase amount is divided by three to calculate the average and the calculated column is called PURCHASE_AMT_3M_AVG.

211

A slight variation, **Variant 1b**, creates a view with the MONTH_ID instead of using the MONTH, MONTH_PLUS_1, and MONTH_PLUS_2 columns. Table 5.8 shows the setup using the month ID.

Node	MONTH_ID mapping in union	Calculation
AGG_MONTH	MONTH_ID	None
AGG_MONTH_1	MONTH_ID_PLUS_1	MONTH_ID + 1
AGG_MONTH_2	MONTH_ID_PLUS_2	MONTH_ID + 2

Table 5.8: Mapping in calculation view with MONTH_ID

Table 5.8 shows how the different MONTH_IDs are mapped for each aggregation node similar to the concept applied in the first calculation view. Based on the MONTH_ID after the union node, the MONTH is joined in the join node JN_MONTH_ADD (see Figure 5.7). This variant of implementing the three month average has the advantage that no additional columns like those in **Variant 1a** have to be stored in the backend.

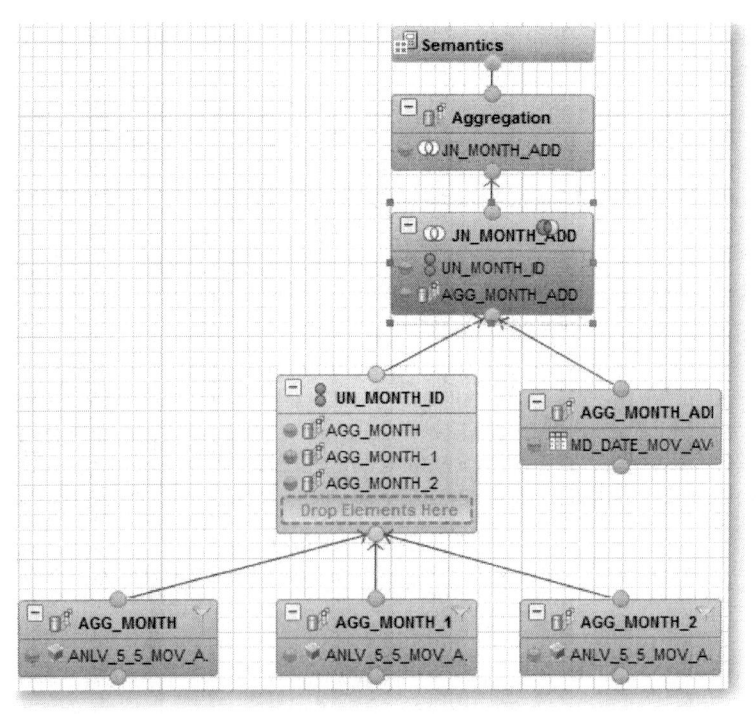

Figure 5.7: Three month moving average with MONTH_ID

The SQL code below shows the scripted calculation view variant, **Variant 2**, for calculating the three month moving average.

```
BEGIN
anlv_data =
CE_OLAP_VIEW("_SYS_BIC"."Advanced_Modeling/ANLV_5_5_MOV_AVG"
,["MONTH_ID","CITY","MONTH", sum("PURCHASE_AMOUNT") AS
"PURCHASE_AMOUNT"]);
VAR_OUT = select MA2."MONTH_ID" as "MONTH_ID" ,MA2."MONTH"
as "MONTH" ,MA2."CITY" AS "CITY",
SUM(MA2."PURCHASE_AMOUNT")/COUNT(MA2."MONTH_ID") as
"PURCHASE_AMT_3M_AVG"
FROM (SELECT "MONTH_ID","CITY", SUM("PURCHASE_AMOUNT") as
"PURCHASE_AMOUNT" FROM :anlv_data GROUP BY
"MONTH_ID","CITY") as MA1, (SELECT
"MONTH_ID","CITY","MONTH", SUM("PURCHASE_AMOUNT") as
"PURCHASE_AMOUNT" FROM :anlv_data GROUP BY
"MONTH_ID","MONTH","CITY") as MA2
WHERE (MA2."MONTH_ID" - MA1."MONTH_ID") >= 0 AND
(MA2."MONTH_ID" - MA1."MONTH_ID") < 3 AND MA1.CITY=MA2.CITY
AND MA2."MONTH_ID">=3
GROUP BY MA2."CITY", MA2."MONTH_ID",MA2."MONTH";
END
```

It supplies the MONTH_ID and CITY as the attributes and the purchase amount three month average. The view only needs two nodes as they create a Cartesian product and cover every combination. The where condition limits the combinations to the result set that is actually required. The first two lines of the condition noted below ensure that the purchase amount of the current month, next month, and the month after are selected. There are two more conditions in the last line. First, the **city** attribute of the two nodes has to equal the selected attribute **city**. This means that a join is executed on **city**. Secondly, the MONTH_ID must be equal to or greater than three. If it is not, a three month average cannot be calculated.

```
(MA2."MONTH_ID" - MA1."MONTH_ID") >= 0 AND (MA2."MONTH_ID" -
MA1."MONTH_ID") < 3 AND MA1.CITY=MA2.CITY AND
MA2."MONTH_ID">=3
```

All these views were queried to supply the same output: the MONTH_ID, MONTH, CITY and purchase amount average of three months columns in the first case. The number of attributes slowly increased for testing purposes (and additional scripted calculation views were created). Table 5.9 compares the query execution time for the three possible implementations.

No. of attributes	Variant 1a (months)	Variant 1b (join)	Variant 2 (SQL)
3	271 ms	271 ms	226 ms
5	5.550 s	4.320 s	3.782 s
10	6.928 s	5.959 s	5.800 s

Table 5.9: Three month average query execution time comparison

The IT department is surprised to find that the view joining the month to the month ID (**Variant 1b**) instead of mapping a different column to each projection (**Variant 1a**) is actually faster. The scripted calculation view is the fastest. However, it only has the option of calculating the average on the exact aggregation level. The graphical views provide the option of calculating the three month average on whatever aggregation level the user chooses in the SQL query being executed. This represents a major advantage compared to the scripted calculation view.

Furthermore, the scripted calculation view indicates the best performance impact for a low number of attributes and is close to the performance of the graphical calculation view for the ten attributes being queried. Based on this result, we recommend the graphical variant. However, we will provide a more detailed recommendation at the end of this chapter.

Six month moving average and weekly average

The same concept as for the three month moving average can be applied to the six month moving average. The graphical calculation view of **Variant 1a** is enhanced by three additional aggregation nodes below the union node. Each of the additional aggregation nodes maps the MONTH_PLUS_3, MONTH_PLUS_4, and MONTH_PLUS_5 columns to the MONTH_ID in the union node. The **Variant 1b** with the join also leverages three additional aggregation nodes calculating the MONTH_ID as MONTH_ID+3, MONTH_ID+4, and MONTH_ID+5. Finally, the scripted calculation view, **Variant 2**, only needs a slight adjustment in the `where` condition, otherwise the script stays the same (see the section Data preparation and architecture):

```
(MA2."MONTH_ID" - MA1."MONTH_ID") >= 0 AND (MA2."MONTH_ID" -
MA1."MONTH_ID") < 6 AND MA1.CITY=MA2.CITY AND
MA2."MONTH_ID">=6
```

Table 5.10 compares the query execution times again with the attributes MONTH_ID, MONTH, and CITY selected, as well as the six month moving average measure. Again, the number of attributes is gradually increased for testing purposes.

No. of selected attributes	Variant 1a (months)	Variant 1b (join)	Variant 2 (SQL)
3	258 ms	245 ms	230 ms
5	8.875 s	6.594 s	4.096 s
10	10.804 s	8.992 s	6.215 s

Table 5.10: Six month average query execution time comparison

As expected again, the scripted calculation view has the fastest performance compared to the other views. It becomes clear that the view with the join to the MONTH_ID is faster than the one without the join. One of the conclusions from this test is that using a MONTH_ID for the calculation instead of five additional columns saves memory space and even leads to an increase in performance.

Using IDs as in **Variant 1b** is also feasible when looking at weekly averages based on calendars with different holidays. A solution for providing the moving average on the basis of working days only could be that only working days receive a sequential ID. All other dates do not receive an ID. That way, the moving average calculation, as shown in **Variant 2** above, can be performed without having to create a large number of columns for each type of moving average. So instead of the structure shown in Table 5.7, only the following structure is necessary (see Table 5.11).

Column	Description
CAL_DATE	The date (e.g., 01/01/2015)
CAL_TYPE	Indicates the calendar being used (e.g., an ID or a country code)
DAY_ID	Sequential ID of a date starting with 1 for the lowest date (date 01/01/2015 = ID 1)
MONTH_ID	Sequential ID of the year and month starting at 1 (e.g., month 01/2015 = ID 1)

Table 5.11: Date ID structure proposal

The calendar type, together with the date column, has to be joined to the fact table in the analytic view or calculation view. This would allow a different calendar to be used for each country or production site for example, and the moving average is calculated on a seven day basis with the calculation view design as shown in Figure 5.7.

5.3.4 Time-dependent master data

Modeling *time-dependent master data* that performs well in SAP HANA has always been the subject of much discussion and SAP HANA now offers standard solutions for this topic. We will test whether it makes sense to use that solution or to choose a different approach leveraging the tool set supplied by SAP HANA.

Let's start with background information: what exactly is time-dependent master data? Time-dependent master data describes master data that changes over time. Therefore, the data has different values at different points in time. An example is a customer address, which is bound to change over the course of the customer's life. There may be different requirements for using this type of master data in reporting. In certain cases, the business should be able to choose, during runtime, which state of the master data is applied to the transactional data and in other cases the historical truth should be shown. Historical truth means that the master data that was valid at the point in time when the transaction took place is used. Another requirement could be that only the latest version of the master data should be shown. As this only requires updating the master data table with the newest set of values and does not require keeping a history, this scenario will not be evaluated here.

To implement the first two cases in SAP HANA (flexible application of time-dependent master data and historical truth), we will consider the following potentially well-performing possibilities:

- Implementation by means of a scripted calculation view with either an input parameter or a join with a between `where` condition (Date >= valid from and Date <= valid to) (**Variant 1**)
- Implementation by means of an SAP HANA history table with a timestamp input parameter (**Variant 2.1**)
- Storage of the master data in the fact table (massive master data duplication) (**Variant 2.2**)
- Creation of a table with **Valid From** and **Valid To** date columns similar to an SAP HANA history table, but in contrast to the history table, the columns are visible and can be used in an SQL query (**Variant 3**)

Table 5.12 shows the implementation variants and the defined test cases in a matrix form with the planned solution in the values section of the matrix.

Master data time dependency requirement	Scripted calculation view (Variant 1)	Graphical design variants (Variant 2)	Master data with validity range (Variant 3)
Input parameter to choose the required master data version (*Case 1*)	Scripted calculation view with an input parameter on valid from and valid to.	HANA history table (**Variant 2.1**): Direct input parameter on table as designed by SAP with an analytic view	Input parameter on valid from and valid to as a greater than/less than condition
Historical truth (*Case 2*)	Scripted calculation view with a join on valid from and valid to and the normal master data record ID	Storage of the master data with the fact data (**Variant 2.2**)	Inner temporal join on customer ID and with the purchase data and valid from and valid to as the time columns

Table 5.12: Time-dependent master data implementations

The scripted calculation views are based on SQLScript (**Variant 1**). The SQLScript performs the joins between the fact table and the master data table and executes an aggregation at the end. **Variant 1** for **Case 1** includes an input parameter filtering on all values greater than or equal to the valid from date and all values smaller than or equal to the valid to date. The second variant compares the purchase date to the valid from and valid to dates as explained above.

All of the graphical implementations are based on analytic views (**Variants 2** and **3**). **Variant 2.1** is based on a history table which can be created via an SQL statement (shown below) and the corresponding attribute view and analytic view have to be enabled for history by setting the ENABLE HISTORY option in the view PROPERTIES pane. A *history table* is a construct specific to SAP HANA which automatically creates a delta tracking for this table. The tracking is created using a COMMIT_ID and a COMMIT_TIME for each insert or update. These are written into a separate public table called TRANSACTION_HISTORY.

```
CREATE HISTORY COLUMN TABLE
"AM_DML"."MD_CUSTOMER_HIST_TABLE" ("CUSTOMER_ID" BIGINT
CS_FIXED NOT NULL , "GENDER" NVARCHAR(6), "FIRST_NAME"
NVARCHAR(11), "LANGUAGE" NVARCHAR(25), "LAST_NAME"
NVARCHAR(10), "STREET_NAME" NVARCHAR(16), "STREET_NUMBER"
DECIMAL(8, 1) CS_FIXED, "CITY" NVARCHAR(22), "ZIP"
NVARCHAR(11), "STATE" NVARCHAR(20), "COUNTRY" NVARCHAR(13),
"PHONE" NVARCHAR(15), "EMAIL" NVARCHAR(45),
"CREDIT_CARD_NUMBER" NVARCHAR(21), "TYPE" NVARCHAR(25),
"FULL_NAME_CREDIT" NVARCHAR(42), "STATE_ID" BIGINT CS_FIXED,
"LOGON_LANG" VARCHAR(1), PRIMARY KEY ("CUSTOMER_ID"))
```

Variant 2.2 uses massive master data duplication by adding the master data to the actual transaction in the fact table. As shown in Chapter 3, this leads to a significant storage overhead.

Variant 3 for **Case 1** requires implementation of the master data table in the data foundation of the analytic view, otherwise no input parameter can be set in the analytic view. This results in a reduction in flexibility as a table change leads to a change of all analytic views where the table is included in the data foundation. Figure 5.8 depicts the data foundation of this analytic view with the input parameter INP_MD_DATE.

ADVANCED MODELING TECHNIQUES

> **"When I traveled through time"**
>
> When you search for "SAP HANA history table" on the Internet, one of the first results you will find is the following link:
>
> http://scn.sap.com/community/developer-center/hana/blog/2013/02/12/when-i-travelled-through-time-using-sap-hana
>
> It contains a very good description of how to use SAP HANA history tables, although the "Enable History" flag for information views is still missing (this feature was only added recently).

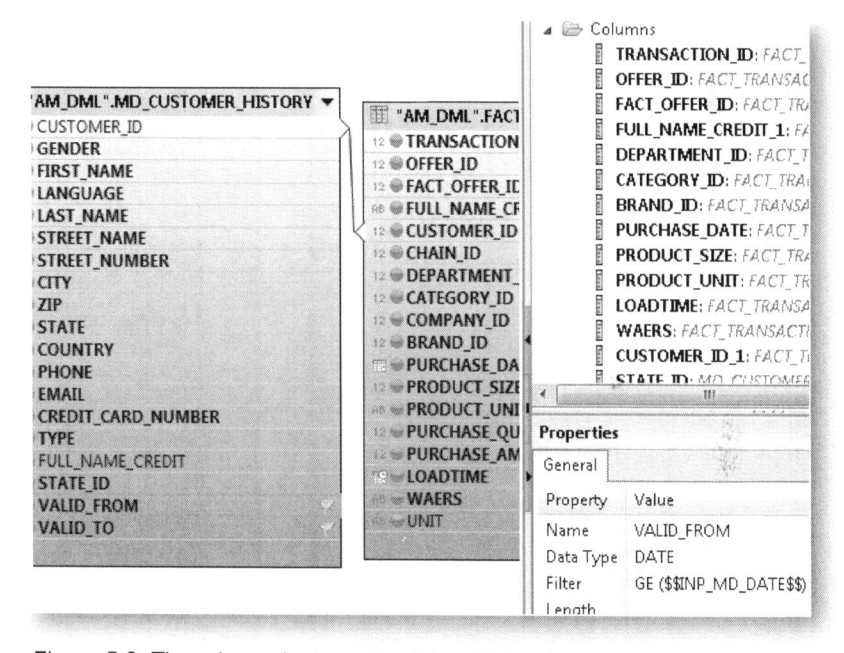

Figure 5.8: Time-dependent master data with input parameter

Finally, implementing time-dependent master data with valid from and valid to columns when you want to depict historical truth can be achieved using a temporal join (**Variant 3, Case 2**). To implement this, an analytic view is used with an inner join between the master data and the fact data. The purchase date from the fact data is added as the temporal column and the valid from date as the FROM column, as well as the valid to date as the TO column.

219

ADVANCED MODELING TECHNIQUES

Table 5.13 reflects the execution times for the variants and cases shown in Table 5.12 again in a matrix form.

Master data time dependency requirement	Scripted calculation view (Variant 1)	Graphical design variants (Variant 2)	Master data with validity range (Variant 3)
Input parameter to choose the master data version (*Case 1*)	40.497 s	9.695 s	11.880 s
Historical truth (*Case 2*)	No execution possible: memory allocation failed	10.148 s	10.890 s

Table 5.13: Time-dependent master data variants execution time

The result that is most clear in Table 5.13 is that the scripted calculation views are slow compared to the other variants. In our first attempt at designing the scripted calculation view with CE functions, the **Case 1** execution even returned an out of memory error. In our second attempt with SQLScript for **Case 1,** the execution worked but delivered the performance results noted in Table 5.13 of around 40 seconds. Our project experience has also shown that using CE functions, although recommended by SAP, the performance was not as fast as expected and in most cases, not even as fast as SQLScript code. Furthermore, the functional possibilities of CE functions are very limited, raising the question of whether they should be used at all, especially since the syntax has to be learned. For further details, please refer to Section 4.3.18.

Another interesting finding for the IT department is that using a standard SQL statement via SQL CONSOLE for Case 1 was quite fast. The resulting performance was comparable to the graphical views. However, the selection on the scripted calculation view or SQL column view leads to a significant performance loss. This indicates improvement potential in the SAP HANA SQL optimizer.

Secondly, as shown by the execution times in Table 5.13 for **Case 1,** the graphical variants are quite fast, although the variant of using a history table in SAP HANA is a little faster.

This result makes the case for using the SAP HANA history table in SAP HANA. However, there are some disadvantages of the history table with Rev. 91 that put the performance gain in perspective:

1. Inserts receive the timestamp of the insert operation and not of the valid from or valid to value as delivered by the source system.
2. No overwrite or update of a committed dataset. Each update creates a new version.
3. Input parameters can only be a COMMIT_TIME or a COMMIT_ID.

It becomes clear that using a history table for reporting can only be achieved by providing a second set of master data to the user. For example, one possibility could be the implementation of a table that provides on one hand the COMMIT_ID, and on the other hand a transparent versioning concept for master data for the end user. This could then be used in the frontend where the commit ID is the key and the master data version is the description. Only the key (COMMIT_ID) is passed to the input parameter.

The results for the second case make a clear argument for using temporal joins. Although storing master data with the transactional data resulted in a slightly better performance, the additional memory required amounted to 40%. Temporal joins can only be based on a referential or inner join. This has to be taken into account of course when an outer or text join is required.

5.3.5 Summary

This chapter started with an explanation of the aggregation behavior of SAP HANA information views and the resulting impact on calculations. The main elements for influencing aggregation are:

- Aggregation and projection nodes in calculation views
- The keep flag property which queries a certain column even though it is not included in the SQL query
- Counters which can be compared to a keep flag in their aggregation behavior
- Joins and unions impacting the aggregation and calculation behavior
- When querying attributes, constant values in union nodes act differently

We then discussed the topic of exception aggregation in SAP HANA information views and came to the following conclusions:

- Exception aggregation is achieved using the keep flag and aggregation nodes.
- Several exception aggregations can require complex calculation view designs with several streams, resulting in a decrease in performance.
- In some cases, realizing the exception aggregation in the front-end can be a valid option.

The next subsection explained how to model moving averages using the example of three and six month averages. It showed that:

- Moving averages can be designed in SAP HANA using graphical calculation views and scripted calculation views
- Graphical calculation views perform nearly as fast as scripted calculation views with a low number of attributes
- Using an ID for dates or months is a feasible alternative to creating an additional column for each time slice (e.g., Month, Month +1, Month +2, ...)

The final part of this subsection illustrated different variants for implementation for time-dependent master data. We evaluated two perspectives: the first consisted of letting the user choose the point in time at which he or she wants to see the master data (1), and the second was to show the historical truth (2). The subsection provided the following insights:

- Scripted calculation views do not show promising results for (1) or (2).
- The best (albeit not the fastest) variant for (1) is based on using temporal joins.
- The fastest variant for (2) is using a history table. However, consider that this has some significant drawbacks in usability.

5.4 Development methods

In this section, we focus on parallel development, agility aspects in design, and the multi-temperature data approach.

5.4.1 Parallel development

In large SAP HANA implementations, there is a strong need for executing developments in parallel. Basic concepts of the SAP HANA development perspective and its supporting environments and tools for SAP HANA developments have been discussed earlier in this chapter. Focusing on the objective of parallel development, we first of all have to accept the fact that, at the moment, an object cannot be modified by several developers at the same time. Thus, parallel development work on SAP HANA views or procedures in the modeler perspective of SAP HANA Studio is not directly possible. Therefore, the challenge for parallel development lies more in slicing the data model and the objects into adequate pieces. Doing so allows each developer to work on a specific part of the data model. When the content of each respective part is activated, it is published and visible to downstream or upstream objects. We will provide information on how to leverage parallel development in this chapter.

The SAP HANA script-based developments follow the default behavior of software implementation in an Eclipse framework. You will also find established features for checking your implementations in or out, version tracking and, therefore, controlling distributed work on specific code snippets. Check the official Eclipse homepage (*http://Eclipse.org*) or the following website for a high-level overview of SAP HANA development tools for Eclipse *https://tools.hana.ondemand.com/*.

> **SAP HANA web-based development workbench**
>
> Since SPS 7 a web-based development workbench has also been available. This environment provides an easy alternative for developing SAP HANA native applications for SAP HANA XS without installing SAP HANA Studio itself. More details and the prerequisites can be found on the following SAP Help page:
>
> *http://help.sap.com/saphelp_hanaplatform/helpdata/en/ 7f/99b0f952d04792912587c99e299ef5/content.htm?frameset=/en/ 5f/eb72f0511e43449f9ad79409a5d259/frameset.htm.* ⇨17
>
> There is also a useful blog in the SAP community network (SCN) on this modeling environment:
>
> *http://scn.sap.com/community/developer-center/hana/blog/2013/12/03/ what-s-new-sap-hana-sps-07-web-based-development-workbench.* ⇨18

From working on large SAP HANA development projects, we have learned that developers sometimes block each other when executing their developer tests on the same SAP HANA index server. On one hand, you can counteract this by restricting the size of an SQL statement in the SAP HANA configuration (for further details see also the SAP HANA administration guide:
http://help.sap.com/hana/SAP_HANA_Administration_guide_en.pdf
or Section 6.7). On the other hand, a distributed development over several SAP HANA instances may also be an alternative. The key challenge here is the non-overlapping slicing of development packages and the merging of various developments back into a common model on the target SAP HANA system. A solution statement, which is not yet provided by SAP, uses various SAP HANA instances in the overarching, version control system (Concurrent versions system (CVS)). Thus, you have the option of also maintaining objects in your repository over several SAP HANA systems. At the moment, the SAP features provided only work locally. Check the SAP roadmap for possible upcoming features in this regard.

5.4.2 Agility aspects in design

Performing BI projects according to the waterfall approach has been state of the art for a long time. Today, the demand for an agile development approach has also reached BI projects. Businesses do not want to wait weeks or even months until a BI system change or enhancement is implemented. Leveraging agile concepts in developing BI systems is not really a new concept, but it was also somehow hindered due to historically grown, complex, and cumbersome BI systems. The acceptance of the BI solution provided was therefore often low. Agile development enables an explorative way of moving forward to the intended target, as well as receiving early feedback on the results per sprint. This can significantly help to achieve a better solution tailored towards the original requirement. The change in the technological platforms also fosters agile BI development.

Starting with the beginning of a BI project or change request, a key element for leveraging BI concepts (which you may be familiar with from scrum or other agile development methods) is adequately slicing your requirement. In data-driven projects like BI projects, the standard agile approach using user stories is often not applicable on a one-to-one basis. That may be one of the reasons why today we are still struggling to really run BI projects using an entirely agile approach. Nevertheless, there are reasonable and well-established ideas on how to apply agile concepts in a BI environment. From our perspective, the key driver for leveraging agile methods in BI projects is again correctly slicing your requirement by focusing on the data needed for reporting. Slicing can take place in both directions—vertically as well as horizontally. As an example, the vertical increment concerns a specific reporting domain (e. g., controlling) or focuses on a specific analysis scenario that can be broken down to a set of linked key figures (e. g., sales measures). The horizontal slicing approach looks at the layers of a typical BI project (e. g., staging or extraction layer, business transformation layer, or the reporting layer). Assuming that these layers are still valid in an SAP HANA native environment, the increment per sprint can be also performed based on these layers. It would appear to be highly practical to combine these two ways of slicing data. Some helpful questions to ask yourself in regards to data slicing are:

- ▶ What kind of business or respectively reporting scenario should be supported? (E.g., analysis of sales volume for a specific year in a selected region by revenue only)
- ▶ What set of key figures are needed and how can they be detailed further? (E.g., support only basic key figures in an increment in the first sprint, calculated key figures are added at a later point in time)
- ▶ How can the set of data be divided into useful bundles? (E.g., by region, by time, by source system)
- ▶ What are the essential or key data flows you have to focus on for the initial start? (E.g., minimum of required master data or basic data at transactional level to enable a correct view on the selected reporting/business scenario)
- ▶ How is the data provided? (E.g., provide reports first of all only with basic functionalities in one specific tool, add further functionality or support additional ways of accessing the data/the report in subsequent sprints)

Once you have answered these questions and are in agreement on the scope of your sprint, you should also ensure that your architecture and data model are suitable for agile development. Thanks to the developments and enhancements of in-memory computing (and in this regard also to SAP HANA), you have a lot more options available for developing a BI system using an agile approach. Historically grown, heavy-weight, and complex BI systems are still alive and do not really allow for flexible enhancements or a fully supported agile method of implementation. However, it is clear that the demand for developing new BI systems or migrating and re-designing existing BI systems using agile concepts is steadily increasing (this is especially true for SAP HANA native systems). Looking at the BI architecture supporting an agile method of implementation, we recognized a number of solution statements in our daily work and also evaluated them. From our perspective, the foundation lies in the segregation of a centrally governed part of the data model and a flexible, decentralized part. Figure 5.9 shows this concept.

ADVANCED MODELING TECHNIQUES

```
┌─────────────────────────────────────────────────────────┐
│          Reporting Tools and 3rd Party Access           │
└─────────────────────────────────────────────────────────┘
                            ↕
┌─────────────────────────────────────────────────────────┐
│     Union of centralized and decentralized data model   │
│  ┌──────────────────────────┐                           │
│  │  View Propagation Layer  │                           │
│  ├──────────────────────────┤                           │
│  │  View Transformation Layer│                          │
│  ├──────────────────────────┤  ┌──────────────────────┐ │
│  │  View Acquisition Layer  │  │ Flexible View Acquisition Layer │
│  └──────────────────────────┘  └──────────────────────┘ │
│   Centralized governed data model  Flexible, decentralized data model │
│                                      Joint SAP HANA instance │
└─────────────────────────────────────────────────────────┘
```

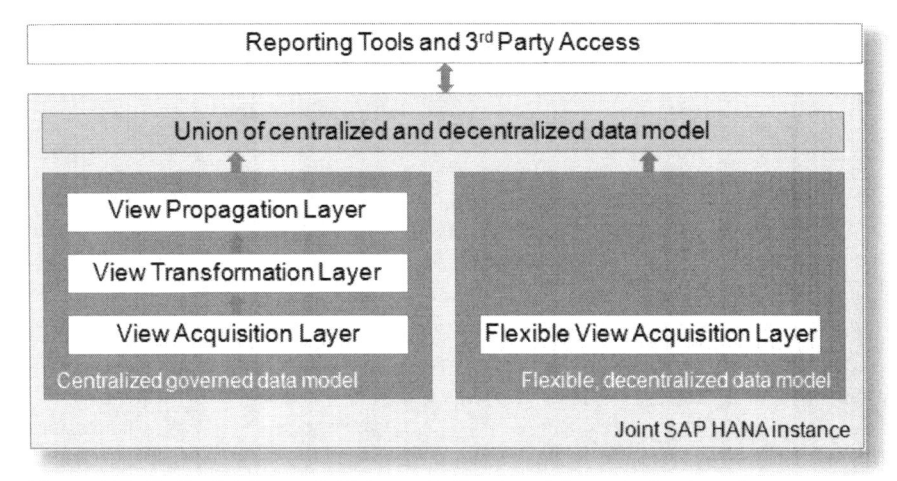

Figure 5.9: Split of data model into centralized and decentralized portions

On the left-hand side, you have an (often globally valid) data model that is managed by a BI competence center for instance. This part delivers data following aligned principles such as data coverage, data accuracy, data correctness, and data availability, as well as the guarantee of commonly valid calculation rules (e.g., for key figures). We call this area the **stable and governed** part of your BI system. On the right-hand side, you will find a lightweight area providing a space for flexible, locally owned data modeling. It is a kind of playground for quickly uploading data and preparing it for running quick analyses (e.g., from a CSV or Excel file). This part of the data model is for **flexible and ad-hoc** enhancement to your BI system (you can consider this area an alternative to SAP's workspace concept). A virtual union layer (which can also cover a join operation) brings both worlds together. This highest layer is the commonly agreed upon point of access for any kind of data consumption either via a reporting frontend tool or any third party tool receiving data through a pull mechanism.

On the left-hand side of the model, please deploy layers fitting to your architecture scenario. Each layer should be handled in separate development packages to ensure that they are independent from developments (e.g., when it comes to transportation). Please consider the number of layers as one of the possible options for your data model. Depending on your scenario, more or less layers may be appropriate. No matter how many layers you plan to establish for your scenario, the important difference to existing BI solutions is that you should consider using virtual concepts (and SAP HANA provides some really good ones as we have

227

learned). Thus, identify the best mix of layers using virtualization, planned persistency, or even a combination of both (see Chapter 3).

A business case for a mix of both approaches could be a real-time reporting requirement also demanding some complex transformation logic. In that case, a complete virtualization over the entire history and volume of data is hardly possible even in an in-memory landscape. In many of our SAP HANA projects we recognized at the beginning that there was a clear motivation to have a maximum of two layers. However, as the systems grew over time, occasionally some additional layers were added. Our strong recommendation is to concentrate on the minimum number of necessary layers and not to run into the same old story of complex and heavy-weight BI systems again. If the business logic forces you to extend your view model, think about outsourcing the logic to an ETL tool, or a separate view in the same layer.

We recommend distinguishing at least between *public* and *private* views per layer (similar to the SAP HANA Live views, see Section 7.5). A public view has an aligned and stable (or at least commonly agreed upon) interface and can be officially consumed from any consecutive layer. Private views are used for encapsulating specific calculation or transformation logic. Thus, the logic can be replaced without changing the structure of the outbound interface of the public view. The intention for private views is to use them (and therefore their calculation result) in a public view. Private views must not be used outside by any consumer except public views. This concept is valid per layer. The top layer of your SAP HANA native BI system should be a virtual layer that functions like an API with a stable and jointly agreed upon interface. Figure 5.10 illustrates an example of this concept.

Taking all these concepts into account, you can easily slice your development work and provide the intended business value per sprint. Thus, it is absolutely possible to enhance your BI solution in an agile way. Furthermore, with this type of development pattern in your SAP HANA landscape, you can assign manageable working packages to your developers.

ADVANCED MODELING TECHNIQUES

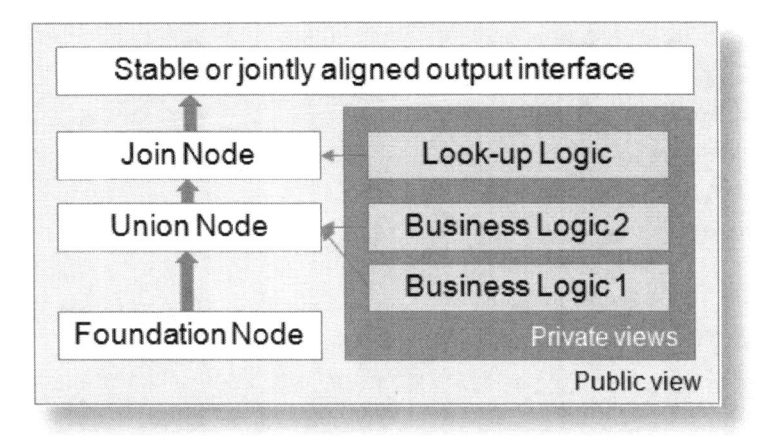

Figure 5.10: Segregation of public and private views

Last but not least, testing is an important cornerstone of each software development project. Testing should accompany (and run in parallel with) the development, especially when you are working in an agile mode. The architectural concepts based on modularization are well-suited for building up a solid test framework starting from unit and integration tests and going right up to user acceptance testing.

Before summing up this section, it is only fair to mention an important downside to the agile development approach of an SAP HANA BI environment. The evolutionary design of your SAP HANA model, that is, enhancing it per sprint, always requires an update and *governance* of your intended SAP HANA target model. Continuously enhancing your data model might lead to formerly established artifacts becoming invalid. For instance, some business logic might become so complex over the course of the sprints that an on-the-fly calculation is no longer possible, meaning you have to adjust this layer in the next sprints, e.g., by using an ETL tool to realize more complex transformation logic. Therefore, you should establish the role of an overall architect and governance lead who is responsible for taking care of these adjustments or corrections in your data model so that it still fits with your architectural guidelines.

Looking at the ideas and concepts provided in this section, you can see that agile development in SAP HANA is possible and can lead to a sustainable architecture in the following situations:

- Defining and aligning appropriate increments supporting a specific business scenario
- Introducing and governing a clearly structured data model consisting of layers with clear purposes
- Using the concept of public and private views to encapsulate developments and support parallel development
- Establishing a technical governance role to bring all the developments and changes in your BI system together

5.4.3 Hot, warm, and cold data

When you start looking into introducing an SAP HANA system, you will quickly come across the *hot*, *warm*, and *cold data* concept (also known as the **multi-temperature** concept). This concept helps you to use your SAP HANA memory space more effectively, meaning that you only keep data that is absolutely necessary in memory and accept, for instance, some longer runtimes for historical data. But let's start at the beginning so that we can briefly explain this approach.

- Hot data is accessed frequently (read or write operations) and should therefore remain completely in memory in your SAP HANA instance. All of the features for leveraging the in-memory capabilities are available.
- Warm data is needed only on an occasional basis and should not eat up your costly SAP HANA memory. Warm data is typically stored on a disk in your SAP HANA instance and loaded into memory when needed. All SAP HANA features are also available for this type of data.
- Cold data is rarely accessed but needs to be archived for a particular reason. This data should not consume your SAP HANA disk space. We recommend that you move this type of data to a nearline storage system (e. g., based on Sybase IQ). Access to this data is restricted to the capabilities of your nearline storage system.

Overall, this approach helps you to reduce your total cost of ownership and to optimize the use of your available SAP HANA resources. According to theory, the data volume of warm data should be less than the data volume in your nearline storage. In our projects, we have noted that many customers do not leverage this concept as intended. An alternative approach is to concentrate only on hot and warm data. Cold data is often no longer considered for reporting.

Taking the previously introduced layer concept into account, the multi-temperature concept can be easily applied. Hot areas should be that part of your data model on which the reporting runs or SAP HANA native operations are executed. Hot data should meet critical SLAs on query performance and data access. For warm data, you should identify areas of your data model with limited reporting access. Cold data is tied to areas of archived and seldom used data. Keep in mind that for cold data, different SLAs for data access generally apply.

Looking at the SAP HANA native approach in our case study, the IT department can leverage the hot and warm data concept by defining unload priorities for column store tables. In order to optimize the use of your SAP HANA memory and to free up memory resources when additional memory space is needed, you can unload column store tables from your SAP HANA memory. For each table, you can define the unload priority in the create statement. To do so, just add `UNLOAD PRIORITY [0-9]` to the end of your create statement. The general idea of this concept is to give SAP HANA a hint about which tables can be unloaded from memory when needed. The unload factor is an integer value between 0 and 9 with 0 meaning no unloading at all. The highest value (9) signals to SAP HANA that this table can be unloaded first. You can view this parameter as a weighting factor to create a ranking on your tables that have to reside in memory. From our field experience, reloading a complete database table even with several million records can be performed quickly. Thus, declaring data as warm is definitely a reasonable way to leverage SAP HANA memory as effectively as possible. Unloading activities can be detected by looking at the diagnosis files in your SAP HANA server. Search for the key word **unload** in the file name.

With regard to the SAP HANA cold data concept, refer to the latest release notes for the options and features available. The preferred solution in an SAP HANA native scenario is to implement a Sybase IQ database with a constantly increasing number of features for the interplay with SAP HANA native.

SAP HANA memory use

This article provides good insight into and a solid explanation of SAP HANA memory use:
http://scn.sap.com/docs/DOC-60337.

Unloading cached objects

If you want to prevent the unloading of cached objects, maintain the parameter unload_lower_bound in the memoryobjects section of your indexserver.ini file.

6 Best practices and recommendations

Now that we have evaluated the various design options in SAP HANA views, we are ready to explore best practices and recommendations for your high-performing SAP HANA data model. The findings of the previous chapters are synthesized and combined with new test cases.

6.1 SAP view strategy

To begin this chapter, we first discuss the general direction that SAP appears to be taking (from our perspective) with regard to SAP HANA information views. Looking at the options that SAP now delivers with calculation views, it appears that SAP is moving towards a future without analytical and attribute views. Introducing the star join node in calculation views appears to be the first step towards replacing analytic views. Furthermore, the dimensional calculation views used in the star join calculation views appear to be a step towards replacing attribute views. Finally, in SAP HANA Live, SAP uses only calculation views. Master data is joined in calculation views and there are different layers with private and reuse views (see Chapter 7).

In our experience on projects where SAP has conducted implementations for customers, the SAP HANA Live concept was used as well. All of the views were calculation views, including private, reuse, and query views.

The question is: are there still use cases for analytical and attribute views? From our perspective, there are still several use cases and we will present them in the following sections.

If you are considering focusing on calculation views only, you should also make use of further governance guidelines. Instead of a clear split between master data implemented via attribute views and transactional data implemented via analytic views, all of the data will be implemented with calculation views. This of course has an impact on governance as master data is no longer easily identifiable in the form of views. Use special naming conventions for the views in order to ensure that master data and transactional data are distinguishable.

SAP HANA table design

The biggest challenge in SAP HANA table design is ensuring data integrity. SAP HANA offers only the typical database concepts such as primary keys, foreign keys, and triggers. As triggers are outside the scope of this book, we analyzed primary and foreign keys and their impact on performance. The positive aspect of primary and foreign keys is that they do not impact query performance. However, it is problematic that the foreign key constraints can only be designed based on whole primary keys. Thus, if there is a composite key using several columns and the foreign key relationship is only supposed to refer to one of these columns, it is not possible to create the constraint. On the positive side, the reference between artificial IDs based, for example, on integer values works as expected. Apart from this, it is difficult to ensure integrity in HANA and additional checks through the ETL loading logic may be required.

As discussed in Chapter 3, adding primary keys and foreign keys to your tables has a significant impact on the loading performance. Each additional index further increases the time required to load data, which may cause issues in the data loading cycles. Therefore, we strongly recommend testing whether or not a primary and foreign key concept is applicable to your company. If this concept is not applicable, we recommended running integrity checks in the ETL logic.

Secondly, we tested the best way to design the data model. Although SAP HANA has high compression rates and the compression is done by columns, a star schema model is still required in order to save space. In our test, adding the master data to the fact table resulted in a significant increase in memory consumption.

Finally, we performed a data type test in order to test the impact on storage. The results are similar to other databases and the number values deliver the best compression, whereas text types deliver the worst compression.

Also, on a database level, table partitioning according to a certain logic leads to a clear performance increase as demonstrated by our test scenarios. If there is a solid partitioning logic in place and SAP HANA can query several tables in parallel, the performance increase is palpable. The best performance was delivered by using the round robin table partitioning algorithm. The disadvantage of the round robin approach is that you cannot set a primary key on the table. If a primary key is necessary in your environment, you will have to revert to hash or range partitioning.

Another topic that SAP is currently putting more focus on is database indexes. As for complex calculation models, the performance can sometimes decrease significantly and customers are requesting database indexes again in order to improve performance. Therefore, we recommend that you leverage indexes to improve performance where necessary.

> **How to design your HANA tables**
>
> - Use artificial keys instead of composite keys to ensure referential integrity.
> - Design your tables according to the star schema approach—it is still the best.
> - In our experience, joins have the highest impact on the performance of your views. Design your tables with this in mind.
> - If your load performance is impacted too much by primary and foreign key relationships, think about integrating the integrity check into your ETL process.
> - Choose integer data types over text data types where possible—this increases load performance and the compression rate.
> - Layers of persistency are still necessary in an SAP HANA data warehouse environment.
> - Think about table partitioning in the SAP HANA design layer.
> - Use further indexes for strongly queried columns in order to improve performance.

6.3 Joins

There are several topics that we need to discuss when considering the results of this book in the context of joins:

1. Joins deliver the best performance when they use ID columns as join partners.
2. A star join, when compared with a series of join nodes in a calculation view, performs equally well.

In addition to these two insights, we will now compare join performance when the views that contain the join are used in a further calculation view. In this calculation view, we add a calculated column in order to ensure that the data is transferred from the OLAP engine to the calculation engine. Furthermore, we compare the following four variants for joining data based on the two insights mentioned above. These four variants consist of:

1. The analytic view with no attribute views
2. The analytic view with attribute views
3. The star join
4. The join path leveraging only tables and no additional views.

The join type used here is the referential join.

The calculated column added here has a constant value of 1 and is of the type **integer**. Furthermore, we perform the test for the execution in the calculation engine (A), in the SQL engine (B), and also with the calculated column included in the select (A1, B1) without the column in the select (A2, B2). See Table 6.1 for the results of the test.

Let's discuss the impact of these findings for modeling SAP HANA information scenarios. To begin with, it makes sense to use analytic views to perform joins. Even when transferred to the calculation engine and with the addition of a calculated column, doing so still delivers a performance gain compared to the calculation view join. This supports the argument for continuing to use analytic views. The next finding derived from the results shown in Table 6.1 is that using star joins or a join path in a calculation view is the slowest variant for implementing joins in SAP HANA in all cases. The join path variant is almost as fast as implementing joins in the analytic view, but when an additional calculated column is implemented on top the picture changes again. In that case, even when the views are executed in the SQL engine, the performance difference is significant enough to suggest joining the data in the analytic view.

View type/test scenario	Analytic view with tables (Variant 1)	Analytic view with attribute views (Variant 2)	Star join in calculation view (Variant 3)	Join path in calculation view (Variant 4)
Full select in calculation engine (A1)	10.723 s	10.452 s	17.012 s	16.554 s
Select w/o calculated column (A2)	9.299 s	9.033 s	9.527 s	9.306 s
Full select in SQL engine (B1)	7.529 s	7.502 s	8.235 s	7.907 s
Select w/o calculated column in SQL engine (B2)	9.173 s	9.076 s	9.682 s	9.550 s

Table 6.1: Join comparison over the SAP HANA views

Furthermore, when implementing the join in the calculation view, adding a calculated column on top, and executing the query in the calculation engine, the decrease in performance is significant. The reason for this seems to be an issue in the SAP execution plan optimizer because the data is joined twice in this scenario, once for the original tables and once for the temporary table created for the intermediate result. You can see the execution times for the join path in Figure 6.1. CEAGGREGATIONPOP is the node where the additional join is performed and performance loss occurs.

BEST PRACTICES AND RECOMMENDATIONS

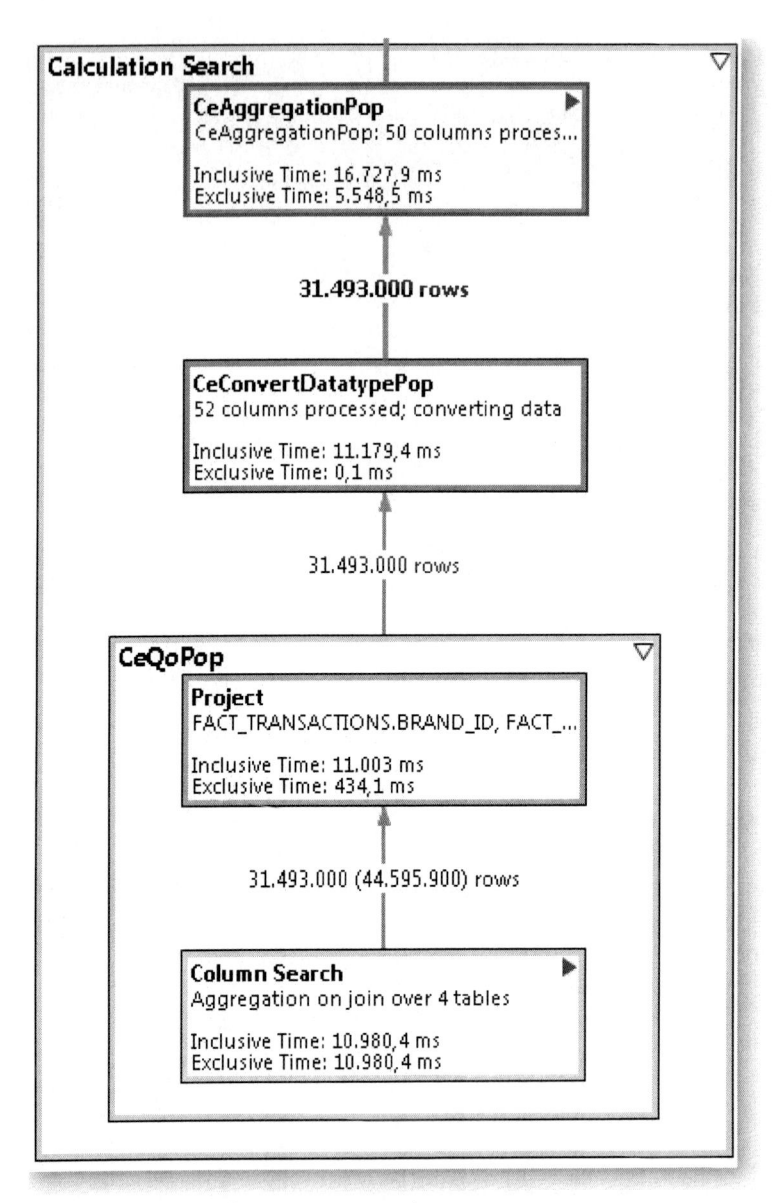

```
┌─────────────────────────────────────────────────┐
│ Calculation Search                            ▽ │
│    ┌──────────────────────────────────────┐     │
│    │ CeAggregationPop                   ▶ │     │
│    │ CeAggregationPop: 50 columns proces… │     │
│    │ Inclusive Time: 16.727,9 ms          │     │
│    │ Exclusive Time: 5.548,5 ms           │     │
│    └──────────────────────────────────────┘     │
│                     ▲                           │
│              31.493.000 rows                    │
│                     ▲                           │
│    ┌──────────────────────────────────────┐     │
│    │ CeConvertDatatypePop                 │     │
│    │ 52 columns processed; converting data│     │
│    │ Inclusive Time: 11.179,4 ms          │     │
│    │ Exclusive Time: 0,1 ms               │     │
│    └──────────────────────────────────────┘     │
│                     ▲                           │
│              31.493.000 rows                    │
│                                                 │
│  ┌───────────────────────────────────────────┐  │
│  │ CeQoPop                                 ▽ │  │
│  │   ┌──────────────────────────────────┐    │  │
│  │   │ Project                          │    │  │
│  │   │ FACT_TRANSACTIONS.BRAND_ID, FACT_…│   │  │
│  │   │ Inclusive Time: 11.003 ms        │    │  │
│  │   │ Exclusive Time: 434,1 ms         │    │  │
│  │   └──────────────────────────────────┘    │  │
│  │                  ▲                        │  │
│  │       31.493.000 (44.595.900) rows        │  │
│  │                                           │  │
│  │   ┌──────────────────────────────────┐    │  │
│  │   │ Column Search                  ▶ │    │  │
│  │   │ Aggregation on join over 4 tables│    │  │
│  │   │ Inclusive Time: 10.980,4 ms      │    │  │
│  │   │ Exclusive Time: 10.980,4 ms      │    │  │
│  │   └──────────────────────────────────┘    │  │
│  └───────────────────────────────────────────┘  │
└─────────────────────────────────────────────────┘
```

Figure 6.1: Join performance comparison

Additionally, for joins in calculation views, the OLAP engine is used. The only difference from a performance perspective lies in the parallel aggregation node which aggregates the data from different joins. This is not as fast as when the join is modeled in the analytic view.

The final result of the test as per Table 6.1 is that the addition of a calculated column (Test type B1) when executing the view in the SQL engine leads to a performance increase compared to the execution of test type B2. Based on our understanding of how SAP HANA works, the result was not understandable as there should be no performance impact at all. Therefore, we tried to understand the result using PlanViz functionality.

Using PlanViz we realized that the attribute Street_Number affects the way the query is executed. When the calculated column is not included in the query, the attribute Street_Number appears to be handled as a key figure with a fixed number of decimal places. Indeed, the street number was implemented as a number attribute of data type **decimal** with a length of eight. This appears to cause the longer execution time in the SAP HANA engine.

In addition to this test case, we evaluated the influence of the data type on the join performance. The outcome was that a join on a numeric basis led to a much better performance than a join based on alphanumeric values. Therefore, we recommend using (artificial) IDs based on integer values. However, if the integer is not sufficient for storing all your ID values, you should think about using NVARCHAR/VARCHAR types as the performance here was comparable. As our tests in Chapter 4 indicated, the join based on a numeric value stored in a VARCHAR or NVARCHAR field was just as fast as when the value was stored as an integer. The only disadvantage of storing IDs in character-based fields is the additional memory consumption. In addition, the join type influences the join performance. The referential join is the fastest join variant followed directly by the inner join. The left and right outer joins deliver the slowest performance. Of course, you cannot always guarantee that an inner join or a referential join will suffice for your requirements. In that case, we recommend ensuring referential integrity artificially, for example by adding an artificial entry to the master data if an entry does not exist. For example, there is a join to the customer table which is based on the customer ID but the customer ID in the fact table does not yet exist in the master data table. In this case, the data load includes an entry for this ID with only null values in the additional columns in the customer master data table.

Setting cardinalities for inner and referential joins also led to a large performance improvement. However, as additional tests indicated, setting cardinalities does not affect left or right outer joins.

> **Join performance summary**
>
> From the results of this test, we recommend the following approach:
>
> - If you plan to execute reporting on calculation views, it may make sense to use only calculation views as they appear to align with SAP's future strategy.
> - For the best performance, continue to leverage analytic views.
> - Additionally, execution in the SQL engine can lead to a performance improvement, but this should be tested for your specific scenario.
> - Use the referential join and create artificial entries in the master data where necessary to ensure referential integrity.
> - Set cardinalities for referential and inner joins.
> - Use integer IDs for joining data. If an integer is not sufficient to cover all of your IDs, you should think about switching to an NVARCHAR number instead of BIGINT.

6.4 Calculations

In this section, we will take a more in-depth look at calculation before aggregation and calculated columns. We will provide clear recommendations on using these features.

6.4.1 Calculation before aggregation

As shown in Section 4.2, performing a calculation before the aggregation degrades performance and should be avoided when possible. The question is always what aggregation level you really need. A higher aggregation level may be sufficient to perform the required calculation. In this case, you can leverage the normal calculation view and set the keep flag to true instead of using calculation before aggregation. However, if you really do need a calculation before aggregation, we recommend using the analytic view. The easiest way to use the calculation before aggregation feature in calculation views is to set the keep flag to true for the key column(s) in the transaction table (if this is the most detailed level). However, in an additional performance test, the performance loss was significant compared to the analytic view. A star join currently does not permit a calculation before aggregation.

Otherwise, as discussed in Chapter 5, you should revert to the existing SAP HANA elements such as the keep flag, counters, or projection/aggregation nodes to influence calculations and the related aggregation behavior. Another option is to store the calculation result in the physical data.

> **Calculation before aggregation**
>
> - Use the calculation before aggregation in the analytic view only if necessary.
> - Otherwise, perform calculations on the necessary aggregation level using keep flags.
> - The aggregation behavior and the calculations are also influenced by other elements in HANA such as joins, unions, projection, and aggregation nodes. Refer to Chapter 5 for a detailed explanation.

6.4.2 Calculated columns

Calculated columns are important when building the basis for reports containing business KPIs. In most cases, the standard measures delivered by the source system are not enough. Our tests regarding calculated columns and calculated columns of type attribute led to some interesting results.

The first finding was that calculated columns of type attribute are very bad for performance. In contrast, calculated measures do not affect performance quite as much. We also tried moving the calculated columns of type attribute to an attribute view or dimensional calculation view, but even that did not result in a better performance. It seems that SAP HANA only calculates the measure after the joins have been performed. This leads us to the conclusion that calculated columns of type attribute should be avoided whenever possible. It may make sense to calculate these in the reporting tool directly instead of using SAP HANA.

A second interesting insight regarding calculated columns was that splitting a complex calculation into two calculated columns actually led to a performance loss. We expected that it would not make a difference, but apparently SAP HANA treats the split as two different calculations.

We now want to explore how moving calculations to a calculation view instead of an analytic view impacts performance.

> **Calculated columns**
>
> *eg* The IT department wants to find out if they should use analytic views where possible and implement calculated columns there, or move the data from an analytic view to a calculation view first and then implement the measures there.

For this purpose, we will perform a test with a calculation view that is based on an analytic view and in the first case has only one calculated measure, in the second case three measures, and in the last case five calculated columns. We then apply the same approach to an analytic view. See Table 6.2 for the test results:

No. of calculated columns	Analytic view	Calculation view
1	13.576 s	14.762 s
3	16.028 s	16.465 s
5	20.157 s	19.445 s

Table 6.2: Calculated columns in analytical and calculation views

As the results shown in Table 6.2 demonstrate, compared to the analytic view, the calculation view has poor performance only for one calculated column, but it improves for three calculated columns, and finally, the calculation view is faster than the analytic view for five calculated columns. This gives a clear picture: if you have a large number of calculated columns, do not implement them directly in the analytic view.

> **Calculated columns**
>
> ▶ Avoid using calculated columns of type attribute if possible, as well as data type conversions to VARCHAR or NVARCHAR.
>
> ▶ Only split complex calculations into several calculated columns if you need to improve maintainability (as doing so decreases your performance).
>
> ▶ When faced with a high number of calculated columns, use calculation views for calculated columns instead of analytic views.
>
> ▶ As noted in Section 4.2.11, refrain from using restricted columns.

6.5 Currency and unit conversion

In addition to joins, currency conversion is one of the two topics that propagate the use of analytic views. As our tests showed, the currency conversion in calculation views is much slower than in analytic views.

Currency defined as:	Analytic view	Calculation view
Input parameter	24.063 s	32.367 s
Fixed currency	23.850 s	31.723 s
Selected column	23.842 s	32.016 s

Table 6.3: Currency conversion comparison

Table 6.3 compares analytical and calculation views extracted from the test cases in Sections 4.2 and 4.3. The first column shows how the target currency is added (as an input parameter, as a fixed column, or defined by a column) and the second and third columns show the results for analytical and calculation views. It is clear that the analytic view is much faster than the calculation view.

However, in this book we suggest a completely different approach to currency conversion. The question is, why can't you accomplish the same thing with a simple conversion table? Depending on the number of measures in your view, this promises to be much faster. You can simply use a central table for storing conversion-related information such as dates, currency, etc. Depending on what conversion you want to use, you can either filter directly or set an input parameter on the table and push the filter down to the conversion table so that no data duplication in the join to the transactional data is created (e.g., through several conversion rates applicable to one transactional dataset). To avoid doing calculations twice, the approach is implemented on the lowest level meaning that the view uses the transactional table directly. At this level, all measures that should be converted to another currency are transformed through calculated measures. The calculated measure contains the measure value multiplied by the conversion rate and the factor for the potential decimal shift.

All other information views based on this view only use the calculated measures with the target currency. Furthermore, using a central table has the advantage that reporting in local currency can also be accomplished using this table. In addition to your source and target currency columns, you can add a further column storing either the local currency as a value or the actual target currency value. Table 6.4 depicts a simplified example with the currencies EUR and USD. The first column represents the *source currency*, i.e., the transactional currency for which the conversion should take place. The *target currency* is the currency that the source currency will be converted to and the *currency selection* is the column for the user selection. The user can now select three currencies in reporting: euro, US dollar, and local currency. Depending on the selection, the column **Currency selection** (see Table 6.4) is filtered and only the relevant rows are joined to the transactional data.

Source currency	Target currency	Currency selection	Conversion rate
USD	EUR	EUR	0.93
EUR	EUR	EUR	1
EUR	USD	USD	1.08
USD	USD	USD	1
EUR	EUR	Local currency	1
USD	USD	Local currency	1

Table 6.4: A simplified example of currency conversion

> **Manual currency conversion**
>
> The IT department wants to test if the currency conversion is actually faster for simple measures performed with a manually created table or when performed with the tables provided by SAP. Therefore, it tests the approach in an analytic and calculation view.

As explained in the example above, the test case is executed with a similar table with the currencies, a conversion type, a conversion rate, and a conversion date. Furthermore, this table, in addition to the other master data tables, is joined to the transactional table and uses an input parameter to define the target currency. Finally, a calculated column is implemented which multiplies the measure with the conversion rate. The IT department tests the approach with a left outer join. In the analytic view, the join is executed based on the data foundation; in the calculation view, the join is performed after all other attribute views have already been joined and thereby their attributes added to the data.

Table 6.5 compares the manual currency conversion with the automated conversion from the previous test scenario which used an input parameter and which is depicted in Table 6.3.

	Analytic view	Calculation view
Manual currency conversion with one measure	15.456 s	17.288 s
Manual currency conversion with two measures	16.440 s	17.321 s
SAP HANA currency conversion with one measure	24.063 s	32.367 s
SAP HANA currency conversion with two measures	26.543 s	38.167 s

Table 6.5: Manual currency conversion scenario

There are two notable outcomes of this test. The first is that a currency conversion with a table that you create is much more efficient than a conversion using the tools that SAP provides. Furthermore, even when additional measures are added to the test, the currency conversion as designed in SAP HANA is significantly slower than the conversion with the table created manually. Adding calculated measures in the calculation view does not make a significant difference in the performance of the calculation view. The only reason why it may make sense to use the currency conversion as designed by SAP is that you can build on predefined tables in SAP HANA without having to store further data, e.g. in ERP systems. However, as the volume of currency conversion data at most companies is very small compared to the transactional data, we see no hindrance to using your own currency conversion table. However, you should consider establishing a comprehensive update process for your currency conversion information as this is available through standard SAP processes.

Our field experience shows that these findings can also be adapted to unit conversion.

> **Currency/unit conversion**
>
> ▶ Build your own conversion table.
>
> ▶ Perform the currency/unit conversion on lower levels so that all additional calculated measures can be created based on the converted columns.
>
> ▶ It may still make sense to map the original columns in case you want to filter values greater than 0, for example. Filtering on the original column will be faster in that scenario.

6.6 Filters

Filter pushdown in SAP HANA is one of the most important concepts for keeping memory use at a reasonable level—the most significant memory consumption issues are caused by join operations. Therefore, filtering data directly before executing a join achieves the goal of low execution times and low memory use. Early filtering helps to reduce the space consumed by intermediate results in SAP HANA. The intermediate result cache grows when the amount of data is increased by a join, for example, when there are several master data combinations for one transactional dataset. This can happen with time-dependent master data that is not filtered on the database level, for example. In addition, the calculation of the join itself requires memory and CPU time. Thus, these facts all emphasize that early filtering on the table level helps to optimize execution significantly.

The theory of this concept is easy enough, but the actual implementation is much more difficult in reality. There are often users who do not want to filter data at all, or if you want to satisfy several users with one SAP HANA view, the user groups may want to use different filters. Furthermore, not using a filter at all can lead to an expensive SQL statement being executed on the database. Finally, if the number of result rows is too high, the client tool may not be able to display or calculate the result correctly.

Filter concept

The IT department is considering how to implement a solid filter concept. To do so, they check the results from the previous tests (see Chapter 4) and also come up with a new test for checking the filter pushdown options in SAP HANA. For this test, they build several layers of SAP HANA views and then review the performance.

SAP introduced the concept of input parameter mapping for dependent calculation views with SPS 8. Thus, for example, you can map the input parameter from view A which is used in view B to an input parameter in view B that has the same data type format. However, attribute views do not support variables or input parameters and therefore, the concept requires testing.

	With input	With variable	With SQL
On constant column with integer	17.074 s	17.134 s	17.110 s
On constant column with string	17.489 s	17.419 s	17.392 s
On certain city and state	4.110 s	4.120 s	4.119 s

Table 6.6: Performance testing for filtering

247

The test for the filter concept delivers similar results to the tests in Chapter 4. First, it is clear that the different variants do not actually make a significant difference in performance behavior. As the test shows, filtering just using a `where` clause in the SQL query is just as fast as using variables or input parameters. This raises the question of whether variables are still required. Variables are only definitely a valid option for use in frontend tools, such as Analysis for Office. In general, you should test whether relying solely on the SQL `where` clause also works in large scenarios.

The second interesting finding from this test is that filtering on integer values is better than filtering text. This is due to the fact that SAP HANA needs to process the string first. To apply this concept to your entire database, for each text column used for filtering there could be an additional (artificial) key column. The key is then an integer value and the text column (label column of the key column in an SAP HANA view) is the value shown to the user. SAP HANA does not support label columns for variables, for example, as yet. This could be very valuable for performance improvements in the future.

Another interesting finding from the test was that the SAP HANA index server needs more time to generate a constant column with text than it needs to generate a column with integer values. When filtering on a certain city and state and including the constant columns, the server needed a much longer time to generate the result with constant columns containing text than it needed for the integer values.

Finally, the last test where a certain city and state were filtered showed that SAP HANA can identify which projection to use in the union. A projection that does not contain the correct values is immediately filtered out. Indeed, when running the same query in our standard calculation view, the performance is the same.

Filtering in SAP HANA

- First, determine a solid filtering concept. If in doubt regarding a certain parameter, implement the filter in the `where` clause of the SQL statement as this works just as well as using input parameters and variables.
- Use integer columns for filtering wherever possible. When using constant columns, use integer values. String values result in a loss of speed, both in filtering and in result generation.

6.7 General SAP HANA design aspects

This subsection discusses advanced design elements and specific SAP HANA settings for improving the performance of your overall architecture.

6.7.1 Result cache

First, we recommend using the SAP HANA caching mechanism for user-intensive queries. To activate the result cache, go to the perspective HANA ADMINISTRATION and then the CONFIGURATION tab. You will find a section called CACHE in the indexserver.ini, as shown in Figure 6.2.

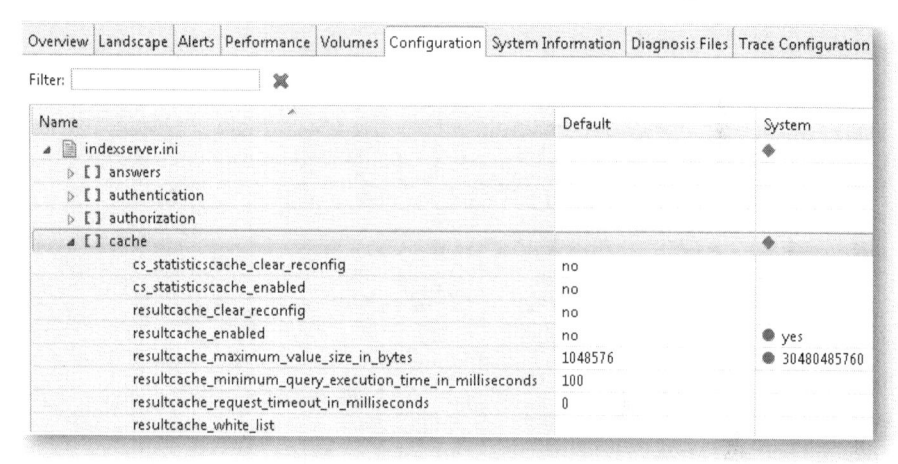

Name	Default	System
▲ 📄 indexserver.ini		◆
▷ [ ] answers		
▷ [ ] authentication		
▷ [ ] authorization		
▲ [ ] cache		◆
cs_statisticscache_clear_reconfig	no	
cs_statisticscache_enabled	no	
resultcache_clear_reconfig	no	
resultcache_enabled	no	● yes
resultcache_maximum_value_size_in_bytes	1048576	● 30480485760
resultcache_minimum_query_execution_time_in_milliseconds	100	
resultcache_request_timeout_in_milliseconds	0	
resultcache_white_list		

Figure 6.2: Parameters for the result cache

The result cache stores the results of frequently used queries in a temporary table. There are some additional limitations/prerequisites for the query, such as result set size and query duration, which have to be fulfilled in order for the query to be loaded to the cache.

The database administrator can set these parameters. The most relevant parameters for activating the result cache are the ones where the setting was changed in Figure 6.2, i.e., resultcache_enabled and resultcache_maximum_value_size_in_bytes. The default setting is that the result cache is deactivated and the default cache size is 1 MB. Furthermore, you can add an additional parameter resultcache_white_list to the cache section and specify the views relevant for caching directly.

You can also change the parameters directly in your Linux environment in the indexserver.ini file. You will find further information in the SAP Notes listed in the ResultCache tip box below.

> **ResultCache SAP Note**
>
> To activate the result cache, use SAP Note 1833049, which is available in SAP Service Marketplace. If you have a distributed SAP HANA environment, you will also need to follow the instructions listed in SAP Note 1833049.

The result cache is not automatically enabled by SAP because caching may lead to data being outdated, especially if you want to implement real-time reporting. This is also the reason why you can set cache invalidation for each view separately (in the view properties). You can set the cache invalidation period to hourly or daily, signifying that the cache is reloaded hourly or daily respectively.

6.7.2 Statement memory limitation

A second useful parameter can be found in the GLOBAL.INI section of the SAP HANA administration configuration section: a parameter that allows you to limit the amount of memory allocated to each query. In a normal production environment, especially in a transactional SAP HANA system, this parameter is an absolute necessity for managing the amount of memory that can be used by a single query. In operational systems, it must always be possible to perform inserts or updates in the SAP HANA database. The parameter statement_memory_limit can be found in the configuration section under GLOBAL.INI and the subsection MEMORYMANAGER, as shown in Figure 6.3. The parameter is set in gigabyte.

▲ [ ] memorymanager	
allocationlimit	
async_free_target	95
async_free_threshold	100
gc_unused_memory_threshold_abs	0
gc_unused_memory_threshold_rel	-1
global_allocation_limit	0
minallocationlimit	0
statement_memory_limit	
statement_memory_limit_threshold	0

Figure 6.3: Statement memory limit

6.7.3 Table type parameter

In SAP HANA, information view development is performed on the column store tables; if you use the SQL create table statement, you should create column store tables and not row store tables. However, the default SAP HANA setting is that the create table statement creates row stores unless explicitly specified otherwise. You can change this setting to column store in the ADMINISTRATION view on the CONFIGURATION tab in the indexserver.ini and subsequently the SQL section. There is a parameter called DEFAULT TABLE TYPE. If you change the value to COLUMN, you will automatically create column store tables.

6.7.4 SQL engine in calculation views

We explained the **Execute in SQL engine** feature in Chapter 4.3. We tested the flag for several scenarios, for example, joins in the SQL engine as discussed at the beginning this chapter. We also executed a comparable test to the one in Section 4.3.2 using the SQL engine. Even in that case the results were inconclusive. In some cases, the performance was worse than in the column engine. If the SQL engine execution is selected for a calculation view, one large SQL statement is generated and executed in the SQL engine. However, as we do not know how these statements are generated and optimized, we are not able to provide any hints on when to use or not use the SQL engine. In general, we recommend testing your view in the normal column engine and in the SQL engine to compare the performance.

6.7.5 Further design recommendations

As explained in Chapter 3, think about using Core Data Services to create and alter tables. As discussed, there are some distinct advantages, including integrity checks and inherent documentation.

Furthermore, if you have a large number of records that have to be loaded into SAP HANA daily and you experience trouble with the load performance, you should adhere to some basic load optimization best practices. There is a very good presentation on this topic in the SAP SCN forum.

BEST PRACTICES AND RECOMMENDATIONS

> **HANA load performance optimization**
>
> For HANA loading performance optimization, please refer to the following SCN entry:
>
> *http://scn.sap.com/community/hana-in-memory/blog/2013/ 04/08/best-practices-for-sap-hana-data-loads* ⇨ 19

As proposed in Chapter 5, we recommend using a *modular view concept* or encapsulating views into small units with limited functionality. The modular approach allows many people to develop in parallel.

Implement a layered approach as with other data warehouses as well. This applies not only to tables, but also to HANA views. Views have to be clearly linked to a certain layer if you are using them for more than just reporting. Also, if you encapsulate a view, think about a naming concept for the modularization so that you can easily identify bottom layer views, views based directly on tables, and also views using other views. The naming concept used by SAP with private and reuse views is a simple but good example.

When using analytic privileges, you should consider the solution proposed in Chapter 5, which segregates packages with private views (not visible to the end user) and public views (visible to the end user). You can then provide rights to the end user on a package level and do not need to consider the view level if you do this correctly. This approach also enables you to improve performance by ensuring that the analytic privileges are disabled on all private views. The fact that each view is checked for analytic privileges leads to a performance decrease. The analytic privilege defined for a user or user group also has to be enhanced to include a restriction for each view that is enabled for analytic privileges.

Finally, think about the agile methodology proposed in Chapter 5. This ensures a high business value, especially in an innovative business environment.

> **General SAP HANA design aspects**
>
> - Consider enabling the result cache.
> - Leverage CDS for SAP HANA table design.
> - Test your views with the SQL engine.
>
> ▶ Optimize your load performance if necessary, especially for your SAP HANA entry layer.
>
> ▶ Divide your package structure into private and public views and only activate analytic privileges for public views.
>
> ▶ Modularize your views to enable higher development parallelization.
>
> ▶ Build a layered architecture with a clear purpose for each layer. Leverage SAP HANA to increase agility in your company.

6.8 Summary

This chapter summarized findings from our previous chapters and compared different view types. We discussed the following general topics:

- SAP HANA view strategy
- SAP HANA table design
- Analytical and attribute views
- Joins
- Calculations
- Currency and unit conversions
- Filters
- General SAP HANA design aspects

7 Operational reporting on SAP HANA

After the IT department implements the complete reporting solution based on an SAP HANA native data warehouse, they realize that a large number of reports are run on transactional data. The IT Director believes that it may be beneficial to run these reports directly on the underlying operational system and move the operational system to an SAP HANA environment.

7.1 Operational versus strategic reporting

Through research, the IT department comes to the conclusion that there are large differences between operational and strategic reporting which not only influence the report layout, but also the level of detail used in the reports and further non-functional requirements (see Table 7.1).

Topic area	Operational	Strategic
Stakeholders	Operational management	Top and middle management
Content use	Day-to-day activities, production planning, and tracking	Long-term strategic planning, external or internal reporting
History	< 3 months	Several years
Level of data aggregation	Low	High
Data volume	Large data volume on a transactional level	Low data volume on a high aggregation level
Data transformation complexity	Low - medium	Low - high
Main HANA storage type	Column store	Column store

Table 7.1: Operational vs. strategic reporting

The comparison between operational and strategic reporting in Table 7.1 highlights the differences in the data as well as in the target group. It further emphasizes that it is very hard to use the same report and meet the reporting needs of both groups. However, this situation is unlikely to be new to the reader as these problems have been discussed in common literature for quite some time now. So what makes this topic worth bringing up again?

To answer this question we have to look at the operational systems themselves. The goal of an operational system differs from the goal of a BI system. The system owner of an operational system has to ensure high availability and a fast response time. This in turn guarantees that new entries can be created at any point in time and the core business can run smoothly throughout the year. The production system downtime due to maintenance or failure reasons at large companies can be measured in the thousands or millions of euros.

It is clear that running reports with a large volume of data in an operational system puts the system under additional strain. Creating further load on the productive systems was not viewed as a good idea at a point in time when in-memory databases did not exist. This is because the extra workload might lead to a breakdown of the entire system. For that reason, operational reporting had to be shifted to the data warehouse.

Now, the availability of in-memory technology enables companies to run their operational systems on an in-memory database, in this case SAP HANA. The expectation is that this will result in a higher performance, not only for creating new entries in the system, for example, a new customer purchase, but also in faster response times for reports running on that system.

Furthermore, there are significant differences in the target audiences and types of reports shown in Table 7.1. These arguments make a clear case for operational reporting being executed completely in the operational system. This has the following advantages:

- ▶ Reduction of redundancy because transactional data no longer has to be duplicated to the data warehouse
- ▶ Real-time reporting in the source system as the transactional tables can be utilized for reporting directly
- ▶ Fast implementation time as operational reports can be built leveraging the agility of SAP HANA views

However, SAP HANA is still an evolving technology and we recommend testing this approach thoroughly first before moving the transactional environment and operational reporting to SAP HANA.

7.2 Specifics of operational reporting

The IT Director decides to move directly to SAP HANA. After having done so, he discovers a whole new set of problems arising from the fact that there are now two systems for reporting: the operational system on SAP HANA and the existing data warehouse solution. Many of the problems are related to governance rules and processes. A small selection of the issues is illustrated in Figure 7.1.

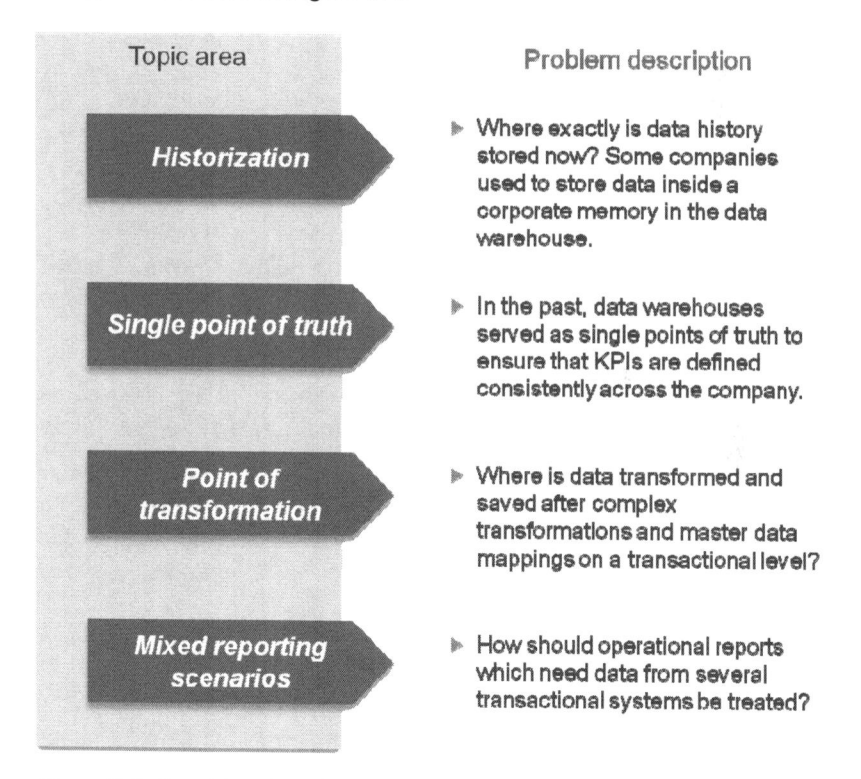

Topic area	Problem description
Historization	▶ Where exactly is data history stored now? Some companies used to store data inside a corporate memory in the data warehouse.
Single point of truth	▶ In the past, data warehouses served as single points of truth to ensure that KPIs are defined consistently across the company.
Point of transformation	▶ Where is data transformed and saved after complex transformations and master data mappings on a transactional level?
Mixed reporting scenarios	▶ How should operational reports which need data from several transactional systems be treated?

Figure 7.1: Considerations for operational reporting

The issues illustrated in Figure 7.1 should be analyzed for each company individually as a different solution might be required for specific reporting needs. The following sections briefly discuss which solutions can be applied, along with their respective advantages and disadvantages.

7.2.1 Historization

When considering reduction of redundancy as one of the main advantages for running operational reporting in the operational system on SAP HANA, historization is again an important topic. Many companies used to store data according to a *Layered Scalable Architecture++* (LSA++) in the corporate memory of the data warehouse. To reduce redundancy, however, one solution is to store old data in a separate table or even the same table in the operational system. To avoid using costly SAP HANA memory, the best practice is to leverage nearline storage for this purpose (see also Section 5.4.3). For example, Sybase IQ can be a suitable enhancement for nearline solutions in an SAP HANA environment.

A second solution is to copy transactional data to the data warehouse and store the history there. This defeats the purpose of reducing redundancy, but it can also be argued that historical data is not relevant for operational reporting anyway, so why should it be stored in the operational system?

A further question to evaluate is whether or not redundancy can be completely avoided. If there is a need to prove that certain data was available at a given point in time and in a specified format (e. g., for external reporting purposes), then redundant storage might be unavoidable.

In conclusion, there is a clear case for maintaining history in the data warehouse and not in the source system, but this leads to another problem regarding the single point of truth.

7.2.2 Single point of truth

A *single point of truth* (SPoT) means that Key Performance Indicators (KPI) and master data are only stored and accessible from one location. This location serves as the single point of truth for this data (write once, read many times). However, if reporting takes place in the operational system as well as in the data warehouse, it is hard to ensure that logics are kept synchronized.

One solution for keeping logic synchronized across systems could be that the results of calculations performed in the operational system may be reused in the data warehouse. Also, recalculation is not allowed in the data warehouse. This implies that a data history of the raw transactional data is only kept in the operational system. This is because basic calculations are performed in the operational system, and so the history has to be kept in that system. In the case of calculation errors, the results can be recalculated easily and subsequently moved to the data warehouse. Another approach is that all tables used in the operational system are replicated one to one in the data warehouse (even with the same schema). In this situation, transformations performed or views built in the operational system can be regularly exported to the data warehouse and reused one to one.

One problem with both of these approaches (data history in operational system versus replication into the data warehouse) is that if views or tables for extraction into the data warehouse are not stable, then it is very hard to build further transformations on top. This has to be considered as a major drawback and should be reflected in the solution design by building a solid foundation of views which are then used in further views (similar to the SAP HANA Live concept explained later in Section 7.5). Furthermore, each reporting requirement needs to undergo a governance process to allow an estimation of the impact on the system(s).

7.2.3 Point of transformation

As argued in Chapter 3, there will always be cases where data has to be stored physically. Therefore, an issue closely linked to the single point of truth problem is the point of transformation. Where does the transformation take place and where are the intermediate results stored?

As a starting point, there are several scenarios that need to be considered:

1. Transformations that are based purely on data from one single operational system and the results are made available for reporting in this system.
2. Transformations that map data from two or more operational systems on a transactional detail level.
3. Transformations that are performed on aggregated (combined) data before writing the results to the data warehouse. This scenario can be covered by the data warehouse and will therefore not be discussed here.

Figure 7.2 shows a possible architecture option including the transformations scenarios noted above.

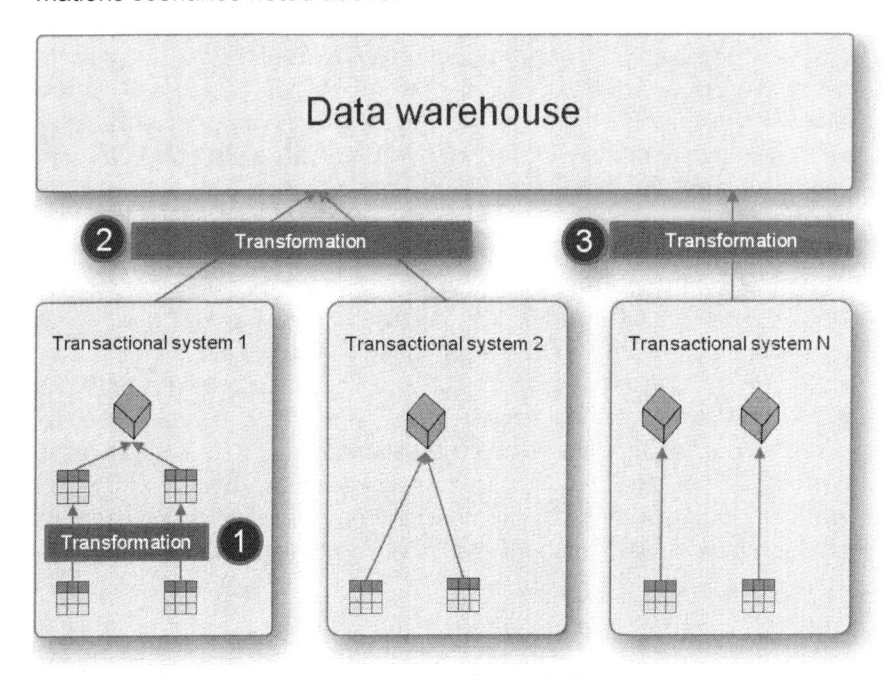

Figure 7.2: Operational transformations in SAP HANA

Scenario 1 has no downside in terms of the SPoT as the intermediate results are stored in the operational system itself (or in the nearline storage to save SAP HANA memory space). As no recalculations of KPIs are allowed in the data warehouse, the calculated KPIs of the source system have to be transferred to the data warehouse in another way.

Scenario 2 poses the most difficult transformation approach because it requires data on a transactional level but cannot be performed in one single operational system. There are several possible solutions for this problem:

1. Storage of intermediate results in the data warehouse
2. An intermediate storage solution, e.g., in the database of the ETL tool used for data transformation

Solution 1 for Scenario 2 is storage in the data warehouse. This has the disadvantage that intermediate results on the transactional level are physically stored in the data warehouse. This defeats the purpose of storing transactional data in the operational system and aggregated (combined) data in the data warehouse. Furthermore, the data is then stored twice, albeit with added master data.

The intermediate storage solution delivers much better performance in this regard (Solution 2). The data is only saved to the database for a limited period of time and then deleted. This ensures that the intermediate data cannot be misused in the data warehouse, nor in any operational system for reporting. Furthermore, this intermediate solution guarantees that the single point of truth for transactional data is kept in the operational systems and the single point of truth for aggregated (combined) data in the data warehouse. An intermediate storage solution could be the database of an ETL Tool, for example.

7.2.4 Mixed reporting scenarios

When looking at Scenario 2 in the previous section for combining data on a transactional level, another use case comes to mind: one operational system might not be enough to perform operational reporting; instead, the transactional data has to be combined with the data of other operational systems to obtain an accurate picture.

> **Leading operational system**
>
> A production manager wants to see which SAP sales orders convert to which production orders and where these orders are in production. SAP ERP is not used to track production orders and a separate system has been implemented.

As the example shows, cases for this scenario exist and this raises a whole new set of challenges. If each operational system runs on SAP HANA and redundancy should be avoided, how then can an operational manager merge the data from several operational systems?

The mixed reporting scenario cannot be solved easily due to the fact that redundancy is hard to exclude. There are several options for delivering combined reports:

1. Define a leading operational system for each case.
2. Supply the data for the reports using virtual tables or smart data access (SDA) – see Chapter 3.

3. Create an operational data warehouse.

See Figure 7.2 for an overview of these solutions.

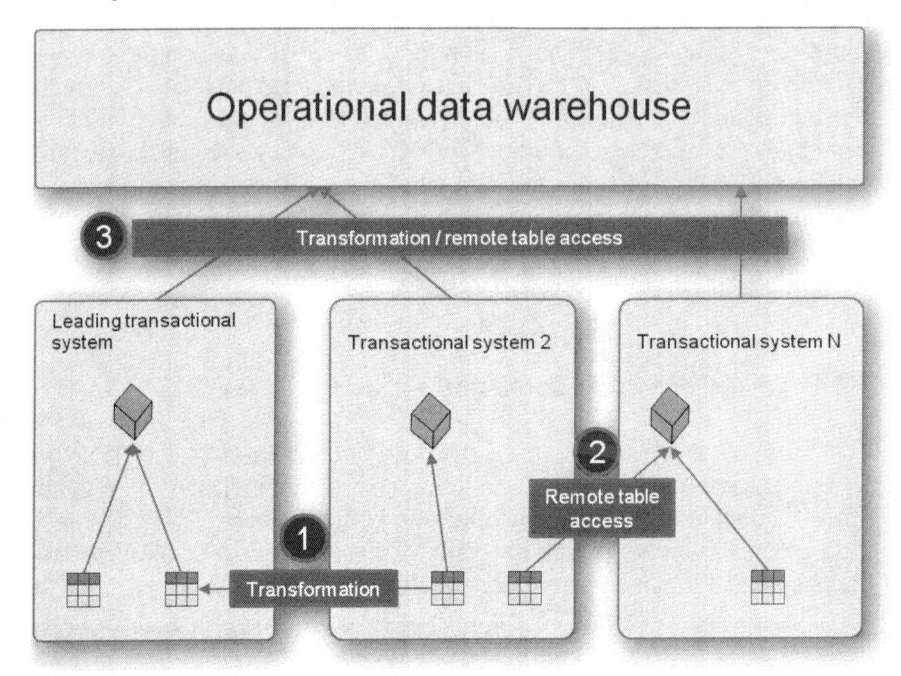

Figure 7.3: Mixed reporting scenario solutions

Each solution has its own merits and pitfalls and is highly dependent on your company. The definition of a leading transaction system implies that one system can be defined as the master operational system.

Leading operational system

Before looking at this implementation option let us look at a simple example.

Example of a leading operational system

Using the example of an SAP ERP system and a separate production system, we could say that the ERP system is the master system because it manages the entire process from order intake to invoicing, whereas the production system represents just one step in this chain.

Of course, defining a master system will still lead to redundancy, but the reporting can be performed in the leading operational system and the data warehouse only uses aggregated (combined) data. This approach only makes sense when there is one leading system and the number of operational systems in the company represents a manageable framework.

However, there are some challenges to overcome. If the operational reporting requirements are based on systems where no system can be specified as leading, the approach may result in an unmanageable number of duplications. Furthermore, if the report requires an enhancement with transactional data from another system, the volume of data exchanged between the systems requires high traffic and high redundancy.

Finally, it may be difficult to realize the correct leading operational system in each case. When the first reporting use cases are requested by the business users, a decision is made to use a certain operational system as the leading system. New requirements may lead to a rethinking of the old decision as suddenly the leading operational system cannot fulfill all the reporting requirements.

Remote table access

Supplying master data through remote table access (e.g., SDA or virtual tables, see Chapter 3) can be a solution when mixing data for reporting from one system with master data from another system. The master data is provided virtually and joined with the transactional data easily. This has the advantage that no data needs to be stored physically in a location separate to the original operational system. Furthermore, it offers a high level of flexibility in data provisioning. From the perspective of providing a single point of truth, the transactional data is still in the original system and only master data is offered in several systems. You must ensure though that the master data is not used for further calculations.

On the other hand, this approach in an in-memory database brings up new issues. First, using data virtually increases network traffic, especially if data is loaded frequently from another operational system. Furthermore, if master data is exchanged between operational systems, the load on each system increases with the increasing volume of master data loaded virtually.

Finally, and this is probably the most critical point, there is no provisioning of transactional data. This means that if data should be joined on a transactional level from two systems or data is even merged for one large report, there is no reporting solution available in this scenario. However, depending on the company this may be necessary.

Summing up the solution mentioned above via remote table access/table virtualization, it quickly becomes clear that some redundancy may be unavoidable. Under strict governance and a clear definition of KPIs across the company, it might still be possible to provide even transactional data virtually between the operational systems and thereby enable complete mixed reporting scenarios.

Operational data warehouse

The third and final solution consists of creating an operational data warehouse. In this context, an operational data warehouse serves the purpose of providing data on a transactional level for mixed reporting scenarios. This data warehouse could be completely virtual, thereby eliminating the need for storing additional data. If only mixed reporting scenarios are provided on this machine, the use could be reduced to a limited number of use cases.

If we argue that exchanging transactional data between two operational systems is not feasible, then this especially holds true when data is now loaded from two operational systems virtually. The operational systems do not have to carry the additional load as data is transferred directly in-memory, but joining data on a transactional level is also costly. This may lead to reduced performance and if additional complex logic is required, the user may have to wait a while even in an SAP HANA-based environment.

Finally, depending on the use case, redundant storage of transactional data in an operational data warehouse may be required. For example, if complex calculations are required, a completely virtual approach will fail (see also Chapter 3.1).

Additional storage in an operational data warehouse, even if kept to a minimum, eliminates the requirement for operational reporting directly on the operational system except for real-time reporting. Therefore, the question has to be raised about the level of detail required when combining data from two operational systems: is it necessary to join several months of data from two operational systems or can a filter be applied? Storing data physically in a separate operational data warehouse would eliminate the purpose of reducing redundancy.

7.2.5 Summary of operational reporting specifics

The previous section contained several discussion points which are summarized in Table 7.1:

Topic area	Solution proposal	Benefit	Challenge
Location of data history	Operational system	No data redundancy	Little use in the operational system
	Data warehouse	Supports mixed operational reporting scenarios	Possibly missing data for operational reporting
Single point of truth implementation	Operational system with view data export to data warehouse	Calculations performed only once	No solid data foundation due to changing views
	Operational system with table data export to data warehouse	Copying of views 1:1 from the operational system to the data warehouse	Redundancy through one to one data duplication
Point of transformation	In the transactional system	Direct use in operational reporting	Possible requirement for additional information from other systems
	Between transactional system and data warehouse	Combination of data from several operational systems possible	Multiple executions of transformations
Mixed reporting scenarios	ETL between operational systems	Fast report performance	Achievement of SPoT difficult
	Smart data access between operational systems	Easy supply of master data to another operational system	Additional processing for the exchange of data
	ETL to operational data warehouse	No additional load for transactional system	Necessity of reporting in transactional systems

Table 7.2: Summary of operational reporting specifics

265

7.3 Operational reporting scenario

The test scenarios from the previous chapters become far more relevant when you are working with transactional data as reports are run on a higher level of detail and in turn, require a larger number of rows. Therefore, it is necessary to optimize reporting performance. In the reporting scenario below, created for our case study, the concepts shown in the previous chapters are applied to operational reporting.

> **Store management report (I)**
>
> One of our store managers would like to view the quantity of each product sold on a weekly basis so that he can replenish accordingly. Also, he would like to see how product sales have increased or decreased in comparison to prior weeks. For the sake of this example, we are making the assumption that the store does not have a vendor-managed inventory.

If this scenario is translated into an IT requirement, it includes the following design requirements:

1. The user must be able to define the timeframe for which the report is run. Alternatively, the timeframe must at least be supplied according to user requirements (here the most recent week).

2. To view how sales have decreased or increased, the data from the previous week must be compared to the sales from the weeks prior to that.

3. In order to adjust the replenishment processes, the store manager will only be interested in a large increase or decrease in sales as products that sold in the same quantity can continue to be ordered at the same levels. The store manager therefore needs to define a threshold.

4. Finally, there may be products for which sales have decreased or increased very slowly over time, meaning that the threshold was never reached. Therefore, it may be worthwhile to have a comparison with the last month.

As the report is built on the operational system itself, we will take into account findings from the previous chapters. A data model redesign is not an option for a transactional system. Therefore, we will propose an architecture optimized for reporting on the transactional system.

First, we need to select and correctly align the design elements. To be able to make that choice, we first look at the detailed steps for achieving that goal.

1. In order to allow the user to define the required timeframe there are three possibilities: variables, input parameters, and a clause in the `where` statement. As discussed in the previous chapters, the input parameter is the most efficient variant for filtering data. One input parameter is sufficient to define a period of one week.

2. In order to perform comparisons, the data from the same table has to be split up into several data slices partitioned by time spans which then have to be merged to perform the required calculations. This can be achieved using a combined solution of projections and union nodes.

3. As thresholds have to be defined after the calculation of sales increase or decrease, this can only be done after the union node. The filter on the threshold value itself will have to be applied in another projection or union node.

4. A comparison with the last month can simply be interpreted as another data slice created by filtering on a start and end date. There must be a common understanding across the company of what a subtraction of one month signifies. The business requirement is that four weeks equals one month.

See Figure 7.4. It implements the principles already discussed earlier. So what is new? First, the report is performed on the product level, which represents a higher level of detail compared to the previous chapters. Also, it is very important that the data is filtered on a low level of the views with a start and end date of the period entered by the user. The same applies to the threshold value mentioned above. This significantly reduces the volume of data provided to the end user, which in turn increases report performance.

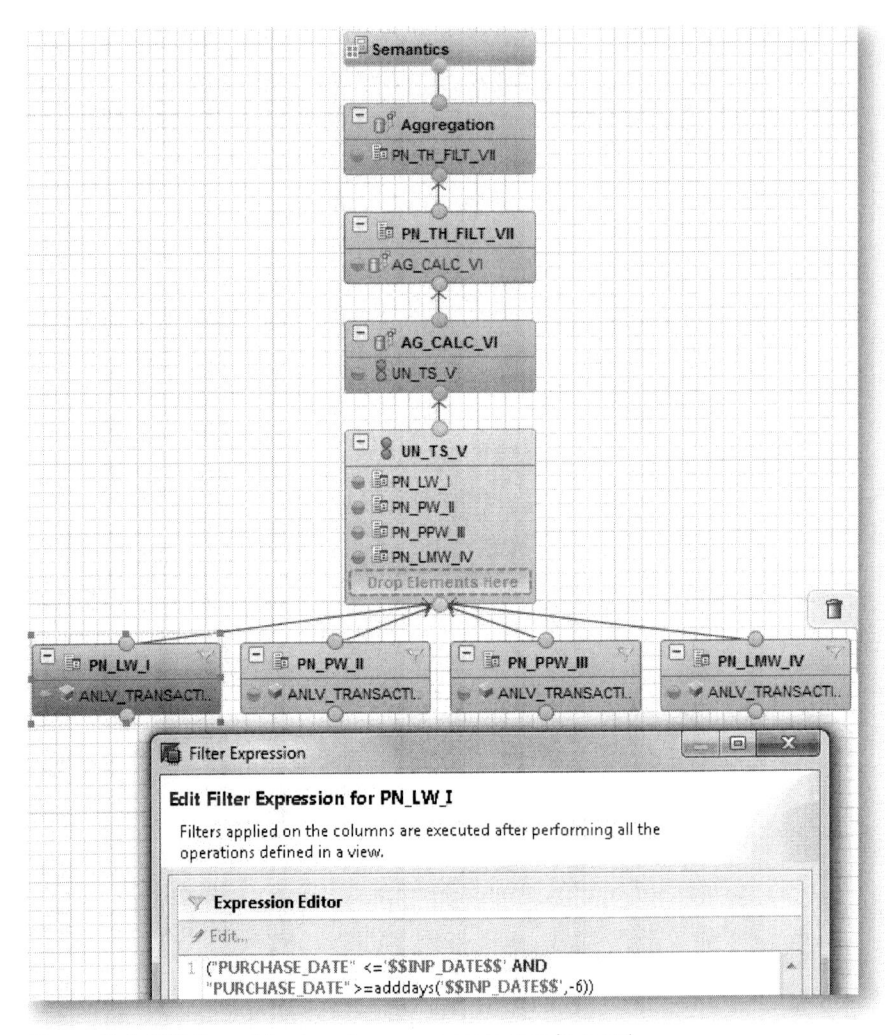

Figure 7.4: HANA architecture for an example requirement

The projection nodes I to IV each represent a certain period of time defined by a start and end date (also visible in the lower half of Figure 7.4). If defined chronologically from left to right, then the projection nodes can be defined as:

1. Purchase date lies in the input week.
2. Purchase date lies in the input week – 1.
3. Purchase date lies in the input week – 2.
4. Purchase date lies in the input week – 4.

In each of these projection nodes, the key figures need to be renamed according to the projection node name. This means that for projection (I), the key figure is renamed PURCHASE_AMOUNT_LW. This is necessary so that the key figures from the different projection nodes can be subtracted from one another.

As many readers will know, defining time slices can be very complex. For example, some users may require a production calendar that contains only the working days for a certain country (check back to Chapter 5 to refresh your memory on the overall concept).

After filtering on these periods of time, a union combines the time slices shown under (IV) of Figure 7.4. Attributes are mapped to the same columns and key figures as per the new names.

The aggregation node (V) ensures that the products can be aggregated at the level required for calculation. The union combines the different time slices, but the aggregation node is required in order to merge datasets with the same attribute sets from different time slices. Also, the calculations for the product purchase ratio between the time slices are performed here. The seven to fourteen days ratio, for example, is calculated as PURCHASE_AMOUNT_LW/PURCHASE_AMOUNT_PW. To ensure that these key figures are calculated on the product level, the keep flag (see Chapter 5) for product is set to true.

The projection (VI) before the final aggregation filters via an or connection on the calculated key figures with the defined threshold value. In order to give the user more options for interaction, the threshold can be defined as an input parameter. We implemented this filter formula for the calculated measures in our calculation view:

```
("CC_SALES_INCR_LMW_LW">1.05 or "CC_SALES_INCR_LMW_LW"<
0.95) AND ("CC_SALES_INCR_PPW_LW">1.05 or
"CC_SALES_INCR_PPW_LW"< 0.95) AND
("CC_SALES_INCR_PW_LW">1.05 or "CC_SALES_INCR_PW_LW"< 0.95)
```

7.4 Operational reporting optimization

To discuss the optimization of operational reporting, we will build on our example of a store management report.

> **Store management report (II)**
>
> *eg* After implementing the report, the store manager of our company notices that discounts impact the sold quantity, which leads to an artificial increase in the product quantity sold and to an incorrect change in the replenishment process.

This new example highlights two main points the IT department has been coping with for a long time:

1. The existing report serves the required purpose but needs to be adjusted to incorporate the new requirement, which implies a view change in the backend and possibly, a complete redesign.
2. Requirements constantly change as the business environment adjusts and therefore agility is necessary in the IT design.

Bringing these two points together with the intention of keeping operational reporting performance high, the team considers the recommendations in Figure 7.5.

(I) Use input parameters to filter time spans

(II) Prefilter the maximum timespan directly

(III) Keep the number of views to a minimum

(IV) Consider joining in calculation views

(V) Store precalculated values if necessary

(VI) Aggregate before calculations

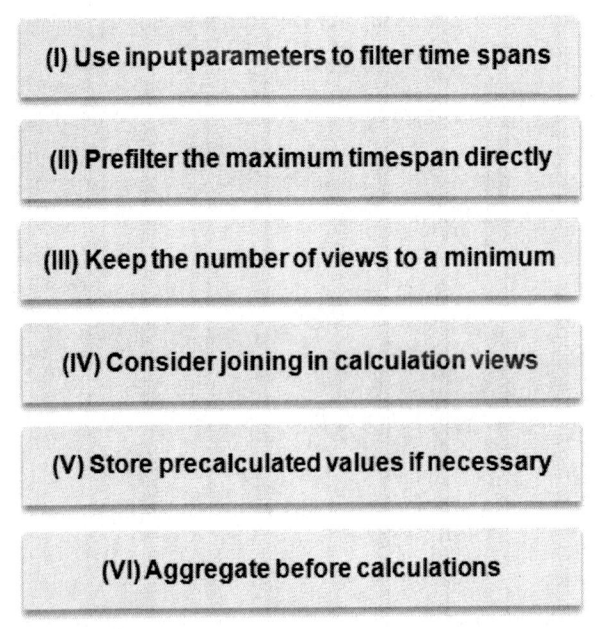

Figure 7.5: Performance optimization in operational reporting

The first piece of advice (I) has already been discussed and emphasizes the importance of filtering at the earliest point in time possible, thereby limiting the volume of transactional data used for the reporting.

Recommendation (II) reflects the same intention of limiting the volume of data before performing calculations. Prefiltering the maximum time span directly means researching how much data history is necessary for operational reporting. As pointed out at the beginning of this chapter, operational reporting often only uses three to six months of data history. For each view therefore, you have to ask the users what timeframe they require for their reporting purposes. The volume of data used can then be limited directly when integrating the fact table into the view.

As the volume of data used impacts performance significantly, a higher number of views impacts the available memory throughout the systems. Therefore, reducing the number of views in the system leads to a reduction in memory consumption through view calculations (recommendation III). Thinking back to the initial discussion on how an operational system is different to a data warehouse, even on SAP HANA the fact remains that operational systems have to guarantee high availability. As each table is stored in-memory and each view result has to be kept in-memory for at least some period of time, the impact of a large number of views on the operational system should not be underestimated. Furthermore, we can postulate that each view allocates its own memory when queries are executed. Every time a user executes a query on a calculation view, the system uses additional memory for calculations. At peak times, the system may reach its limit. In order to ensure high availability of your system, the number of views should be kept low. Join operations should be executed on only a number of limited rows (recommendation IV). Instead of joining in a predefined join path or joining a star schema, consider first calculating the result set on the required aggregation level and then performing the join to the master data. This makes sense in particular when several aggregation levels are necessary for the calculations which have a much higher level of granularity than the master data being joined.

Storing a precalculated dataset (recommendation V) is especially useful when complex operations have to be performed in order to obtain the required result set. The more complex the calculations in the view, the more memory is needed. In that case, precalculation can reduce the amount of memory consumed. However, be aware that storing results eliminates the advantage of real-time reporting in operational systems. If you want to store results and you require real-time reporting, consider using an ETL tool which loads data every 10 seconds, for example.

Finally, to improve performance, the data in the views should aggregate before a calculation as much as possible (recommendation VI). This improves performance as far fewer rows have to be accessed.

To summarize our learnings from this chapter, there are clear use cases for adapting the common recommendations provided by SAP to your scenario.

7.5 SAP HANA Live

The IT department has now seen what a complex task creating SAP HANA views for operational reporting can be. They need another way to implement requirements faster to fully satisfy business requirements. The IT Director discovers SAP HANA Live on the SAP homepage and implements it directly as it is free of charge on most SAP HANA machines (see also *http://www.saphana.com/docs/DOC-2923*).

7.5.1 Introduction to SAP HANA Live

What is SAP HANA Live? *SAP HANA Live* represents a prebuilt number of views that are used for operational reporting. The views are based on the standard transactional tables that can either be replicated from the operational system into a data warehouse or used directly in the operational system. The prebuilt views are not only available for SAP ERP systems, but also for some industry-specific solutions. The architecture has four main view types, as shown in Figure 7.6.

1. *Private views*
2. *Reuse views*
3. *Query views*
4. *Value Help views*

The private views are based directly on the physical tables and as per SAP's recommendation, should not be edited. However, as we will see later, this may sometimes be necessary.

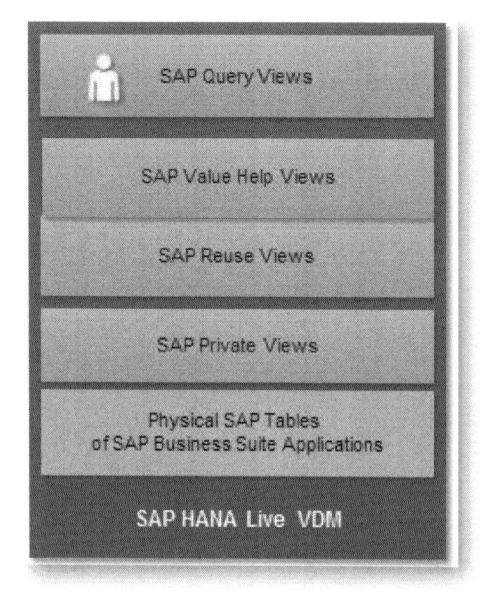

Figure 7.6: SAP HANA Live view types (source: SAP[8])

The reuse views are based on private views. They can be reused for further modeling of additional views for reporting at your company. SAP recommends either copying the reuse views before modifying them, or directly creating a query view on top of the existing reuse views.

The query views represent views that can be directly consumed by reporting applications and used for the reporting done by the business users.

Finally, value help views provide data for selection, for example, if the end user wants to select a certain region, then the value help view will provide all the regions available for selection.

Each of the four view types are used in a standard SAP HANA Live installation. As shown in Figure 7.7, there are a high number of views in the installation itself.

---

[8] http://scn.sap.com/docs/DOC-59928

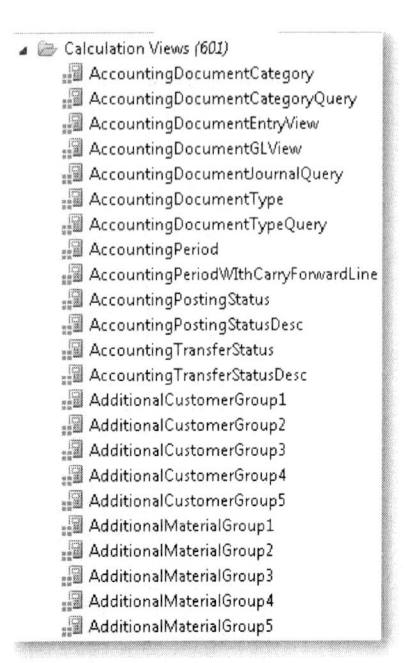

```
▲ 📂 Calculation Views (601)
    📄 AccountingDocumentCategory
    📄 AccountingDocumentCategoryQuery
    📄 AccountingDocumentEntryView
    📄 AccountingDocumentGLView
    📄 AccountingDocumentJournalQuery
    📄 AccountingDocumentType
    📄 AccountingDocumentTypeQuery
    📄 AccountingPeriod
    📄 AccountingPeriodWIthCarryForwardLine
    📄 AccountingPostingStatus
    📄 AccountingPostingStatusDesc
    📄 AccountingTransferStatus
    📄 AccountingTransferStatusDesc
    📄 AdditionalCustomerGroup1
    📄 AdditionalCustomerGroup2
    📄 AdditionalCustomerGroup3
    📄 AdditionalCustomerGroup4
    📄 AdditionalCustomerGroup5
    📄 AdditionalMaterialGroup1
    📄 AdditionalMaterialGroup2
    📄 AdditionalMaterialGroup3
    📄 AdditionalMaterialGroup4
    📄 AdditionalMaterialGroup5
```

Figure 7.7: SAP HANA Live views

SAP HANA Live was built solely on calculation views and the private, reuse, value help, and query views can be differentiated by their name.

The SAP HANA Live rapid deployment solution offers the option to use predelivered reports directly in SAP Lumira or Analysis for Office. For this purpose, you can use *SAP HANA Live Browser*.

SAP HANA Live Browser is an SAPUI5-based tool for looking at all the relevant SAP HANA Live views and their dependencies to other views or tables. A screenshot of SAP HANA Live Browser is shown in Figure 7.8.

OPERATIONAL REPORTING ON SAP HANA

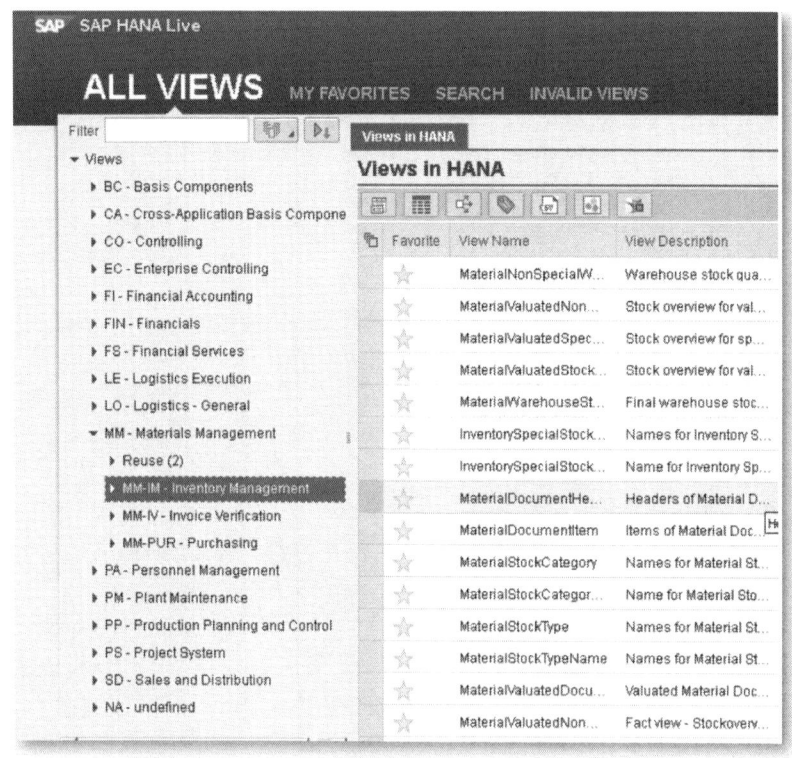

Figure 7.8: SAP HANA Live Browser (source: SAP[9])

7.5.2 Controversial SAP HANA Live

As illustrated above, the structure of SAP HANA Live view types is straightforward and the number of views indicates that a large number of reporting cases can be covered with the standard delivered by SAP. From this perspective, SAP HANA Live does not seem as controversial as indicated by the heading of this subsection. However, Table 7.3 provides a different picture when it comes to the strengths and weaknesses of SAP HANA Live.

---

[9] *http://scn.sap.com/community/hana-in-memory/blog/2014/02/11/sap-hana-live-on-the-rocks*

Strengths	Weaknesses
▶ Prebuilt reporting views installed easily ▶ No licensing costs, delivered automatically with SAP ECC ▶ Predefined analysis possibilities ▶ Enhancement of prebuilt views for individual reporting purposes possible ▶ Structured view layer ▶ Good documentation ▶ Out-of-the-box reporting functionality	▶ Limited coverage of actual reporting needs ▶ No connection to reporting domains in the views themselves ▶ No easy customization possible ▶ Usage of calculation views only ▶ High number of views

Table 7.3: Strengths and weaknesses of SAP HANA Live

SAP HANA Live strengths

The whole concept of SAP HANA Live is to deliver prebuilt SAP HANA views for operational reporting. In itself, this is a huge advantage, as customers installing SAP HANA Live do not have to build their own views. Furthermore, the installation can be completed easily as it is no more than an enhancement package to the existing SAP HANA instance. Finally, SAP HANA Live is free of charge, which is a further incentive to customers to install the enhancement package. After all, what is there to lose?

The predefined analysis possibilities offered by SAP HANA Live present the interested business user with predefined information views. Some of the analysis possibilities offered through SAP HANA Live Sales and Distribution (release 1.0 SPS 10) query views as documented in the official SAP Help portal are:

- ▶ What is the proportion of quotation items with the status accepted, rejected, open, and expired? (View: SlsQuotationValueTrackingQuery)
- ▶ Will I reach my business goals this year? What are my sales revenue values from the last 12 months? What is the sales revenue this year compared with same period last year? (View: SalesOrderItemNetAmountQuery)

If there are special analysis questions that the business user would like answered, then it makes sense to look up the question in the SAP Help portal and see if there is an SAP HANA Live view covering the requirement.

In some cases, the SAP HANA Live views may already cover the reporting requirements of the business user completely. In other cases, query views can also be enhanced with other reuse or private views to cover a specific reporting need. This option is provided through SAP HANA Live. A final variant is to use the existing or enhanced query or reuse views to build a new view on top.

Another advantage of SAP HANA Live is that it offers a predefined structure through the different view types. That means that if you are building new reuse or query views, you can adopt the existing naming convention and therefore, the structure remains transparent to the end user as well as the IT department.

When we started writing this book, SAP HANA Live was relatively new on the market and we noted missing documentation as a significant weakness. Now, with SAP HANA Live Browser, the documentation provided is comprehensive. You can see what fields are included in each view and which view or table is referenced therein. To use SAP HANA Live, for example in a scenario where the basic tables are replicated to an SAP HANA system, this kind of documentation makes it much easier to identify exactly which tables are necessary in order to use this view.

Finally, the SAP HANA Live query views can be opened by the end user directly in SAP Lumira or Analysis for Office.

SAP HANA Live weaknesses

The first weakness of SAP HANA Live is that views built by your IT department can address a far more specific use case than that offered by SAP HANA Live. Normally, and this is another weakness, the prebuilt views cover only one reporting use case at a time and other use cases are not covered at all. This means that the business requirements are not fulfilled and additional effort has to be invested.

These business requirements increasingly require the merging of certain domains as depicted in the example below.

277

> **Merging business domains**
>
> An example for merging business domains is comparing sales and delivery orders in reporting. For example, an operational manager would like to track a customer order from entry into the system up to the final delivery. One of the common questions in this scenario is: what sales orders are ready for delivery but have not yet been shipped out? This requires the merging of sales and delivery order information.

SAP HANA Live does not deliver functionality for merging different business domain data out of the box. The user can see information on sales orders or deliveries, but certainly not on both ERP domains — or rather, this is at least not possible with the prebuilt views offered by SAP HANA Live. The joins that are required between SAP HANA Live views to allow this information to be delivered have to be built by the user and will most likely decrease reporting performance significantly.

Experience shows that all SAP customers have customized content in their SAP system. Because SAP does not know about your specific content, they cannot implement the adjustments specific to your SAP instance in the prebuilt views. This results in the following complications:

1. If your system is heavily customized, the SAP HANA Live views may not work the way you expect them to.
2. If you want to add certain custom fields to query views, you first have to analyze which private views the query view is based on.

The solution to the second complication above involves several steps. The first step consists of checking whether the table with the additional custom field is in one of the private views included in this query view. After this analysis, either the field has to be mapped through the view layers, or a new private view may need to be created if the field is in a custom table. If, for example, the field is not in a private view used by the query view, you will have to search for the private view that supplies the information and add it to the query view structured. For the sake of completeness: SAP recommends that you do not change private views. From our perspective, it may make sense to change the basic private views if your SAP operational system is highly customized. However this customization may mean that you are not able to benefit from patches and upgrades. For example, when an SAP HANA Live private view is changed in a newer version, you will not be able to upgrade to the new version without manual adjustments.

As discussed in Chapter 6, SAP's strategy appears to be to use only calculation views. Therefore, all operations in SAP HANA Live are performed in calculation views and no additional persistency, i.e., storage of intermediate results in tables is delivered. Looking at the reporting speed, joins on a huge volume of data as shown in Figure 7.9 are quite common in SAP HANA Live views. If you have large dimensions or fact tables, this can lead to a serious deterioration in performance. Furthermore, if you use the standard views and need to build another layer or even several layers on top, each join will lead to a decrease in performance.

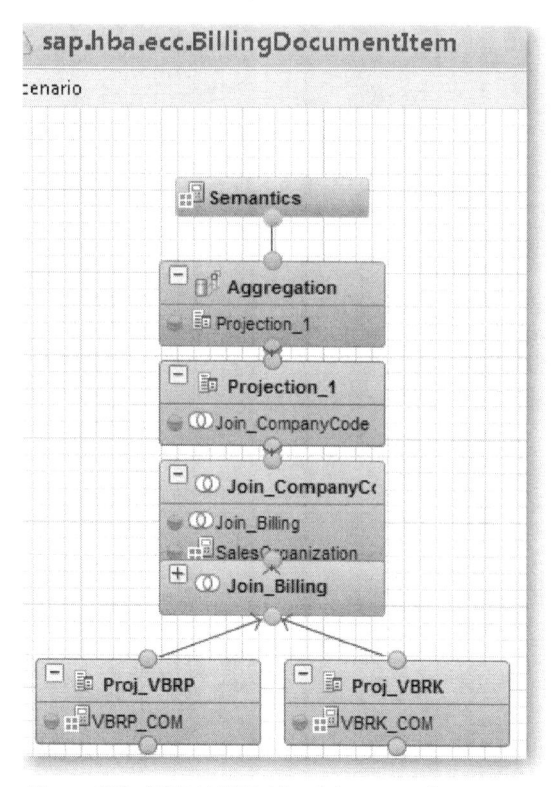

Figure 7.9: SAP HANA Live join example

Finally, the number of views as seen in Figure 7.7 is very large. This leads to significant maintenance efforts for IT when it comes to problems in reporting and especially when additional views are built for further reporting use cases.

7.5.3 Summary: SAP HANA Live

All in all, as seen from the arguments illustrated above, the decision to install and use SAP HANA Live in your SAP HANA system needs to be based on the following factors:

- How many of the reporting requirements can be covered with the query views in SAP HANA Live?
- How much customization exists in your SAP ERP system?
- How much data do you have in your transactional system? Could the joins in the views cause issues?

Therefore, when looking at these questions and at the arguments above, you should consider whether it makes sense to implement SAP HANA Live at your company at all. In our experience with customers, the majority do not implement SAP HANA Live and if they do, they enhance it significantly.

7.6 Summary

This chapter focused on operational reporting and the factors that should be considered when implementing operational reporting in a transactional SAP HANA system. We discussed the pitfalls of implementing operational reporting in an SAP HANA operational system and uncovered new problems on the road to performing operational reporting only in the operational system. We discussed:

1. Where does the historization take place for data on a transactional level?
2. Where is the single point of truth for transactional and master data, including calculations?
3. Where are transformations performed on transactional data from different sources?
4. How are mixed reporting scenarios handled where data from several operational systems is needed on a transactional detail level?

Furthermore, we continued with an example for a reporting scenario based on our sample company which led directly to a set of best practices for implementing operational reporting. Our recommendations included the following:

- Use input parameters for filtering as the filter is pushed down to the physical table level.
- Aggregate your data before executing a join.
- Store precalculated values after complex transformations to improve the query performance.

Finally, we discussed the advantages and disadvantages of SAP HANA Live.

8 Conclusions and outlook

This chapter summarizes the content and key finding of this book and gives an outlook on topics for further research.

8.1 Conclusions

Our goal in writing this book on advanced modeling in SAP HANA was to provide you with deep insights on SAP HANA data modeling techniques. The case study in Chapter 2 provided an initial use case for developing an SAP HANA native solution. We also provided an overview of the key software components and hardware of our SAP HANA system. Derived from the ERM model in our case study, we started to build our SAP HANA data model (see Chapter 3). In that chapter, we emphasized that virtualization is vital for keeping the data model simple and flexible. However, virtualization is limited when it comes to more complex transformations. In this case, persistency helps in handling complex data transformations, providing historical data and/or historical truth. It is crucial to find a balance between performance, data model complexity, and memory consumption.

For analysis and performance optimization, PlanViz is the tool of choice. It helps you to analyze the execution plan and identify bottlenecks. We also analyzed data types, primary and foreign key constraints, as well as partitioning with regard to performance and memory consumption.

As we clarified the fundamentals of data modeling in SAP HANA, we implemented and tested different SAP HANA design elements with regard to their performance in the chapter on high-performing information views (see Chapter 4).

In the first section of our test series, we turned our attention to **attribute** views. We emphasized that you should use referential and inner joins. Using filters to reduce the result set improves performance.

In the **analytic view** section, we had several unexpected test results. Our prior assumption, i.e., that an analytic view based on attribute views and a fact table would result in the best performance information model, was incorrect. The analytic view based solely on tables had a similar runtime. The test results also underscored that the recommended join type is the referential join.

In addition, we showed that variables or constraint filters used to reduce the result set had a positive performance impact. We also recommended leveraging input parameters when implementing currency or unit conversions. In general, the conversion functions were quite slow. The runtime of an information model is impacted by the introduction of counters and restricted columns.

In the **calculation view** section, we had several important findings, including that a star join is a reasonable alternative with slightly reduced performance compared to standard joins. Furthermore, we found that the functionality of hierarchies is less rich than in SAP BW and that not all frontend tools can leverage hierarchies completely. We established that the exception aggregation can be realized using the keep flag property. Looking at scripted calculation views, the SQL-based variant is preferable to the CE functions. Finally, we demonstrated that procedures help to structure your scripted views.

After focusing on the information views, we discussed several issues resulting from our daily work on SAP HANA projects (see Chapter 5). In the section on advanced modeling techniques, we analyzed using CDS for the table design and discussed the advantages of doing this. Furthermore, we provided a clear guideline on how to influence the aggregation behavior in SAP HANA. We also explained how to solve complex modeling challenges such as moving averages, exception, and time-dependent master data. At the end of the chapter, we discussed development methods.

The next stop on our SAP HANA journey was Chapter 6, which gave best practice recommendations. It covered the overall comparison of HANA information views and also explained where to use which feature. We analyzed the common queries such as joins, calculations, and filters. We also pointed to a set of SAP HANA parameters which can be maintained in order to improve performance.

The final chapter highlighted the specifics of operational reporting in an in-memory reporting environment (Chapter 7). Furthermore, we evaluated the current SAP HANA Live package delivered by SAP. To conclude this chapter, we presented a simple reporting use case for operational reporting.

8.2 Outlook

Up until now, we have focused solely on SAP HANA native and performance-optimized implementation of information models. However, this reflects only one part of a performance-optimized system landscape.

To design and run SAP HANA-optimized solutions, further building blocks such as ETL, frontend reporting, big data with Hadoop, and predictive analytics have to be considered. We would like to provide you with an outlook and some ideas for thinking about your own system landscape further and the options available to you for enhancing and optimizing your landscape.

Figure 8.1 provides an overview of the topics we will look at in this chapter.

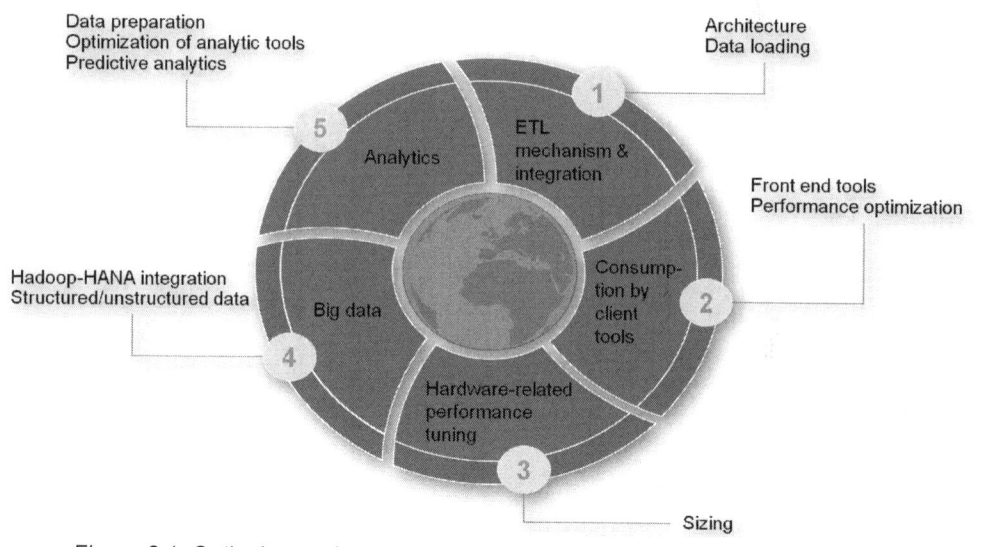

Figure 8.1: Outlook overview

Let's start with **the ETL mechanism and integration:** SAP HANA native SPS 9 itself has an ETL functionality with limited features. This component is called SAP HANA EIM and is on the strategic roadmap of SAP. Thus, further enhancements are to be expected. Consider this as one option for realizing complex logics and persistency.

Another approach is to install a separate ETL tool which communicates directly with your SAP HANA system. Today there are multiple SAP HANA certified ETL tools on the market.

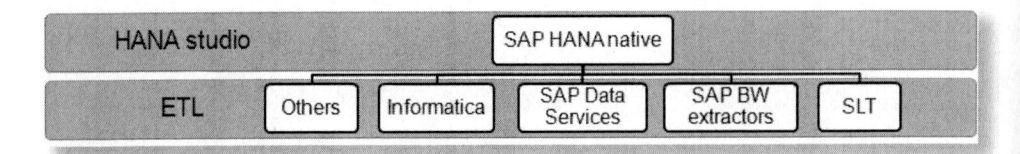

Figure 8.2: ETL tools overview

From an integration perspective, SAP Data Services appears to be a good choice. You should also think about implementing real-time functionalities with SAP Data Services available in the latest version.

Transformation features in SAP HANA native are limited and very complex to solve with information view functionality only.

This leads us to some research topics for a holistic SAP HANA architecture.

- Which design principles should I follow for my ETL processes?
- How can I best combine the features of my ETL tool with the possibilities offered by SAP HANA native?
- How do I optimize ETL processes for in-memory databases?
- How do I deliver data in real time while executing complex transformation logics?
- Which is the best approach for combining my ETL tool with replication mechanisms like SLT and SRS?
- What is the use case for integrating SDA with an ETL tool?
- How can my ETL tool support the update and storage of intermediate results in-memory?
- How should I set up my SAP HANA and ETL environment and how much parallelization do I allow within this environment?

All of these questions are very relevant for building an integrated SAP HANA and ETL solution

Frontend tool performance optimization is a relevant topic for IT departments as the requirement for the frontend solution mostly consists of having a modern, fast, easy-to-handle, and flexible reporting solution. Therefore, the question is, how can you design your frontend solution in order to achieve these goals?

There is a huge diversity of SAP HANA connectors, for example:

- JDBC: Java Database Connectivity
- ODBC: Open Database Connectivity
- ODBO: OLE DB for OLAP
- BICS: BI Consumer
- SQLDBC: SAP native database SDK

The important question around connectivity to SAP HANA is the performance and the supported functionalities of the connector. The following topics are also worth considering:

- How do I split the calculation logic of my KPIs between the backend and frontend?
- How do I combine the frontend data provision features with my existing SAP HANA database?
- How do I set up a solid user management and authorization concept considering both backend and frontend? What features can I leverage for single sign-on?
- Does the frontend support standard SAP HANA functionalities such as hierarchies, value help etc.?
- How do I combine SAP HANA with other sources (ERP, BW, and SQL Server) in my frontend?

If you have already come into contact with SAP BusinessObjects (BO), you will probably be familiar with the wide range of possibilities for performance improvement, for example:

- Enable query stripping.
- Set the parameter array fetch size from 10 to max. 1000.
- Ensure query synchronization is performed in SAP HANA and not in the client tool (set Join_by_SQL = Yes in data foundation).
- Create only one query for each report on a universe.

These points can serve as a starting point for further analysis.

Hardware-related performance tuning is a good backbone for your overall SAP HANA architecture. There are several hardware scenarios that allow you to realize your SAP HANA solution. Besides the standard appliance on certified physical SAP HANA hardware, there are also the tailored data center integration and the virtual SAP HANA appliance. This serves as a further topic for research and raises the following questions:

- How do the hardware and its components impact the performance?
- What is the best for me: scale-up versus scale-out?
- What is the best approach for obtaining a reliable sizing?
- Which parameters can be set to improve the performance of my hardware related to SAP HANA?
- Which hardware architecture is recommended?
- How does the operating system impact the SAP HANA performance?

All of these points are worth investigating further in order to build a high-performing and fully integrated SAP HANA native solution.

Big data and Hadoop are closely interlinked and are very popular in the IT world.

According to Gartner, *big data* is defined as: "*high-volume, high-velocity and high-variety information assets that demand cost-effective, innovative forms of information processing for enhanced insight and decision making*"[10].

Big data offers the possibility to gain new insights into your business and your business environment. From a technical perspective, the *Hadoop* framework is one of the key components for realizing a big data architecture.

So what is Hadoop? On the official *Apache Hadoop* internet page[11], it is defined as open-source software for reliable, scalable, distributed computing.

In this context, we came across the following questions:

- What does my reference architecture combining SAP HANA and Hadoop look like?

---

[10] *http://www.gartner.com/it-glossary/big-data/*

[11] *http://hadoop.apache.org/*

- What connectors are there for combining Hadoop with SAP HANA?
- What are the cornerstones of a sound governance model considering SAP HANA and Hadoop?
- How do I handle data transfers between SAP HANA and Hadoop?
- How can I access data from a Hadoop implementation via SAP HANA smart data access?
- Which data should be stored and analyzed in SAP HANA and which should be stored in Hadoop?

> **SAP HANA SPS 9 – Hadoop integration**
>
> Details about the SAP HANA–Hadoop integration are provided at:
> https://hcp.sap.com/content/dam/website/saphana/en_us/Technology%20Documents/SPS09/SAP%20HANA%20SPS%2009%20-%20Hadoop%20Integration.pdf ⇨20

These points need to be considered for building an integrated Hadoop and SAP HANA native solution.

Closely connected to the big data topic is analytics. **Analytics** is defined as *"the scientific process of transforming data into insight for making better decisions"*.[12] A further evolution is called predictive analytics. According to the definition by Gartner, predictive analytics is an *"approach to data mining with the focus on prediction, rapid analysis, business relevance on the resulting insights and ease of use of the tools."*[13]

In connection with SAP HANA, the following questions often arise:

- How can we support predictive analytics scenarios with SAP HANA?
- Where does the data preparation take place?
- Which tools aside from SAP Predictive Analytics 2.0 suite are able to use the possibilities provided by SAP HANA?

---

[12] *https://www.informs.org/About-INFORMS/What-is-Analytics*

[13] *http://www.gartner.com/it-glossary/predictive-analytics*

CONCLUSIONS AND OUTLOOK

- Which reporting tool should I use to leverage all the benefits of predictive analytics based on SAP HANA?

As you can see, all the topics are interlinked and are worth investigating together.

> **SAP HANA SPS 9 – Predictive Analysis Library**
>
> Further information on the Predictive Analysis Library in SAP HANA SPS 9 can be found at:
>
> *https://hcp.sap.com/content/dam/website/saphana/en_us/ Technology%20Documents/SPS09/SAP%20HANA%20S PS%2009%20-%20Predictive%20Analysis%20Library.pdf* ⇨21

We hope we have given you an idea of how you can further develop the insights and learnings gained from this book to unfold the full potential of your SAP HANA solution.

espresso tutorials

You have finished the book.

Sign up for our newsletter!

Learn more about new e-books?

Get exclusive free downloads.

Sign up for our newsletter!

Please visit us on *newsletter.espresso-tutorials.com* to find out more.

A About the Authors

Dominique Alfermann

Dominique Alfermann is a Consultant in the global Insights & Data Practice at Capgemini Deutschland GmbH. He is an information systems graduate (M.Sc.) of the University of Leipzig. Dominique is a skilled and experienced architect in particular in SAP HANA environments. He has performed several proofs of concept as well as development projects to demonstrate the power and capabilities of native SAP HANA design elements. His deep SAP HANA knowledge helps him in successfully leading SAP HANA implementation or transformation programs. Dominique is SAP BW and SAP HANA certified.

Dr. Stefan Hartmann

Dr. Stefan Hartmann is Principal Solution Architect in the global Insights & Data practice at Capgemini Deutschland GmbH. He has designed and implemented Business Intelligence applications based on SAP NetWeaver BW for more than 13 years. The development of transformation strategies towards sustainable business intelligence services is one of his areas of expertise. Thus, his focus is on SAP BW and SAP HANA architectures.

Stefan is SAP BW and SAP HANA certified. He has worked on several proofs of concept, SAP HANA feasibility studies, as well as SAP HANA transformation programs.

Benedikt Engel

Benedikt Engel is Senior Consultant in the global Insights & Data Practice at Capgemini Deutschland GmbH. Since his graduation in information systems (B.Sc.) at the University of Applied Sciences in Munich, he has been working on innovative business intelligence applications based on SAP NetWeaver BW and native SAP HANA. In addition to his profound knowledge of designing and implementing custom-specific business intelligence solutions, he has solid experience in combining SAP Business Warehouse and SAP HANA concepts.

Benedikt is SAP BW certified. His engagements cover architecture roles, especially in hybrid scenarios leveraging both SAP BW and SAP HANA.

B Index

A

Aggregation 45, 198, 200, 203, 204, 221, 255
Aggregation node 134, 157, 184, 200, 203, 210, 241
Agility 18, 225, 253
Analytic view 45, 51, 98, 233, 236
Attribute view 45, 54, 88, 233, 247
Average aggregation 198, 200

C

Calculated column 92, 113, 116, 117, 126, 127, 134, 137, 154, 157, 204, 241
Calculation before aggregation 113, 199, 240
calculation engine 53
Calculation engine 55, 56, 62
Calculation view 45, 55, 132, 233, 251
 Scripted 56, 172, 174, 176, 178, 220
Cardinality 90, 109, 110
CE function 172, 175
Constant column 145, 248
Constraint filter 105, 144, 151
Core Data Services 192, 251
Counter 124, 161, 204
Critical path 61
Currency conversion 117, 119, 156, 243

D

Data duplication 180, 217
Data recovery 39
Data replication 47
Data type 68, 70, 71, 85, 113, 121, 235
Date function 155
Denormalization 65
Development perspective 191, 192, 223

E

EIM 37, 38
Engine utilization 53, 60, 62
ETL 40, 51
 Transformation 36, 40, 42, 49, 259
Exception aggregation 163, 206
Execution plan 59, 60

F

Filter 95, 97, 102, 108, 132, 142, 144, 167, 184, 246, 248
 Pushdown 182
Foreign key 79, 82, 195, 234

G

Governance 46, 229

H

Hidden column 129, 170
Hierarchy 158

295

Index

Historization 258
   Historical data 34, 35, 230, 259
   Historical truth 35, 216
History table 35, 36, 218, 219

I

Index server 53
Information view 16
Input parameter 57, 96, 97, 105, 108, 144, 145, 167, 174, 176
   Mapping 58

J

Join 45, 54, 72, 88, 91, 98, 109, 111, 147, 150, 151, 153, 235, 240
   Referential 91, 101, 113, 239
   Star join 148, 150, 233, 235
   Temporal 127, 128

K

Keep flag 163, 164, 203
Key attribute 94, 95

L

Load performance 82, 252
LSA++ 34, 258

M

Master data 35, 263
   Time-dependent 35, 216
Memory consumption 44, 66, 76, 78, 234, 271
Metrics 117, 119, 153, 156
Moving average 207
Multi-temperature concept 230

O

OLAP engine 53, 62, 238
Operational reporting 44, 255, 257, 266, 269, 272

P

Parallel development 223
Partitioning 72
Persistency 33, 34, 40, 46, 52
PlanViz 56, 57, 59, 62
Primary key 72, 76, 79, 82, 84, 193, 234
Private view 228, 252, 272
Procedure 46, 50, 169, 178, 223
Projection node 132, 137, 138, 140, 141, 157, 180, 182
Public view 228, 252

Q

Query view 273, 276, 278
Quick sizer 41

R

Rank node 186, 188
Real-time reporting 11, 36, 38, 40, 228, 250
Redundancy 41, 258, 263
Restricted column 123, 243
Result cache 249, 250
Reuse view 273, 277
Row engine 54, 56

S

SAP Data Services 49, 50
SAP HANA Live 272, 276, 277
SDA 39, 40, 43, 44
Semantics node 138, 166
Single version of truth 38, 258, 261
Sizing 39, 40, 41
SLT 38, 44, 47, 48
SQL engine 55, 56, 148, 236, 251
SQLScript 42, 45, 53, 174, 220
SRS 44, 48, 49

Star schema 45, 55, 65, 234
Statement memory limitation
  parameter 250

T

Table type parameter 251

U

Union node 145

Unique value 74
Unit conversion 119, 155, 243
Unloading 231, 232

V

Value help view 273
Variable 97, 105, 138, 165, 248
Virtual access 43
Virtualization 33, 37, 42, 43, 52

C Disclaimer

This publication contains references to the products of SAP SE.

SAP, R/3, SAP NetWeaver, Duet, PartnerEdge, ByDesign, SAP BusinessObjects Explorer, StreamWork, and other SAP products and services mentioned herein as well as their respective logos are trademarks or registered trademarks of SAP SE in Germany and other countries.

Business Objects and the Business Objects logo, BusinessObjects, Crystal Reports, Crystal Decisions, Web Intelligence, Xcelsius, and other Business Objects products and services mentioned herein as well as their respective logos are trademarks or registered trademarks of Business Objects Software Ltd. Business Objects is an SAP company.

Sybase and Adaptive Server, iAnywhere, Sybase 365, SQL Anywhere, and other Sybase products and services mentioned herein as well as their respective logos are trademarks or registered trademarks of Sybase, Inc. Sybase is an SAP company.

SAP SE is neither the author nor the publisher of this publication and is not responsible for its content. SAP Group shall not be liable for errors or omissions with respect to the materials. The only warranties for SAP Group products and services are those that are set forth in the express warranty statements accompanying such products and services, if any. Nothing herein should be construed as constituting an additional warranty.

More Espresso Tutorials Books

Ingo Brenckmann & Mathias Pöhling:

The SAP® HANA Project Guide

- ▶ Delivering innovation with SAP HANA
- ▶ Creating a business case for SAP HANA
- ▶ Thinking in-memory
- ▶ Managing SAP HANA projects

http://5009.espresso-tutorials.com/

Janet Salmon & Ulrich Schlüter:

SAP® HANA for ERP Financials, 2nd edition

- ▶ Basic principles of SAP HANA
- ▶ The idea behind SAP Accounting powered by SAP HANA
- ▶ HANA applications in ERP Financials
- ▶ Implications on business processes

http://5092.espresso-tutorials.com/

Rob Frye, Joe Darlak, Dr. Bjarne Berg:

The SAP® BW to HANA Migration Handbook

- ▶ Proven Techniques for Planning and Executing a Successful Migration
- ▶ SAP BW on SAP HANA Sizing and Optimization
- ▶ Building a Solid Migration Business Case
- ▶ Step-by-Step Runbook for the Migration Process

http://5109.espresso-tutorials.com

Made in the USA
Middletown, DE